VICKSBURG'S LONG SHADOW

The Civil War Legacy of Race and Remembrance

Vicksburg National Military Park:
The Illinois Memorial and Shirley House. Author's photograph.

VICKSBURG'S LONG SHADOW

The Civil War Legacy of Race and Remembrance

CHRISTOPHER WALDREP

ROWMAN & LITTLEFIELD PUBLISHERS, INC.
Lanham • *Boulder* • *New York* • *Toronto* • *Oxford*

ROWMAN & LITTLEFIELD PUBLISHERS, INC.

Published in the United States of America
by Rowman & Littlefield Publishers, Inc.
A wholly owned subsidary of The Rowman & Littlefield Publishing Group, Inc.
4501 Forbes Boulevard, Suite 200, Lanham, Maryland 20706
www.rowmanlittlefield.com

PO Box 317
Oxford
OX2 9RU, UK

Distributed by National Book Network

British Library Cataloguing in Publication Information Available

Library of Congress Cataloging-in-Publication Data

Waldrep, Christopher, 1951-
  Vicksburg's long shadow : the Civil War legacy of race and remembrance /
Christopher Waldrep.
    p. cm. — (The American crisis series)
  Includes bibliographical references and index.
  Contents: War—The meaning of the Civil War in Reconstruction—The generals'
war—The boys from Iowa—The great reunion—A farewell to arms—A new deal—
Herman Lieb's report on Milliken's Bend— "The Battle of Milliken's Bend" / by David
Cornwell—Reported lynchings in Warren County—State monuments on the Vicksburg
battleground.
  ISBN 0-7425-4868-6 (cloth : alk. paper)
  1. Vicksburg (Miss.)—History—Civil War, 1861-1865. 2. Vicksburg (Miss.)—History—
Siege, 1863. 3. Reconstruction (U.S. history, 1865-1877)—Mississippi—Vicksburg. 4.
Milliken's Bend, Battle of, La., 1863. 5. United States—History—Civil War, 1861-1865—
Social aspects. 6. United States—History—Civil War, 1861-1865—African Americans. 7.
Slaves—Emancipation—Southern States. 8. United States—History—Civil War,
1861-1865—Influence. 9. Racism—United States—History—19th century. 10. Racism—
Southern States—History—19th century. I. Title. II. Series.

F349.V6W27 2005   2005002732
973.7'344—dc22

Printed in the United States of America

♾™The paper used in this publication meets the minimum requirements of American National Standard for Information Sciences—Permanence of Paper for Printed Library Materials, ANSI/NISO Z39.48-1992.

CONTENTS

ACKNOWLEDGMENTS

I WOULD never have thought to write this book if Matt Hershey had not suggested it. I could have never completed it had Gordon Cotton and Jeff Giambrone of Vicksburg's Old Court House Museum not directed me to the important sources in their collection. Mary Evelyn Tomlin helped me at the National Archives in Atlanta. Terry Winschel and Dwight Pitcaithley of the National Park Service provided me with important Vicksburg documents. Anne Lipscomb of the Mississippi Department of Archives and History suggested sources I would never have found on my own. Aloha South of the National Archives eased my access to the Southern Claims Commission papers. Kathleen Bellesiles helped with the photographs. Dwight Pitcaithley, Steven Woodworth, Thomas H. Appleton, Jr., Les Benedict, Pamela Waldrep, and James Klotter painstakingly read and commented on the entire manuscript. I am deeply grateful. Craig Zaim, John Rosen, and Rachel Van assisted my research. Brian Chambers of the J. Paul Leonard Library at San Francisco State University did sterling service securing obscure texts through interlibrary loan. The San Francisco State University Foundation facilitated my travel and research. As I learned how to research this book, my wonderful daughters, Janelle Waldrep and Andrea Waldrep, discovered the joys of travel to Mississippi.

INTRODUCTION

GETTYSBURG. For some people, just saying the name brings to mind not only the Civil War but all of American history as well.[1] One writer has called Gettysburg "the most written about battle in world history." This famous battle occurred at precisely the same time as another great Civil War battle, the North's campaign against Vicksburg. To state things too simply, one could say that the battle over Vicksburg tore the South asunder, while Gettysburg foiled a Confederate raid into Pennsylvania. Vicksburg made Ulysses S. Grant's reputation, and Gettysburg challenged that of Robert E. Lee. But while Vicksburg arguably mattered more than Gettysburg, there is little magic in the name Vicksburg. In memory, if not history, Gettysburg matters more. A Gettysburg historian once passed out cards declaring that "the Union was born in Philadelphia 1776, but it was preserved at Gettysburg 1863."[2] As I wrote this book, the bookstore near my campus had a special section titled "Gettysburg." The Gettysburg battlefield, not Vicksburg, moved Michael Shaara to write *The Killer Angels*. Turner Pictures did not make a movie called *Vicksburg*. Presumably, Newt Gingrich could have chosen any battle for his new Civil War novel, but he titled his book *Gettysburg*.[3] That battle dominates the American Civil War memory far in excess of its actual military importance. When memory contradicts history so blatantly, red flags go up (or should go up) for students of memory.

Memory has attracted the attention of a growing band of academic historians. In part, this interest can be attributed to a desire by scholars to reunite academic scholarship with popular history. David Goldfield writes that history and memory are "not distinct" but rather that they "intertwine," "interact," and "intersect." All this intertwining and interacting does not make academic history the same thing as memory. Academic history can seem narrow and technical; memory is big and powerful, the very essence of consciousness, the maker of tradition and identity. David Blight quotes Robert Penn Warren as saying that Americans *feel* their Civil War history, they *live* it in a shared imagination. Blight associates memory with "vision" as though historical consciousness shapes the act of seeing itself.[4] Memory *is* history and incorporates academic writing, but it also draws on movies, novels, poetry, food, gossip, and more to become the national consciousness, the understandings that ordinary people share about their collective past. Culture translates its conceptions of identity into iconography[5] and then carves its icons onto public monuments.[6]

Battlefields are particularly important memory sites. Competing patriotisms have collided in our remembering at Gettysburg but also at the Alamo, Little Bighorn, the Vietnam Memorial, and, more recently, the Smithsonian when officials exhibited the aircraft that dropped the atomic bomb on Hiroshima, Japan. On old battlefields, ideas are redefined, new understandings sought, and fresh lessons from past wars learned; the defeated sometimes win rhetorical victories not possible in war. When Gettysburg hosted its great 1913 Blue-Gray extravaganza, it was "a Jim Crow reunion" held "at a time when lynching had developed into a social ritual of its own horrifying kind."[7] Edward Linenthal has shrewdly observed that Americans quarrel over old battlegrounds for "symbolic ownership."[8]

Stories about the Civil War that include discussion of the postwar Reconstruction period often tell a history of ultimate northern defeat after initial military victory. In *The Romance of*

Reunion, Nina Silber makes it her goal to understand how "the North won the war, but the South won the peace."[9] Congress subjected the South to renewed military occupation and passed a succession of civil rights laws but then lost the will to enforce them and failed to "reconstruct" the South. After the Civil War came segregation, whites-only voting, and a vicious spasm of white racial violence directed against blacks—the American horror story called lynching. The North "retreated" from its efforts to reshape southern society. The Civil War demolished the states' sovereign right of secession, but in its place states' rights proliferated. Some years ago, one of my students read this history in Eric Foner's *Reconstruction* and blurted, "I thought we won that war."[10]

I agreed with my student. I knew that northern soldiers marched off to war writing letters home on stationery that proclaimed "THE UNION, THE CONSTITUTION—AND THE ENFORCEMENT OF THE LAWS."[11] Their vision of law and constitutionalism did not prevail; lynching did. In the long run, I knew, the white South had "won" the Civil War—if that war is understood to pit freedom against racial oppression. Slavery did not return after 1865, but peonage, segregation, and mob violence subjected "freed" people to a different kind of bondage. Widespread respect for states' rights meant that the North allowed the southern states to run their own racial affairs as long as they did not formally reintroduce slavery.

All these views formed my historical knowledge before I began researching who "owned" Vicksburg's battlefield. Looking at the Civil War commemorations in Vicksburg changed my views in ways I never anticipated. At its best, Civil War memory does not merely add to the old political history. Memory records prevailing power, the *structure* of society, the hierarchy of sovereignty, the most fundamental ways a nation organizes itself. Northerners played a decisive and powerful role in shaping Vicksburg's historic landscape and determining its meaning. Southerners did not, after all, monopolize Vicksburg's Civil War memory. The Lost Cause ideology—postwar efforts to sentimentalize the Confederacy—held no "stranglehold" over the white South, even in Mississippi.[12] In fact, in Vicksburg, white northerners rather than white southerners built the Civil War's physical presence and constructed its meaning. In large measure, northerners designed the Civil War's permanent physical presence in Vicksburg, just as they did in Gettysburg and on other Civil War battlefields. In Vicksburg, Iowa veterans made the battlefield into a national park, persuaded Congress to fund it, and operated the park for its first thirty years. Northerners, not white southerners, built a replica of an antebellum mansion on park grounds. The U.S. government, both in World War I and in the New Deal, reawakened the park to its patriotic promise. Southern distinctiveness advanced national power.[13] If landscape really is culture, as Simon Schama has written, then knowing that the national government—northerners—made Vicksburg's Civil War landscape helps us understand how the federal government mobilized the Lost Cause as a tool to advance its power, to cement its presence in ordinary Americans' lives.[14] To study the memory of the Vicksburg campaign is to see its *constitutional* impact. The Civil War shifted sovereign power in a way that, at first, made little difference to be sure. Such is the nature of constitutional change. But sooner or later, the new power arrangement matters.

Such changes do not come without a fight or, rather, many small fights. Individuals struggled on particular landscapes to shape the Civil War's meaning. It is a mistake to claim that "the South" or "the North" did anything. Some of the best work in print on Civil War memory looks at single battlefields, not whole regions.[15] The Lost Cause was no monolith. Working on this project taught me to watch how individual veterans (and nonveterans) found personal meaning in their wartime experience—or did not. The intoxicating force of war gave life meaning—sometimes. Americans became invested in their Civil War myth, in the idea of a noble, gallant, and romantic war, as a result of many personal, individual decisions. How did that happen?

The place to begin unraveling the significance of northern and national commitment to the Lost Cause is in the Civil War itself. Initially, I wanted to know what northern soldiers thought they fought for and how their thinking changed through the war. Next, I wondered how their ideas evolved after Appomattox as the nation wrestled with whether the war should or could change the national government's role in American society. Federal officials decided to pursue justice not through its courts but bureaucratically, paying off Civil War veterans, black and white, through the nation's first social welfare program. This happened in the last third of the nineteenth century, a time when ordinary soldier-veterans received unparalleled attention. Yet it was the generals who largely focused the nation's Civil War metahistory on military maneuver and strategy over any kind of emancipationist narrative. After World War I, poets and novelists wrote the important books; after the Civil War, memoirs held sway. And as the generals penned their recollections, the country mobilized its memories of Civil War valor for new wars.

Congress authorized the Vicksburg National Military Park in an impulse both jingoistic and pragmatic. Jingoism promotes the martial ideal, seeking experiences that make manhood in an industrialized age. Pragmatists see all narratives, indeed all consciousness, as instrumental; there is no truth, really, just visions, ideas, and imagined principles all available as tools. At the crossroads of Gilded Age masculinity and pragmatism, Civil War memory became an instrument for men seeking to remake themselves through violence.[16] It follows, then, that World War I revitalized interest in Civil War military heroism, while 1920s isolationism sent the Civil War into eclipse. The New Deal again excited interest in Civil War military heroism. Northern historians came to Vicksburg determined to revive the Lost Cause and antebellum romanticism. At every step, American nationalism—more than white southern sectionalism—revived aracial memories of the Civil War, putting reconciliation ahead of racial justice. For every major war or national crisis between the Civil War and World War II, northerners and the national government mobilized memories of Confederate heroism. Civil War gallantry consistently served American militarism, imperialism, and nationalism.

White America imbibed white southerners' racial views and the Lost Cause ideology and committed itself to remembering Civil War valor over emancipation. In Vicksburg, the national government pragmatically absorbed white southerners' racial values as it constructed Vicksburg's landscape and memory. The national park became Vicksburg's hallmark, the defining element in its Civil War consciousness. But while the national government achieved dominance in part by embracing white southerners' racism, it nonetheless crafted a resource available for another, less benighted generation. It did not mean to do so, but that is the very essence of memory: the creators of the iconographic record cannot control the use that future generations will make of their work.[17] Even in repose, this national power would be available when the nation stirred itself to protect civil rights. The study of memory teaches us what political history missed: the North did not, after all, "retreat" from the South after the Civil War.

Notes

1. James McPherson, *Hallowed Ground: A Walk at Gettysburg* (New York: Crown, 2003), 15. Amy Kinsel writes, "The name [Gettysburg] is as rich with meaning for most Americans as any word in the United States historical vocabulary." Kinsel, "'From These Honored Dead': Gettysburg in American Culture, 1863–1938" (Ph.D. diss., Cornell University, 1992), 1.

2. One author who looks at both Vicksburg and Gettysburg writes that "Vicksburg was the key. No matter how much success [Lincoln's] armies in the east might have . . . the Confederates could not be defeated as long as the South held Vicksburg." Duane Schultz, *The Most Glorious Fourth: Vicksburg and Gettysburg, July 4, 1863* (New York: Norton, 2002), 6. See also Benjamin Tarber Dixon, "Gettysburg: A Living Battlefield"

(Ph.D. diss., University of Oklahoma, 2000), 8; Michael B. Ballard, *Vicksburg: The Campaign That Opened the Mississippi* (Chapel Hill: University of North Carolina Press, 2004); Shelby Foote, *The Beleaguered City: The Vicksburg Campaign, December 1862–July, 1863* (New York: Modern Library, 1995); James R. Arnold, *Grant Wins the War: Decision at Vicksburg* (New York: John Wiley & Sons, 1997); Richard Wheeler, *The Siege of Vicksburg* (New York: Crowell, 1978); Earl Schenck Miers, *The Web of Victory: Grant at Vicksburg* (New York: Knopf, 1955); A. A. Hoehing, *Vicksburg: 47 Days of Siege* (Englewood Cliffs, N.J.: Prentice Hall, 1969); Samuel Carter, *The Final Fortress: The Campaign for Vicksburg, 1862–1863* (New York: St. Martin's, 1980); Warren E. Grabau, *Ninety-Eight Days: A Geographer's View of the Vicksburg Campaign* (Knoxville: University of Tennessee Press, 2000); Edwin Cole Bearss, *The Vicksburg Campaign*, 3 vols. (Dayton, Ohio: Morningside, 1986); Terrence J. Winschel, *Vicksburg: Fall of the Confederate Gibraltar* (Abilene, Tex.: McWhitney Foundation Press, 1999); David G. Martin, *The Vicksburg Campaign: April 1862–July 1863* (Conshohocken, Pa.: Combined, 1994).

3. Michael Shaara, *The Killer Angels: A Novel* (New York: McKay, 1974); *Gettysburg*, directed by Ronald F. Maxwell (Turner Pictures, 1993); Newt Gingrich and William Forstchen, *Gettysburg: A Novel of the Civil War* (New York: Thomas Dunne, 2003).

4. David Goldfield, *Still Fighting the Civil War: The American South and Southern History* (Baton Rouge: Louisiana State University Press, 2002), 2–4; David W. Blight, *Race and Reunion: The Civil War in American Memory* (Cambridge, Mass.: Harvard University Press, 2001), 1–2.

5. Nina Silber, *The Romance of Reunion* (Chapel Hill: University of North Carolina Press, 1993), 2–5.

6. Kirk Savage, *Standing Soldiers, Kneeling Slaves: Race, War, and Monument in Nineteenth-Century America* (Princeton, N.J.: Princeton University Press, 1997), 18–19.

7. Blight, *Race and Reunion*, 9.

8. Edward Tabor Linenthal, *Sacred Ground: Americans and Their Battlefields* (Urbana: University of Illinois Press, 1991), 6n6 (quotation); Sarah J. Purcell, *Sealed with Blood: War, Sacrifice, and Memory in Revolutionary America* (Philadelphia: University of Pennsylvania Press, 2002); Sanford Levinson, *Written in Stone: Public Monuments in Changing Societies* (Durham, N.C.: Duke University Press, 1998), 77–90; John Bodnar,

Remaking America: Public Memory, Commemoration, and Patriotism in the Twentieth Century (Princeton, N.J.: Princeton University Press, 1992), 3–20; Jay Winter and Emmanuel Sivan, eds., *War and Remembrance in the Twentieth Century* (Cambridge, U.K.: Cambridge University Press, 1999), 6–39.

    9. Silber, *The Romance of Reunion*, 3.

    10. Eric Foner, *Reconstruction: America's Unfinished Revolution, 1863–1877* (New York: Harper & Row, 1988); William Gillette, *Retreat from Reconstruction, 1869–1879* (Baton Rouge: Louisiana State University Press, 1979).

    11. Samuel H. Glasgow to Emma, August 24, 1862, Samuel H. Glasgow Papers, State Historical Society of Iowa, Des Moines.

    12. Gaines M. Foster, *Ghosts of the Confederacy: Defeat, the Lost Cause, and the Emergence of the New South, 1865 to 1913* (New York: Oxford University Press, 1987), 11–75; Jane Turner Censer, "Reimagining the North-South Reunion: Southern Women Novelists and the Intersectional Romance, 1876–1900," *Southern Cultures* 5 (1999): 64–91.

    13. On this point, see Reynolds Scott-Childress, "Cultural Reconstruction: Nation, Race, and the Invention of the American Magazine, 1830–1915" (Ph.D. diss., University of Maryland, 2004). For the North's success in imposing meaning on the Gettysburg battlefield, see Dixon, "Gettysburg."

    14. Simon Schama, *Landscape and Memory* (New York: Knopf, 1995), 61–211.

    15. Gettysburg and the East, of course, get most of the attention. See Jim Weeks, *Gettysburg: Memory, Market, and an American Shrine* (Princeton, N.J.: Princeton University Press, 2003); George R. Stewart, *Pickett's Charge: A Microhistory of the Final Attack at Gettysburg, July 3, 1863* (New York: Houghton Mifflin, 1959), 281–91; Earl J. Hess, *Pickett's Charge—The Last Attack at Gettysburg* (Chapel Hill: University of North Carolina Press, 2001), 385–403; Kinsel, "'From These Honored Dead'"; Carol Reardon, *Pickett's Charge in History and Memory* (Chapel Hill: University of North Carolina Press, 1997); Stephen Cushman, *Bloody Promenade: Reflections on a Civil War Battle* (Charlottesville: University Press of Virginia, 1999); Dixon, "Gettysburg." For a western battlefield, see Timothy Smith, *The Great Battlefield of Shiloh: History, Memory, and*

the Establishment of a Civil War National Military Park (Knoxville: University of Tennessee Press, 2004).

16. Jackson Lears, *No Place of Grace: Antimodernism and the Transformation of American Culture, 1880–1920* (New York: Pantheon, 1981), 117–39; Louis Menand, *The Metaphysical Club* (New York: Farrar, Straus & Giroux, 2001), 351–75.

17. Maurice Halbwachs, *On Collective Memory*, ed. Lewis A. Coser (Chicago: University of Chicago Press, 1992), 46–51.

PROLOGUE

O
N January 26, 1861, when artillery boomed over Vicksburg, most people reacted with studied indifference. It was the minority white population who cheered and celebrated their state's secession as they did again the next day with fireworks, talking excitedly about the hated Abraham Lincoln, secession, and war. By April, companies of armed whites marched about the public squares, drilling for battle.

As whites chattered about war, their servants continued to work the cotton, produce the food their masters ate, drive the wagons, clear the tables, and wash dishes. With little or no supervision, carpenters worked in the homes of whites as news of the coming war circulated. Hacks driven by unsupervised slaves carried passengers from one destination to the next. They had done so for a generation, but now as they clattered over the streets of Vicksburg, their drivers heard news of secession, Lincoln's call for volunteers to subdue the South, and the attack on Fort Sumter.[1]

On Sundays, carriages and buggies converged at churches all over Warren County. As the whites worshiped, their drivers congregated outside, talking in low tones, exchanging the news they had overheard the previous week while casting quick, hard glances at the church's doors and windows. They speculated about this man Abraham Lincoln and his chances for success at defeating the white South. "We were slaves and did not know much about the causes of the war," one man remembered later. "We thought it was because Mr. Lincoln was elected president—which the South did not want—but the colored people all wanted it."[2] A woman named Matilda Anderson remembered that "all the colored people, myself included, wanted the Union cause to win, because in that event we all would be free."[3] Hack driver Henry Banks "knew the Yankees would whip" the South as they represented the stronger side. Another slave remembered, "We all felt happy whenever the Yankees got a victory and talked about it among ourselves." The drivers also wondered if old Abe might wipe out slave-owning whites and if blacks might get a chance to help fight for their own freedom.[4]

The slaves speculated among themselves about the meaning of freedom, imagining life without slavery. Vicksburg slaves already enjoyed considerable freedom compared to those laboring in the rural cotton fields outside town. Inside the city, a few slaves even operated their own businesses. Urban slaves knew where to go when they wanted a drink and might even buy a gun.[5] Some—perhaps most—knew where to go for a forged pass: a white man named Red Jack. He had sold so many phony passes for a dollar and a half each that slave owners noticed an uptick in the number of runaways. Red Jack's identity, though, had been a closely guarded secret in Vicksburg's slave community until 1859, when authorities persuaded a captured runaway to identify him. Tried and convicted, Red Jack went to prison for twenty years in 1860.[6] But as the war raged and freedom talk grew, the slaves whispered among themselves that they might not need forged passes soon: "We could go where, when, and how we pleased, and our children would no longer be sold and that negro trading would be played out," Henry Banks told his fellows. "I was a slave and had no vote," he explained after the war. Nonetheless, "I was for the Union cause all the time."[7]

For the most part, Vicksburg's slaves kept their conversations secret from whites. When laborer Joseph McFields, the property of William Beatty, said within earshot of Charley Bradford that he would "eat with the Yankees yet," the white man whipped him. More often, the slaves talked about the war "on the sly," that is, secretly, "among ourselves." They talked "in the presence of other colored people—but not in the presence of white people—we did not dare do that." Another slave recalled that "it wouldn't do" to talk in favor of the Yankees within hearing of whites.[8] Whites organized vigilante companies shortly after secession to find and punish the disloyal, including slaves. But with their long access to Vicksburg's underground economy, clandestine places where goods could be bought and sold and information exchanged, Vicksburg slaves had learned how to elude whites years before. The new vigilantes did no better than their prewar predecessors at putting dissident slaves under the lash.[9]

The extent to which this freedom talk penetrated the entire Warren County slave population is impossible to document. Several of the slaves claimed that "all" their fellows privately cheered the North.[10] But Joseph McFields warned that "there were some colored people who did not."[11] Twelve thousand slaves worked as field hands on Warren County plantations outside Vicksburg and may not have had access to the information available to slaves working in town. Perhaps more important, each slave had to calculate the North's chances for success. McFields supported the Union because Henry Banks convinced him that he "knew" the Yankees would whip the South. Those more impressed with the South's chances sided with northerners only cautiously, even when speaking to other slaves.[12]

Probably few Vicksburg slaves, and perhaps few in the outlying precincts as well, failed to understand just exactly

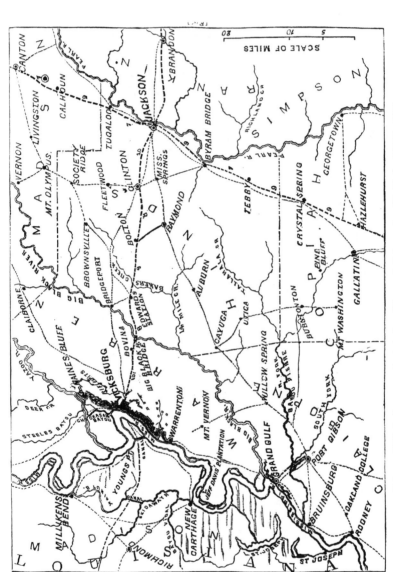

Map of Vicksburg and vicinity. *Harper's Magazine* 27 (July 1863): 272.

what was at stake as the war commenced. For the white population and the attacking Union forces, the meaning of the war would remain in doubt for many decades.

Notes

1. Dora Miller, "War Diary of a Union Woman in the South," ed. G. W. Cable, typescript, Old Court House Museum, Vicksburg, Mississippi; *Vicksburg Daily Evening Citizen*, May 13, 1861.

2. Albert Webster deposition, June 24, 1873, Henry Banks claim 14443, box 207, entry 732, Records of the Accounting Officers of the Department of the Treasury RG 217, National Archives, Washington, D.C.

3. Matilda Anderson deposition, May 20, 1873, Matilda Anderson claim 6935, box 207, entry 732, Records of the Accounting Officers of the Department of the Treasury RG 217, National Archives, Washington, D.C.

4. Joseph McFields deposition, June 24, 1873, and Albert Webster deposition, June 24, 1873, Henry Banks claim 14443, box 207, entry 732, Records of the Accounting Officers of the Department of the Treasury RG 217, National Archives, Washington, D.C.; *Vicksburg Evening Citizen*, May 27, 1861.

5. *State v. Rebecca McCade*, indictment, November 1850; *State v. Catherine Hill*, indictment, April 18, 1849; *State v. Ellen Grandman*, indictment, April 11, 1849; and Patrick Lynch, indictment, June 9, 1852, Warren County Circuit Court Papers, Old Court House Museum, Vicksburg; *Christian Fleckenstein v. State*, bill of exceptions, filed December 11, 1852, case 8810, High Court of Errors and Appeals, Mississippi Department of Archives and History, Jackson.

6. *Vicksburg Weekly Citizen*, October 31, 1859.

7. Henry Banks deposition, June 24, 1873, Henry Banks claim 14443.

8. Joseph McFields deposition, June 24, 1873, Henry Banks claim 14443; Albert Deval deposition, November 1871, Albert Deval claim 6954, box 208, entry 732; and William Green deposition, Dick Green claim 6963, box 210, RG 217, Records of the Accounting Officers of the Department of the Treasury, National Archives, Washington, D.C.

9. *Vicksburg Daily Evening Citizen*, January 3 and 22, 1861.

10. Matilda Anderson deposition, May 20, 1873, Matilda Anderson claim 6935; Albert Webster deposition, June 24, 1873, Henry Banks claim 14443.

11. Joseph McFields deposition, June 24, 1873, Henry Banks claim 14443.

12. McFields deposition, June 24, 1873, Henry Banks claim 14443. Vicksburg's slave population in 1860 was 1,402. The slave population for all of Warren County, including Vicksburg, was 13,763. See Joseph C. G. Kennedy, comp., *Population of the United States in 1860: Compiled from the Original Returns of the Eighth Census* (Washington, D.C.: U.S. Government Printing Office, 1864), 265, 269, 271.

CHAPTER 1

War

The actual Soldier of 1862–'65, North and South, with all
his ways, his incredible dauntlessness, habits, practices,
tastes, language, his appetite, rankness, his superb strength
and animality, lawless gait, and a hundred unnamed lights
and shades of camp—I say, will never be written—perhaps
must not and should not be.

—Walt Whitman[1]

SCHOLARS rarely work from tape recordings or exact
transcripts of past events. Instead, they weave their narratives from recollections of various sorts—letters written
home, diaries, and memoirs. The shards from our past can
be darkly depressing, documenting the depravity of the human
soul, but they can also reveal humankind at its most magnani-
mous and generous. History emerges from this conflict. One reason war so powerfully attracts writers and readers is because it
tests noble sentiments against human nature at its most ignoble
and depraved. War stories soar from stirring rhetoric and plunge
into the abyss of savage depravity.

In the Civil War especially, we seek angelic qualities in our
killers. In 1861, both the North and the South sent bigots and
racists off to war under cover of patriotic sentiment, men just as
prejudiced as the societies they represented. More than 600,000
perished. Did the survivors come back better, morally purer? Did

northerners travel into their heart of darkness to be if not cleansed of their racism by the blood of their fellows then at least enlightened by the slavery they encountered?

The evidence to answer these haunting questions is all too readily available in soldiers' diaries and letters that fill the shelves of libraries and archives across the American midsection. Those diaries and letters allow a search for signs of enlightenment, evidence that war challenged old prejudices. Unfortunately, these manuscripts yield no easy answers. They document all the conflicts, disagreements, confusions, propaganda, dissembling, forgetting, and remembering characteristic of human memory. And they show us that during the Vicksburg campaign, the North's war with the South evolved into a vast conversation about racism, equal rights, slavery, and emancipation.

On April 15, 1861, the day after Fort Sumter surrendered, Lincoln called for 75,000 state troops to overthrow the Confederacy. Across the Midwest, regiments formed. A young Illinois lawyer named James P. Boyd saw the "immense military preparations" in St. Louis and felt "an intense anxiety to participate" even though doing so threatened his budding legal career and risked turning his six children into orphans. "My country calls loud and distinct," Boyd wrote, even as he pondered his family obligations.[2]

Understanding how young men like Boyd could hear the call of his country so loudly has long challenged and fascinated historians.[3] In the midst of the great Union siege of Vicksburg, Rowland Chambers, a dentist trapped in the city, encountered a captured Union soldier. From the perspective of the modern historian, Chambers posed exactly the right question. The Yankee defiantly answered that "he is fighting for the constitution and would rather die than live with ceches [secessionists]."[4] But, really, that constitutes no answer at all. What exactly was the "constitution" that this man imagined himself defending? It had no Thirteenth, Fourteenth, or Fifteenth Amendment. Federally protected equal rights could hardly be imagined. The captured soldier gave no hint of any hostility toward slavery.

Understanding how midwestern soldiers perceived their Constitution requires first realizing that while joining the army separated Boyd and other recruits from their families, they did not abandon their communities or neighborhoods. As young men assembled, they took neighborhood understandings of justice and law with them. In 1861 and 1862, the regiments that organized to march south saw themselves as extensions of their towns, villages, and hamlets. Village leaders organized the regiments. Local women made the uniforms. The young men in those uniforms understood government on local terms. They (or their fathers) served on juries and filled the ranks of posses and vigilante groups. In their world, community made and enforced neighborhood understandings of law.[5]

Yet had these soldiers been thoroughly parochial, they would have let the South go. Boyd thought slavery only a pretext for war, a device to arouse the masses. The real question, Boyd wrote in his diary, asked, "Do we have a Gov with real sinews or only a rope of sand?"[6] These soldiers put in motion a grassroots political constitutionalism. As he prepared to join the army, Boyd remembered Andrew Jackson's refusal to tolerate South Carolina's nullification. Jacksonian democracy had taken root in Illinois, cementing local allegiances to something national, the Democratic Party. The party connected neighborhoods to the nation, creating a real national network for the first time but, many passionately believed, keeping ultimate sovereignty, the power to decide right and wrong, in local hands, not in distant Washington, D.C. Jacksonian democracy hardly threatened race-based slavery. Under Jackson, whites' racial prejudice flourished. For many, including Boyd, Lincoln's inaugural address, delivered only a month before, captured their thinking exactly. Scrupulously avoiding any denunciation of slavery, Lincoln had characterized secession as "the essence of anarchy" and positioned himself and the Union as a proponent of law and order. Secession angered ordinary northerners; they wanted to punish the South. As early as December 1860, Ohio Senator Benjamin F. Wade articulated this when he called for "making the South a desert." Another Ohioan wanted rebel "scalps." Northern soldiers saw themselves as the instruments of true, grassroots popular sovereignty—real law, local law, white people's law—organized to smite the South's lawless insult to constitutionalism.[7]

Even before they marched from their training camps, Union soldiers were determined to punish the "secesh," as they called all white southerners and their northern sympathizers. In Iowa, companies of volunteers threatened to lynch any disloyal men they encountered. Samuel H. Glasgow wrote home that his crowd "gathered a rope" and put it "round the neck" of one Confederate sympathizer. "We . . . was about to elevate secesh when he began to realize his awful condition and he then came to the conclusion that he was a good Union man." Once in camp, officers ordered secesh arrested for aiding Confederate guerrillas. The soldiers darkly whispered that only the presence of their officers prevented them from lynching the captured men.[8] Feelings of community sovereignty perhaps led the 124th Illinois Volunteers to seize civilian property while still stationed in Camp Butler, Illinois. "Perhaps we will get among the secesh pretty soon," one soldier wrote, thinking that then the looting would be more legitimate.[9] Obviously, such taking of property did not represent any command decision; rank-and-file soldiers simply felt empowered by their unit's communal sovereignty. "Unit cohesion" characterizes successful military companies in any war. It is often said that soldiers generally fight for their comrades more than for patriotic rhetoric or great causes or their flag. In the Civil War, soldiers came from communities convinced well before hostilities even began that their neighborhoods and villages had a sovereign authority to determine right and wrong. Such thinking could mobilize lynchers. In 1861 and 1862, it characterized the thinking of many northern soldiers as they learned to equate secession with criminality.[10]

More than their predecessors in earlier wars, ordinary Civil War soldiers earned the nation's respect and admiration. At the same time, Americans have long seen that conflict as decided by eminent generals, even incorporating this thinking into the titles of books: *Grant Wins the War* and *The Web of Victory: Grant at Vicksburg*.[11] Soldiers elected their officers, seeing themselves and their community as the real moral force for right and against wrong. Regimental officers instructed the soldiers not to take civilians' property, but once in Missouri, many soldiers declared anything they wanted "contraband" and seized it.[12] An Ohio soldier noted that while the officers issued strict orders against foraging, "the boys had been out long enough now to know what they wanted and usually found a way to get it regardless of the order." John A. Griffin justified soldiers' seizure of a farmer's sweet potatoes with news that Congress had passed the first Confiscation Act. Congress passed this very limited law on August 6, 1861, which allowed the taking of Confederate, not personal, property actively in use on behalf of the Confederate war machine. Sweet potatoes hardly qualified. Most soldiers' diaries make no mention of this law; they needed no congressional endorsement for their decision. Griffin wrote about the Confiscation Act several times, either deliberately misconstruing its provisions or honestly misunderstanding them. In any case, he seems to have used the law as a kind of rhetorical cover for what he wanted to do anyway. John G. Given also took note of orders against foraging, describing how his regiment found a vacant house, property of a southern soldier, near camp. The Illinois soldiers knocked the weatherboards off to make floors for their tents. When an officer objected, many of the soldiers returned the lumber. Not Given. "Us four boys," he wrote of his tent mates, "kept ours and so we have got a floor in our tent." He went on, "I say hang all the officers who won't let us steal Rebel property."[13]

One officer who did not want Given to steal secesh property was Ulysses S. Grant. Early in 1861, Grant served under Henry W. Halleck, commander of the Department of Missouri and then commander of the Western Department. Halleck's contemporaries considered him a brilliant military theorist and a proven top-flight administrator, but he hesitated to attack even when Lincoln urged him on. Grant reentered the army in June, first commanding a regiment stationed in Missouri. Afterward, he directed a larger force in Cairo, Illinois. From Cairo, the Tennessee, Cumberland, and Mississippi rivers stretched southward.

From Cairo, Grant used these rivers as avenues for attack. In this, he reflected the larger Union strategy of cracking the Confederacy by opening the great Mississippi River to Union traffic. The Mississippi River and its valley had great psychological as well as practical importance. The river connected the heart of the nation to the greater world and provided a highway for internal traffic. Northerners regarded its capture as central to their cause.[14]

After dispatching five regiments down the Mississippi to attack Confederate troops at Belmont, Grant teamed up with Admiral Andrew H. Foote to attack Fort Henry on the Tennessee River, just inside Tennessee. Foote's ironclad gunboats supported Grant's infantry in an amphibious landing. Most of the Confederates fled to Fort Donelson on the Cumberland River, twelve miles away. At Fort Donelson, the Confederates waged a stubborn if brief resistance. Surrounded and outnumbered, they surrendered February 16, 1862.[15]

A few days after the fall of Fort Donelson, the Confederates evacuated Nashville, Tennessee, and Columbus, Kentucky. The Confederates concentrated their forces at Corinth, Mississippi. On April 6, the Confederates attacked Grant's overconfident forces at Shiloh, catching them off guard and ill prepared. The next day, after a hellish night in a thunderstorm, Grant's reinforced troops counterattacked, taking back the ground lost the day before. In May, the Union army captured Corinth.

As the infantry invaded Mississippi, the navy sailed down the Mississippi River. The Union navy organized rams (gunboats with reinforced prows) and steamed into the Confederate navy at Memphis on June 6. Winning this battle gave the Union navy access to the Mississippi River all the way to Vicksburg. The Union army turned Memphis into a base for launching attacks down the river.[16]

The North also made progress at the other end of the Mississippi River at New Orleans. To mount a defense against the North at Shiloh and Memphis, Confederate commanders had stripped their New Orleans garrison down to its essentials, leaving the city only lightly defended. In April, Admiral David Glasgow Farragut, a veteran of the War of 1812, took advantage of the opportunity, silencing Confederate batteries and occupying the city. Farragut dispatched his gunboats up the Mississippi River toward Vicksburg as gunboats from Memphis came down the river.[17]

In May, Farragut's gunboats opened fire on Vicksburg itself. The city sat atop high bluffs on a great bend of the Mississippi River, and the Confederates had made the most of their topographic advantages, placing heavy artillery along a three-mile stretch of the river. Northern gunboats dueled with these emplacements through June and into July. By the end of July, however, the cannonading slackened. July 25 dawned quietly. Farragut and his fleet had departed. "Some of our people," one Vicksburger wrote, slipped over the river and found 700 Yankee graves. That victory, most expected, would be but the opening act of a long play. Confederate troops continued to march into town, reinforcing city defenses. Soon they would be a part of a battle and siege that, to a large degree at least, would help shape the city's subsequent history as well as the lives of those connected to it by memory and word.[18]

Even as Farragut pulled away from the city, great columns of northern troops also moved toward Vicksburg. A look at three regiments can illustrate what thousands of troops in scores of regiments experienced. The 124th Illinois reached Cairo on October 7. The 116th Illinois followed in November, shipping out for Memphis by steamer a few days later. The 23rd Iowa reached a camp near Alton, Illinois, in January, 1863, going to Memphis in April. The 124th occupied Camp La Grange, Tennessee, stripping local farmers of their crops. When a general discovered and seized a cache of sweet potatoes, John G. Given grumbled that the officer probably took them only for his own use. The general explained that the Confiscation Act did not authorize seizure of property except for use by the government. Given concluded that the general must have been a Democrat and a Rebel sympathizer.[19] The 116th Illinois "fell indiscriminately on hogs, sheep, and cattle," one officer recorded in his diary.[20] Iowa troops had already occupied portions of Mississippi. "You would laugh," one Iowan wrote his wife, "to see the soldiers after the secesh chickens." This soldier explained that "they say that a man cannot be a soldier until he first learns to be a good jayhawker." If that be true, Sam Glasgow wrote, "we have a lot of good soldiers in the 23[rd Iowa]."[21] "From Corinth to Grand Junction [Mississippi]," a medical doctor wrote, "we were truly ruthless invaders." This officer concluded that severe discipline and tough punishments had persuaded soldiers to stop their thefts. But in the 116th Illinois, foraging parties continued gathering stock even though officers arrested foragers and hung them by their thumbs.[22] Officers actually policed this looting inconsistently. George Reed Lee wrote in his diary that on one of his foraging trips, he had been seen by a general, "but [he] said ne'er a word."[23]

In Kentucky, the 124th mutinied, refusing to board a train bound for Tennessee as ordered. The soldiers had been issued old French muskets in their training camps. Now, in preparation for combat, some soldiers saw the ancient guns as an insult to their dignity and, more to the point, their safety. "We were willing to fight," Stephen Beck wrote later, "but we wanted guns that would do execution." According to the regimental chaplain, the soldiers found the guns, which had a tremendous recoil, wildly inaccurate with little range. Beck did not think recoil was the problem; most of the guns could not be made to fire at all, let alone recoil. The men pronounced their weapons worthless, and some of their junior officers agreed. As the regiment's chaplain related later, the soldiers "were determined not to be sacrificed by the wilfulness of those whose judgment was no

better than their own." In the end, the regiment shipped out—
with their unreliable old muskets. Military discipline had prevailed over communal sovereignty. According to their chaplain,
the 124th men remembered their mutiny years later with
pride—"the honest manly protest of thinking men"—but, perhaps improbably, the chaplain thought they also recalled their
submission to discipline with equal pride. Stephen Beck's account of how the mutiny ended sounds more plausible than the
chaplain's story. According to Beck, the protest ended only
when the 124th's commander promised to get serviceable arms
as soon as he could arrange it.[24]

In November, the 124th Illinois headed toward the front, traveling to Bolivar, Tennessee, by rail. From there, they joined other
regiments, forming a great column, marching south. Artillery,
cavalry, and infantry filled the roads for miles. As they passed
through the Tennessee landscape, the soldiers seized the stock
they encountered, in one case herding calves into the ranks, covering them with blankets and coats. One captain found that his
soldiers had butchered a cow and buried the head, hide, and en-
trails. As it turned out, this captain could be cheaply bought. For
a piece of beef, he joined the conspiracy. The men kept their secret so well that their colonel indignantly but mistakenly denied
charges that his soldiers had foraged at all.[25]

By December 1862, some Union troops had gotten within
three miles of Vicksburg. At the end of December, however, the
Confederate cavalry, under Earl Van Dorn, had slashed into the
Union supply depot at Holly Springs. Capturing the town with
only a few shots fired, Van Dorn's cavalry set commissary ware-
houses ablaze and exploded an impressive store of munitions.
The Union army had constructed one of its largest hospitals at
Holly Springs, with beds for 2,000 patients. The hospital went up
in flames too. The Union abundance at Holly Springs led the ill-
equipped southerners into an orgy of looting that their officers
could not control. The cavalrymen piled on plumed hats, blankets, blue overcoats, and extra rations. Finding wads of cash, they

took that as well. There were crates of cigars, and the Confederates smoked them by the thousands.[26]

Caught with no supplies, Grant retreated. One soldier wrote to his wife that he had read an account of Grant's mission into Mississippi saying that the soldiers had been put on half rations. However, the men did not need rations at all, this soldier protested; he and his fellows had been plundering "like beasts," looking for something better than army rations.[27] Nonetheless, unaware of the extent to which his army already knew how to supply itself through foraging, Grant felt he had to retreat. Grant told interviewers after the war that if he had known then that he could subsist his army off the countryside, he would not have pulled out. If these words are taken at face value, Grant and his postwar biographers showed an amazing ignorance of a reality known to every private in the army. Grant said that he watched in amazement as his soldiers proved entirely capable of living off the land. "This taught me a lesson," he wrote later. One of Grant's troopers, David Cornwell, wrote in 1908 that Grant's head must have been "exceedingly thick; he was learning fearfully slow and at a terrible expense to the Government." The soldiers cheered that Grant had finally caught on to their policy of deliberately pillaging the southern landscape. DeWitt Clinton Loudon exulted, "What he is doing now our whole army should have done a year ago." Soldiers generally saw their full-throttle foraging after Holly Springs as revenge. "It is really questionable," one of them drily remembered later, "if the vicinity of Holly Springs had much cause to felicitate itself with the results of the Van Dorn burning, when our protracted stay and foraging were taken into the account."[28]

But the lesson Grant learned after Holly Springs marked a change in policy far less dramatic than Loudon and other soldiers hoped. Unlike the rank and file, Grant saw seizure of civilian property as a temporary expedient in the absence of supplies, not as a tool to punish white southerners. Officers still persisted in arresting and hanging unauthorized foragers by their thumbs.

Clinton B. Fisk complained on March 6 that "we cannot make good soldiers of thieves and robbers." Fisk's complaint contained within it documentation that the foraging had become widespread in spite of continued orders against it from headquarters. Fisk issued new orders against looting, insisting, "I will enforce it if I have to shoot men both in and out of shoulder-straps." In other words, he recognized that even some officers had joined in the looting.[29]

In December, William T. Sherman moved his troops down the Mississippi River on an armada of gunboats and transports. As Union troops celebrated Christmas Eve on their transports, singing and drinking whiskey, the Confederate officers at Vicksburg partied at the city's Balfour mansion. A Confederate telegraph operator named Lee Daniel spent his Christmas eve sixty-five miles above Vicksburg sitting in a cold drizzle on the banks of the Mississippi, watching seven Union gunboats and fifty-nine transports steam by. Daniel telegraphed the news to Philip Fall, a Confederate telegraph operator stationed across the river from Vicksburg. In the early hours of Christmas morning, Fall intruded on the festivities, striding amidst the dancers, "muddy and woe begone" from his trip across the river. "Well, sir, what do you want?" Major General Martin Smith, Confederate commander at Vicksburg, irritably demanded. Fall reported that Union gunboats and transports were on the way. Turning pale, Smith exclaimed, "This ball is at an end, the enemy are coming down the river, all non-combatants must leave the city."[30]

In the night, Sherman's force arrived at the mouth of the Yazoo River above Vicksburg. The next day, Sherman moved his fleet up the Yazoo River. On the twenty-seventh, Sherman marched toward Vicksburg in four pincers, each led by a division commander. All four columns ran into Confederate pickets but pushed them back. In his contemporary report and in his memoirs, Sherman described the terrain as difficult both from "nature and art." The Confederates had well fortified a landscape that naturally favored the defender over the attacker. Chickasaw

Bayou could be passed at only two points, on a levee or across a sandbar, each commanded by Confederate sharpshooters. Sherman planned his major assault for four days after Christmas.[31]

Sherman blamed the failure of this December 29 assault on one of his division commanders, George W. Morgan. On the morning of the attack, Sherman wrote in his memoirs, he had met with Morgan and the other division commanders, pointing out on a map where he wanted Morgan's division to pass the bayou. In Sherman's account, Morgan answered, "General, in ten minutes after you give the signal I'll be on those hills." Sherman wrote that "he [Morgan] was to lead his division in person." According to Sherman, Morgan failed to do that, and his attack miscarried. "I have always felt that it was due to the failure of General G. W. Morgan to obey his orders, or to fulfill his promise made in person." Morgan had not made "lodgment on the bluff, which would have opened the door for our whole force to follow."[32]

Morgan himself remembered things quite differently. In his memoir of the battle, he emphasized the difficulty of the terrain, describing Chickasaw Bayou as "tortuous," a "forest intersected by sloughs, more or less filled with water." Sherman chose the worst possible point for his assault, a "mucky and tangled swamp," an area that "bristled with the enemy's artillery and small-arms." After the war, Morgan corresponded with the Confederate commander and quoted the Confederate general's confirmation of his own assessment. "Had Sherman moved a little faster after landing," General Stephen D. Lee wrote, "or made his attack . . . at any point between the bayou and Vicksburg, he could have gone into the city." Instead, Sherman "attacked at the apex of a triangle while I held the base and parts of the two sides."[33]

Henry C. Bear, a soldier in the 116th Illinois Volunteers, explained to his wife that "the way we war to get at them was to go through this narrow road where their whole fire could be centered, and we had to file through just as if we war going through a gate." The Confederates, Bear continued, had occupied hills

George W. Morgan remembered Chickasaw Bayou as a "forest intersected by sloughs, more or less filled with water," the worst possible place for an assault on Vicksburg, in Robert Underwood Johnson and Clarence Clough Buel, *Battles and Leaders of the Civil War*, 4 vols. (New York: Century, 1884–1887), 3:462.

behind a level field that they filled with rifle pits. They had felled trees to clear their field of fire.[34]

After scouting the proposed battlefield, Morgan "regarded an attack from my left, by way of the narrow road or causeway leading across the bayou as impracticable." Morgan passed his opinion up to Sherman and invited Sherman to come see for himself. When Sherman came, "I called his attention to the very narrow and difficult front; to the bayou in its tortuous course on our left; to the mucky marsh beyond the bayou and bridge, all within easy range of the enemy's guns."[35]

According to Morgan, Sherman took it all in and then exclaimed, "That is the route to take!" pointing at the bluffs. Sherman then wheeled away without another word. Later, Sherman sent his adjutant with instructions to "tell Morgan to give the signal for the assault; that we will lose 5,000 men before we take Vicksburg, and may as well lose them here as anywhere else." Morgan remembered sourly responding that Sherman's "entire army could not carry the enemy's position in my front; that the larger the force sent to the assault, the greater would be the number slaughtered."[36]

Morgan depicted himself as the faithful subordinate, launching a suicidal attack with three brigades, commanded by Frank Blair, John DeCourcy, and John H. Thayer. All fought very well, Morgan wrote. On the left, Blair's men forded a stream, climbed a steep bank, and routed the defending Tennesseans. Their victory proved short lived. Within minutes, the Confederates had repulsed Blair, sending his soldiers reeling back across the swamp. DeCourcy's troops ran into a shattering cross fire. Thayer led with the 4th Iowa. As DeCourcy retreated, the Fourth Iowa advanced, running across abandoned Confederate rifle pits. Realizing tardily that no other unit had gone with the Fourth Iowa, Thayer had to call them back. They retreated, taking fire with every step.[37]

According to Sherman, DeCourcy's brigade crossed the bayou but then took cover behind the bank and "could not be moved."

At the time, Sherman said that "withering fire from the rifle-pits and cross-fire of grape and canister from the batteries" crumpled his attack. Sherman intimated that Morgan reported that the failure had not discouraged his men and that they wanted to try again in half an hour. "But," Sherman drily noted, "the assault was not again attempted." In his report, Sherman said, "I assume all responsibility and attach fault to no one." Nonetheless, in his memoirs, he sharply censured Morgan. Sherman wrote that he had always held Morgan responsible for the ill-fated attack since his division commander had not obeyed orders. Had Morgan acted with "skill and boldness," Sherman declared, he could have taken the high ground, opening the door for the whole force. By Sherman's account, Morgan's failure left the 6th Missouri terribly exposed. That regiment fought its way across the bayou farther down, only to be left trapped under a steep bank when Morgan failed to break through. The defenders held their muskets outside their positions vertically, firing straight down on the trapped attackers. The Missouri soldiers desperately sought shelter by scooping mud with their bare hands. Henry C. Bear of the 116th Illinois wrote that after the 6th Missouri reached the bank, the Confederates poured in heavy fire and "we all fell to our bellies." Bear recalled being within eighty yards of the trapped Missouri soldiers but unable to fire for fear of hitting his own men. "So there we all lay from half past twelve till after dark." It rained the whole time, and the Confederates poured their own "storm of bullets" on the hapless northerners. Sherman could get the Missouri soldiers out only after dark, slipping them across the bayou one at a time.[38]

Sherman gave no credit at all to Stephen D. Lee, commander of Confederate forces at Chickasaw Bayou, for the Confederate victory. In white Mississippi, though, Lee would forever be the hero of Chickasaw Bayou. Tipped off by the two Confederate army telegraph operators, Lee had what military commanders always prize: advance knowledge that Sherman was coming. Lee had been assigned to Vicksburg only the previous November, having served before that as an artillery officer on Robert E. Lee's staff in Virginia. Lieutenant General John C. Pemberton, a Pennsylvanian, had departmental command over Confederate forces at Vicksburg, but Confederate President Jefferson Davis, expecting that the fight for Vicksburg would hinge on artillery, wanted an experienced artillery officer to manage the city's defense. When he arrived in November, Lee won over the civilian population "with his plain, free and easy manner." At Chickasaw Bayou, Lee personally commanded his troops, coolly exposing himself to enemy fire. His artillery fire swept Sherman's first wave from the field, and his infantry mowed down subsequent attackers. At one point, the 26th Louisiana and the 17th Mississippi counterattacked, stunning the cowering Yankees and taking more than 300 prisoners. Lee's reputation was made; his victory at Chickasaw Bayou would be long remembered around Vicksburg. Lee then bolstered his reputation even further. Through the night, in sleet and rain, huddled Confederates looked up to see General Lee alone, carrying a water bucket of whiskey and conveying his congratulations to each individual. Lee also ordered litter bearers onto the battlefield. Though fired on by the Union troops who mistook them for attackers, Lee's soldiers rescued eighty injured federals and treated them in Confederate hospitals.[39] Sherman, meanwhile, if Morgan's account is to be believed, felt so humiliated by defeat that he refused for a time to ask for a truce so that the bodies of his dead and his injured could be recovered. That, the defeated Sherman told Morgan, "would be an admission of defeat."[40]

After the Chickasaw Bayou disaster, in February and March, Grant tried to outflank Vicksburg by digging a canal across the bend in front of the city to redirect the river. However, Grant said in his memoirs that he never had much hope that his soldiers could successfully shift the Mississippi River. He pursued the digging, he wrote, only to maintain morale by keeping his men working and to convince northern public opinion that he was making progress toward Vicksburg. In fact, War Department engineers

Stephen D. Lee: the Confederate hero of Chickasaw Bayou. Robert Underwood Johnson and Clarence Clough Buel, *Battles and Leaders of the Civil War*, 4 vols. (New York: Century, 1884–1887), 3:467.

and even Lincoln himself endorsed the plan as entirely feasible. The 5th Minnesota furnished a large contingent of soldiers for the job, digging mud in knee-deep water. The soldiers would never see their labors accomplish anything: the river showed no signs of diverting down the new channel. Nonetheless, Grant kept his men digging through January and February. On February 18, Grant told Halleck that the work progressed well. On March 1, Grant ordered round-the-clock digging. Steam-powered dredges joined the effort. *Frank Leslie's Illustrated Newspaper* ran drawings of the canal, predicting on March 28 that the largest boats would pass through the canal in two weeks.[41]

Such optimistic reports may have encouraged Grant's determination. In any case, the soldiers paid a high price for it. Malaria and other diseases raged through the ranks; floating hospitals along riverbanks were filled with the sick; and Grant buried the victims of his morale program on the levees that walled the river, the only dry ground available. One Minnesota officer remembered later that the levees became "thickly dotted" with wooden markers for buried soldiers. "Such conditions," he observed, "could not contribute to the hopefulness and cheer of men."[42]

While Union soldiers dug and died across from Vicksburg, General James McPherson's corps tried to clear a channel through Louisiana that would also allow transports to skirt Vicksburg, landing troops south of the city for an attack from below. At the same time, Grant and Rear Admiral David D. Porter also tried to navigate through the shallow swamps north of Vicksburg. Advancing on the Tallahatchie River, federal gunboats dueled with the guns at Fort Pemberton, located between the Tallahatchie and the Yazoo, just outside Greenwood. Porter led an expedition hoping to reach the Yazoo and Fort Pemberton, only to bog down short of his goal, hopelessly entangled in log-infested passages defended by Confederate snipers. Porter ignominiously backed out.[43]

Grant had repeatedly tried to get at Vicksburg and, just as repeatedly, had failed. These failures fueled Lincoln's doubts about

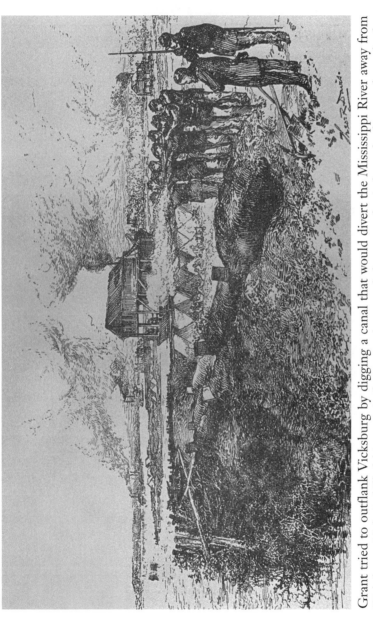

Grant tried to outflank Vicksburg by digging a canal that would divert the Mississippi River away from Vicksburg. Malaria killed his men in large numbers, and they were buried on the levees, the only dry ground available. Robert Underwood Johnson and Clarence Clough Buel, *Battles and Leaders of the Civil War*, 4 vols. (New York: Century, 1884–1887), 3:495.

Grant. On March 12, Secretary of War Edwin M. Stanton named former journalist Charles A. Dana special War Department commissioner to investigate Grant's command. Dana reported back to Stanton in a secret code, doing his own code work, not trusting a clerk with his reports.[44] With his secret code, Dana was prepared to relay his most critical appraisals of Grant to Washington.

On March 22, 1863, as Dana sought transportation south, Grant reviewed his options. Continuous high water and rough terrain made it impossible to assault Vicksburg from the east, he said. The canal project had failed. Admiral Porter and Sherman struggled to get five gunboats to the Yazoo River through Steele's Bayou, but this assault had stalled as well. Grant decided to concentrate his forces and attack Haynes' Bluff, a Confederate artillery emplacement guarding the northern approaches to Vicksburg on the Yazoo River. By the time Dana arrived, Grant had this plan for capturing Vicksburg worked out and ready to implement.[45]

Dana brought something largely absent from Grant's army: determined abolitionism. Confederate commanders routinely referred to Union troops as "the Abolitionists."[46] Charles Dana really merited the moniker; few others qualified, but that was changing. Dana's arrival coincided with a shift that had already begun in the generals' thinking, a move forced on them by Abraham Lincoln's January 1 Emancipation Proclamation. In his proclamation, Lincoln not only freed slaves in seceded and rebellious states but also announced that he would receive the freed slaves into the armed services of the United States "to garrison forts, positions, stations, and other places." On the last day of March, Halleck wrote unofficially to Grant "as a friend." Stop mistreating the slaves and returning them to their owners, he advised. The character of the war had begun to change, and there was no longer any chance of reconciling the sections and returning to the divided house, half slave and half free.[47] Once again, the officers followed their soldiers—some of them, at least.

Months before, Ohio soldier DeWitt Loudon had written home to complain that "slavery is the sacred cat of our butternut brethren." White southerners do not mind seeing northern soldiers die of disease, leaving widows and orphans, "but," he sneered, "let anybody touch a hair of slavery."[48] Another soldier wrote that when the war began, he had been "willing for them to keep slavery where it then was," but no more. Now, he said, he would rather serve out his time than allow slavery in a single state.[49] There were some who did not shift their thinking. A soldier in the 10th Illinois Cavalry wrote home that he approved all acts of the administration—except the Emancipation Proclamation. Julius Allen had "no very great objection to the arming of the blacks . . . if the white and black soldiers are kept distinct and separate." But, he added, "we have plenty of white men to whip the damned rebels." One Iowan was less tolerant, writing that "the idea of arming and equipping Negro regiments for the purpose of making them soldiers is, to my mind, worse than ridiculous nonsense."[50]

In April, General Lorenzo Thomas toured the Union army encampments around Vicksburg, giving speeches on behalf of arming blacks and forming them into regiments. Some officers objected. One soldier wrote home on March 4 that his captain thought that if whites could not fight the war for themselves, they should give up. This soldier had a more practical view: "I think the Nigger might just as well be shot at, and hit, too, as white soldiers."[51] Overcoming such racism was no easy task, and Thomas hardly seemed up to the job. In the opinion of many ordinary soldiers, he made bad speeches. David Cornwell remembered Thomas as so incapable of extemporaneous speech, so tied to his script, that General James McPherson could leave him tongue-tied—"truly pitiful"—simply by anticipating his message when he introduced the older man. Unless the unit commanders backed up Thomas's appeals, the plodding pleas of an abolitionist could hardly be expected to sway rank-and-file skeptics. On April 8, when Thomas spoke to the assembled soldiers of the

124th Illinois, they hissed at the very mention of black soldiers. Then their well-liked division commander, unlike Thomas, a real combat officer, stepped forward. Everyone paused to hear what General John A. Logan, a skilled orator, would say. The general began by confessing that he had once "loved" slavery himself.

Logan had "loved" slavery as an Illinois state legislator and congressman. Elected to the Illinois legislature in 1852, Logan had promptly proposed a new state law preventing immigration of free blacks into the state. This racist measure proved so popular among Logan's constituents that it made his reputation statewide as the leading spokesman for "Egypt," as the southernmost portion of Illinois called itself. Logan became Stephen A. Douglas's lieutenant, accompanying him to the Lincoln–Douglas debates. As a Douglasite, Logan vigorously favored the fugitive slave law and its enforcement. In one memorable speech, he called the hunting down of escaped slaves "dirty work" but pronounced himself and his fellow Democrats ready to do it. The Confederate bombardment of Fort Sumter left the voluble Logan uncharacteristically silent. Months slid by, and still he said nothing. Illinois boiled with rumors that Egypt might secede, joining the Confederacy. Secessionists organized military companies, and some said Logan would lead them. Logan finally announced his position on secession in the most dramatic fashion possible. Colonel Ulysses S. Grant, fearing that his regiment might go home rather than reenlist, had called on John McClernand to make a patriotic appeal. When McClernand showed up at Grant's camp, he had brought Logan along. Knowing Logan's reputation for sympathizing with the South and slavery and his silence on Sumter and secession, Logan's presence made Grant uneasy. Grant greeted Logan warily. To Grant's enormous relief, when Logan spoke, he appealed so vigorously to the soldiers' manhood and patriotism that hardly a soldier left the colors.[52] Logan had chosen his side.

Once he decided to side with the Union, Logan had stumped his state, recruiting Illinoisans to fight the Confederacy. Logan had formidable political skills; it was said he knew most voters in his district by their first names. His efforts seemed to make a difference. Southern Illinois, once doubtful in its support for the war effort, sent more soldiers to the army than any other part of the state. Logan had personally recruited many of the soldiers who sat waiting for him to talk about slavery, about the black people he once sought to bar from his state. In his booming voice, Logan told them that the war had opened his eyes. "Slavery had struck at the life of the Republic, and there remained no alternative but to strike slavery." Logan declared that "we must hurt the rebels in every way possible," a sentiment even the most prejudiced soldiers would not dispute. Logan knew how to lead, how to articulate his soldiers' inchoate thoughts with his own words. Rather than pleading, he told the soldiers what they should think, something he could do because he had faced battle at their side. You are "willing even a colored man should shield you from rebel bullets," he announced. Logan told the soldiers they would unite behind the new policy, "putting the one who is the innocent cause of this war, who has everything to gain or lose . . . in the first rank." After that speech, the 124th's chaplain said he heard little further complaint about Negro troops.[53]

Union commanders did not plan to put black men in command of the new regiments. In a move intended at least partly to win over reluctant white soldiers, the white officers in charge of the new units would come from the enlisted ranks of white regiments. Assembling black regiments allowed white enlisted men a chance for promotion they would not have had in the white army. "This was my opportunity for a hundred and ten per month, instead of thirteen," David Cornwell wrote about his transfer from his Illinois unit into the 9th Louisiana Volunteers (African Descent). "Loathe" to leave his Illinois comrades, Cornwell saw "no hope of advancement" if he did not make the move. Cornwell could never learn not to disparage African Americans as "coons" or "darkeys," a habit he continued for the rest of his life. Others made the shift for more altruistic reasons than Cornwell. Some white soldiers volunteered to lead black units out of missionary zeal for abolitionism or a more general patriotic devotion to the war effort.[54]

Whites desiring positions in black regiments had to pass an oral exam administered by a board of examiners. Boards asked candidates about army regulations, history, geography, and mathematics. Some 60 percent passed. Proponents thought the process produced superior officers, better than could be found in white regiments. But this was not always the case. Frederick Roziene had been a sergeant in the 72nd Illinois Infantry when that regiment organized in Chicago early in the war. He suffered from diarrhea and fevers so severely that by June 1863 he was no longer fit for active field service in the judgment of army doctors. The army made him a hospital clerk, and his doctor told him he would never recover. Long separation from the 72nd weakened whatever bonds Roziene had originally forged with his white comrades. Yet in 1864, Sergeant Roziene, too sick to fight with white troops, became a commissioned officer in the 49th U.S. Colored Infantry.[55]

At the same time Lorenzo Thomas toured Union camps around Vicksburg, Grant gave up his plan to attack Haynes' Bluff. Such an attack would result in a an "immense sacrifice of life," Grant finally realized. Grant's last hope of making a conventional attack on Vicksburg had disappeared. He now had to do something more creative. Within a few days Grant had decided on a new plan. The navy would run past the Vicksburg batteries, placing gunboats and transport craft below the city. The army would march by Vicksburg on the west side of the river. Once below the city, the transports would ferry the soldiers across the river so they could attack Vicksburg from the south and east. Grant's plan represented a dangerous gamble. The navy told him that once below Vicksburg, they could not turn back, as going against the current would slow their boats down too much to pass Confederate gunners safely. Disconcertingly, while Confederate deserters reported the Vicksburg garrison well supplied, with plentiful food, Grant's plan ran the risk of cutting his own supply line. Grant's friend and confidant William T. Sherman advised against the plan and years later, in his memoirs, still insisted that an overland attack through northern Mississippi would have more efficiently defeated the Confederates at Vicksburg.[56]

In April, Dana found Grant's immense army at Milliken's Bend. Dana later described the scene as he passed down the Mississippi as "most imposing." Grant's army sprawled across the riverbanks and onto the plantations, white tents mingling with roses, oaks, magnolias, and plantation mansions.[57]

Grant and his officers openly and freely confided in Dana, explaining their new plan to skirt Vicksburg and attack it from below. The abolitionist and idealist could have sunk the pragmatic Grant's career with his encoded reports back to Washington. Instead, he defended not only Grant but all his trusted subordinate officers as well. Dana thought Sherman a genius. McPherson had a "fine natural ability . . . a man without any pretensions." Dana found Porter "active, courageous, fresh-minded."[58] As Grant, Sherman, McPherson, and Porter drew Dana into their circle, the envoy, sent to spy on Grant, soon began to share Grant's officers' doubts about the one corps commander Washington did trust, Major General John A. McClernand, an Illinois politician. Under Grant's plan, it would be McClernand who would take charge of the march down the Louisiana side of the Mississippi River. Dana heard Sherman and Porter plead with Grant not to entrust this critical responsibility to McClernand. Grant answered that McClernand, as senior corps commander and "an especial favorite of the President," could and should do the job. By now, Dana had so allied himself with Grant's officers that he too implored Grant not to trust McClernand and conveyed his doubts about McClernand back to Stanton. McClernand, Dana decided, was "merely a smart man," lacking the steady judgment that marked a truly effective general.[59]

On the night of April 16, Porter's fleet made preparations to run past the Vicksburg guns. Sailors piled cotton bales, hay, and sandbags around the vulnerable points on their gunboats and transports. Shortly before midnight, the vessels began to quietly slip downstream. Admiral Porter on the *Benton* thought his boats looked like phantoms as they drifted silently down the river. Maybe, but they were not invisible. In the dark quiet, an alert Confederate sentry spotted the fleet. Confederates set fire to abandoned buildings and stacks of tar barrels so the fires would illuminate the fleet. Vicksburg's artillery—twenty smoothbores and seventeen rifled cannon commanded by Colonel Edward Higgins—opened fire on the brightly lit targets.[60]

Porter planned to hug the Louisiana shore until spotted and then steer for the Mississippi side, hoping the Confederate gunners would have trouble shooting down on targets so close. With barges lashed to either side, the gunboats lumbered across the river with difficulty, but they got very close to the eastern shore. Porter's *Benton* passed within forty yards of the city, its guns firing point blank into downtown buildings.[61]

Thundering Confederate cannon fire blasted the *Mound City*, the *Pittsburg*, and the *Louisville*. The *Henry Clay* caught fire, and its crew abandoned the ship. The *Tuscumbia* ran aground, backing off, only to collide with a transport. The *Tuscumbia* took a hit below the waterline but stayed afloat through furious pumping. Confederates disabled the *Forrest Queen*, and it drifted away, taking water but still afloat. Once Porter's boats had passed downstream of Vicksburg, both sides realized an awesome truth: Vicksburg's big guns had failed to stop Porter's flotilla. Grant had his transports south of the city, ready to move his troops across the river. Northern sailors and soldiers cheered. Inside Vicksburg, Confederate gunners expressed dismay that their artillery had accomplished so little.[62]

While the navy had a hair-raising run past the Vicksburg river batteries, the infantry passed quietly through its own valley of the shadow. The army marched across Louisiana, penetrating enemy territory on a single road. Major Isaac Harrison commanded Louisiana troops at Richmond, the town halfway between the

The Union navy running past Vicksburg's guns. Admiral Porter's *Benton* leads the way. Robert Underwood Johnson and Clarence Clough Buel, *Battles and Leaders of the Civil War*, 4 vols. (New York: Century, 1884–1887), 3:496.

Union base at Milliken's Bend and New Carthage on the river. Harrison's small cavalry unit retreated in front of the advancing Yankees, trying to understand what the advance meant. Harrison reported the advance to General John Bowen, commander of Confederate forces at Grand Gulf, Mississippi. Harrison thought the Union troops might be on a foraging mission or a raid. If so, Bowen had little to worry about. But Harrison worried about a "foraging party" so far from home. Bowen kept his superior, Pemberton, informed. By April 6, the Union had occupied New Carthage, and Bowen finally realized what was happening, but he could not convince Pemberton that the occupation threatened Vicksburg.[63]

Grant's corps commanders based their troops in three Louisiana towns above Vicksburg. McPherson occupied Lake Providence, farthest from Vicksburg. Milliken's Bend hosted John McClernand's XIII Corps. Sherman's XV Corps took over Young's Point, closest to Vicksburg. Grant had ordered McClernand's Corps to march through Louisiana to New Carthage first. Grant instructed McClernand to land his troops at the Mississippi town of Bruinsburg, south of any territory occupied by Confederate troops protecting Vicksburg.[64]

On May 1, the invading Union army engaged and defeated the Confederates at Port Gibson. At 4:00 A.M. on May 3, Porter could hear the Confederates detonating their powder magazines at Grand Gulf. Porter fired up the *Benton* and headed up the river, finding the town abandoned by the Confederacy but not yet occupied by Union troops. The fall of Grand Gulf made re-supply much easier. Grant still had to ship supplies down to Milliken's Bend, then through Louisiana, and then across the Mississippi River again, but now he had a good place for a supply depot on the Mississippi side.[65] Although Grant had not outrun his supply lines, he had stretched them considerably and decided to make the country supply required forage. He still tried to keep his troops under control, telling Stephen A. Hurlbut, commander of the XVI Corps (still in Memphis), to keep his cavalry out of people's houses. Grant did want his soldiers to destroy crops, take stock, and disable agricultural implements. "In other words," he said, "cripple the rebellion in every way, without insulting women and children or taking their clothing, jewelry, &c." Grant explained to Sherman that it would be impossible to supply his army without constructing additional roads. The army would provide bread, coffee, and salt "and make the country furnish the balance."[66] For their part, captured Confederates seemed well fed and clothed. They had blankets and guns.[67]

On May 12, Grant's soldiers captured Raymond and then turned east toward Jackson and away from Vicksburg. Union army troops so thoroughly destroyed the state capital, burning and razing the buildings, that the town site looked like an orchard of chimneys. People began calling it "Chimneyville." Union troops broke into the state penitentiary, freeing the prisoners, including John McGuiggan, also known as "Red Jack," serving his twenty-year sentence for selling forged passes to Vicksburg slaves. Unexpectedly out of prison, he took to the countryside, eventually making his way back to Vicksburg, where he would work for the Union army as a civilian employee.

Sherman still scrambled to control his rampaging troops, complaining that he had heard that his provost marshals had been allowing the troops to loot merchants. "This, if true, is wrong," Sherman fumed, adding that "the private rights of citizens should be respected."[68] Yet everyone below the rank of corps commander seemed to know what was happening. Even Grant's twelve-year-old son preferred eating with the troops. His father's army rations tasted awful, young Fred Grant said later, while the rank and file set an infinitely better table, thanks to their foraging.[69] Half a century later, when aging Union army veterans returned to Vicksburg for a reunion, a northern governor still joshed the town folk. Better lock up your chickens, he advised them.[70]

Grant's army turned west and began advancing toward Vicksburg. Sherman's corps stayed to the rear, McPherson took the center, and McClernand placed his corps on the left. The Confederates made a stand at Champion's Hill on May 16, but by the end of that day the Confederates again retreated, beaten. They tried again to resist Grant's advance at the Big Black River. Once again, Union troops sent them flying, this time into the city of Vicksburg itself. Civilians turned out to watch the disheartened army retreat into town; the soldiers looked beaten and demoralized. Women called out to the troops, asking who would defend them from the Yankees.[71]

Grant's victorious army swept toward Vicksburg, feeling unbeatable. "We expected to make short work of Vicksburg," one soldier remembered later.[72] On May 19, when Grant ordered a frontal assault on the city's defenses, it hardly seemed necessary to do much coordination or advance planning against such an obviously defeated enemy.

Years later, a member of the 113th Illinois would remember that the day started as a beautiful, cool morning. Then the troops flung themselves against Vicksburg's perimeter. John Jackson Kellogg recalled the "leaden hail from the enemy" as "absolutely blinding." So many bullets hit the earth around him that Kellogg could see the sticks and chips on the ground dancing at his feet. Henry C. Bear of the 116th Illinois, veteran of the Chickasaw Bayou disaster, remembered running across 500 yards of open field against bullets "flying thick as hail." Even so, "Some of the boys went clear to the brest works but could not get over." The sight of his friends struggling and failing to get over the Confederate line haunted Bear: "It was awful. I don't want to see another such a time." Vicksburg's defenders bloodily repulsed the attacking northerners. Bear himself went down, shot in the side. Kellogg remembered watching the "slender blue line" advance and then retreat, "leaving the field thickly strewn with the blue sheaves Old Death had gathered so quickly." Sherman wrote that his troops fought their way to the top of the Confederate parapet but could not cross it.[73]

On May 22, Grant made a second attempt, planning the assault with more care than he had on May 19. An awesome can-

nonade opened the battle. One Confederate thought Union artillery set the air "ablaze with burning and bursting shells, dart-
ing like fiery serpents." The earth shook. After the war, another
Confederate waxed eloquent: the artillery resembled "a sublime
orchestra, playing a dreadful chorus of death. Long tongues of
fire flashed from the mouths of 300 cannon[s]." Federal troops
came out of the woods formed in three lines. Vicksburg's defenders waited in silence until the attackers came within rifle range.
Then the Confederates opened up with their rifles and artillery,
tearing bloodily into the advancing soldiers. The Union troops
amazed the Confederates by maintaining formation and not faltering.[74]

Volunteers carried ladders to the Confederate parapets but
could not scale the walls. One contingent, led by the 11th Missouri, charged down the Graveyard Road, one of the main routes
into the city of Vicksburg. From their formidable earthworks
looking down the road, the Confederates commanded the terrain. As the 11th Missouri advanced, one officer remembered
later, Confederate gunfire from the front and flanks "literally
melted down" the attackers. So many died that heaps of bodies
became obstacles for the troops following the first wave. A hand-
ful of soldiers actually made it to the ditch that fronted the fort,
among them the color-bearer who placed his flag on the fort.
They hung there, trapped for a time, until retreating back across
the battlefield, exposed to withering fire the whole time. More
blue-uniformed bodies covered the fields in front of Confederate
positions.[75]

Vicksburg is now so famously associated with the battlefield
park and national cemetery that it seems odd that the North at
first did so little to care for its fallen. Like Sherman at Chickasaw
Bayou, Grant would not ask for a truce to bury the dead. Frustrated by this, on May 24, John Jackson Kellogg and a friend
slipped out onto the battlefield after dark, without orders and
with no truce, to bury fallen comrades. It was a dangerous business: the two soldiers could be shot by pickets from either side.

"We could only bury them by throwing dirt upon their bodies," Kellogg remembered later. After Vicksburg surrendered, Kellogg went to the spot where he had tried to bury his fallen friends. Their feet and heads stuck out of the ground, perhaps exposed by rain and wind. The day after Kellogg made his unauthorized sortie into no-man's-land, the Confederates asked for a truce so that squads from both armies could venture onto the killing grounds and bury their dead. Stephen Beck thought the Confederates asked for the truce because most of the dead lay closer to their lines and the stink affected them more than the Union soldiers. Like Kellogg, these burial details had time only to throw some earth on the fallen men. Kellogg saw soldiers looting the dead, ripping open pockets and taking money, watches, and other valuables. Kellogg himself picked up a photograph he found lying about.[76]

After his setback at Chickasaw Bayou, Sherman castigated a subordinate. Now, following the May 22 attack, Sherman perhaps more justifiably turned on his fellow corps commander, McClernand. When the Confederate defenses bloodily repulsed Sherman's attackers, the general consulted with Grant. As the two officers surveyed the battlefield, a staff officer approached with a dispatch indicating McClernand had captured the Confederate parapet in his sector. He called on Sherman and McPherson to renew their attacks so his men would not be trapped. Sherman and McPherson launched new attacks, only to be beaten again, with further loss of life. In the end, it turned out, McClernand had captured not the Confederate parapet but only one or two minor positions outside the main perimeter. This affair led to McClernand's dismissal after he issued a self-serving message to the press claiming his men had broken through the lines, falling back only because Sherman and McPherson had declined to do their part of the overall plan.[77]

After the two failed assaults, Grant dug in around the city, laying siege. This emboldened Mississippi's black population. The slaves became more openly restless, scarcely concealing their meetings from whites. "Think the meetings ought to be stopped," Elizabeth Ingraham fretted in her diary, but she knew that was not going to happen. "We won't meddle with them, it is certain." One white property owner had already been burned out by his own slaves, Ingraham knew, and she confessed that she feared "the blacks more than I do the Yankees." By the end of May, some of the slaves around Vicksburg went on strike. "The negroes are as idle," Ingraham wrote, "as darkies only can be."[78]

Grant hardly noticed if the slaves worked or did not. He was fully focused on Vicksburg. He regularly rode the lines, reassuring his soldiers that the Confederates had been trapped and would soon surrender. "We have them right where we want them," he said, or, "It is only a question of time, they must surrender soon or starve." Grant and his officers so concentrated their resources on Vicksburg that they left their long-attenuated supply line through Louisiana exposed. On May 7, General Francis Blair had left Milliken's Bend weakly defended, calculating that a few troops, backed by navy gunboats, could guard the supply base.[79]

The commander of Confederate forces threatening Grant from the west was Edmund Kirby Smith. His command included General Richard Taylor, son of President Zachary Taylor and a brother-in-law of Jefferson Davis, and John G. Walker's Texas division. Kirby Smith and Walker understood that Grant's exposed supply depots represented an excellent opportunity to strike a blow against Grant's Vicksburg campaign, but they convinced Taylor only with difficulty. Taylor had commanded Louisiana troops under Robert E. Lee and Thomas "Stonewall" Jackson in Virginia before winning a promotion and a command in Louisiana. Before leaving Virginia, Jefferson Davis and his secretary of war had instructed Taylor to attack and retake New Orleans. At the time Davis hatched this plot, it seemed feasible, as the North had stationed a small and untested force in the Crescent City. After that plan became impracticable, Taylor and his commanding officer, Kirby Smith, focused more on relieving northern pressure on Vicksburg.[80]

Through May, the Confederates struggled to maneuver their forces into position so they could attack Grant's supply line. As they did so, Union officers tried to persuade recently freed slaves to join the army. David Cornwell remembered later that he could not draw his officer's pay until he recruited enough black soldiers to make the unit viable. Until then, he drew his old pay only. As he remembered it later, Cornwell relied on Big Jack Jackson, an African American sergeant with only a half dozen "darkeys to boss over and crazy to get more of them." Cornwell and Jackson went to plantations, lining up the former slaves like so many tenpins. Jack marched them away, even though "the wenches . . . set up a terrible howl." One former slave remembered later that "the Union Infantry . . . came along and took me with them to Greenville, Washington Co. Miss . . . and kept us colored folks about 3 months." When John Gordon said that "I was enlisted," he almost suggests an involuntary enlistment. John Howard, on the other hand, told interviewers that he had been "sold and put to Louisiana" before the war. "I ran away and joined the Yankees at Grand Gulf and enlisted at Milliken's Bend," Howard said, sounding like a genuine volunteer. The recruits varied in age greatly; Cornwell remembered weeding out at least one older than the age of seventy. That still left a wide range; the new soldiers' ages ran from sixteen to forty-five. Though almost all came from Louisiana and Mississippi plantations, they had been born all over the Southeast, a testament to southerners' migrations and the slave trade.[81]

Cornwell took charge of training his new recruits, finding that "they taught about as easily as white men." The first camp commander allowed discipline to go slack, permitting freed women to flock onto the camp grounds. Soon Colonel Herman Lieb took command, "running things with some system." Cornwell set up target practice. When a recruit missed, "I would call him a wooly headed nincompoop, aim his gun correctly . . . and tell him if he did not do it right the next time I would kill him." Cornwell bluffed, "I had no recruits to spare and knew he would learn after a while."[82]

On June 5, the 10th Illinois Cavalry and the 9th Louisiana (African Descent) probed westward, looking for Walker's Texas Division. Two miles from Richmond, Louisiana, the Union soldiers ran into Confederate pickets. Lieb ordered a company of black troops to attack the Confederates. As they did so, the Union officer detected Confederate cavalry skirting a wooded area, planning to attack the Union forces from behind. Lieb ordered his men to move to the rear to meet this new threat. As the blacks moved back, they appeared to be in retreat to the white Illinois soldiers, unaware of the threat to their rear. The white soldiers made disparaging remarks about the apparently retreating "niggers." According to Cornwell, when the black infantry actually attacked the Texans, the Illinois troopers piteously bawled, "Save us, save us, save us." After the fight, the white soldiers "boil[ed] over with gratitude," exclaiming that "they saved our lives." Cornwell no doubt exaggerated, but as a conversion narrative it differs little from other white officers' memories of their time in black units. They had crossed the color line, been ostracized, and felt vindicated when their new commands fought well.[83]

After this skirmish, Taylor ordered Walker to attack the Milliken's Bend depot. In addition to Lieb's 9th Louisiana (285 officers and men), the 1st Mississippi (153), the 13th Louisiana (108), and the 11th Louisiana (680) guarded Milliken's Bend. One Iowa unit of white soldiers provided the only trained veteran troops on the Union side: only a hundred or so officers and men remained in the 23rd Iowa, battered from battles at Champion's Hill and the Big Black.[84] The stage was set for what northern newspapers would describe as a decisive test of the new black troops' courage.[85]

On June 7, at daybreak, some 2,000 Texans attacked Milliken's Bend. One white officer remembered later that the Confederates advanced over the smooth field in front of the Union line "as if on parade." They flanked the defenders, "and they swept our line away with the greatest ease." Confederate gunfire crashed into the bodies of the black soldiers, leaving some permanently disfigured.

A musket ball passed through the palms of Mike Caston's hands; he would never again grasp anything without pain. Gunshot wounds to his left leg and right arm took down John Brown. A rifle ball struck nineteen-year-old Randall Davis in the hip, leaving him limping for the rest of his life. William Marshall, the same age as Davis, caught rifle balls in both legs; poor medical attention left his legs oozing an offensive pus for twenty years. Samuel Morris lost the use of his right arm when a rifle ball shattered a bone. Attackers and defenders battled ferociously, fighting hand to hand with bayonets and the butts of muskets. John Brown, already down from his gunshot wounds, took bayonet thrusts to his head and midsection, leaving his left eye permanently inflamed and watering. A saber thrust into John Howard's left cheek split open his face, knocking out teeth. The Confederates succeeded in outflanking the black defenders, pouring murderous gunfire into their ranks from the sides. Cornwell remembered later that Lieb rode up on his horse, the only mounted officer in the battle, a conspicuous target, and called for a retreat to the river—we can't stand this any longer, he said. Union troops retreated to a second levee. Up to this point, Cornwell emphasized in his memoir, the two Union gunboats had not fired a shot. They sat so low in the water that they could not see over the levee to intervene effectively. With the Union troops pushed back to the water, though, they now fired. Their artillery went over the heads of the attacking Confederates, according to Cornwell, but "gave them a plausible pretext to give up the fight."[86]

Dr. Sylvester Laning remembered later having nothing in the camp to care for the wounded. He loaded the injured onto a small boat and floated them down the Mississippi. As he drifted downstream with his load of wounded, Laning found another injured man in the water and fished him out for treatment too. A gunboat took some of the injured, as did a field hospital farther downstream. Years later, as an old man, Laning told stories about performing 112 operations after the battle. "There was no white man to assist me in my duties except our chaplain," he recalled.[87]

The North had defeated the Confederacy. One question, though, was, Who got the credit: black infantry or the gunboats manned by white sailors? An officer present wrote that the gunboats assisted "but very little; because every rebel who had sense enough to be a soldier must have known they could do *them* no harm, without injuring us more." Postbattle accounts presented varying interpretations. On June 12, the *New York Times* relied on "an unofficial telegram from the Vicinity of Vicksburg" to report that "colored troops" had "decisively" defeated attacking whites. The *Times* explained that at first the blacks had fallen back but, hearing that the Confederates were killing black prisoners, "rallied with great fury and routed the enemy."[88] The *Chicago Tribune* initially reported the story in the same fashion: blacks had retreated, only to be galvanized by Confederate barbarism. Horace Greeley's *New York Tribune*, trusting a report published in the *Richmond Dispatch*, first claimed that the Confederates had captured Milliken's Bend, leaving Grant cut off from his supply line. But two days later, the *Tribune* got on board with the other papers and told the same story of white cruelty and black courage.[89]

Newspaper reports of Confederate cruelty reflected suspicions widespread in northern society. One rumor claimed the Confederate commander vowed to "take the d——d nigger camp or wade in blood to his knees." Many years later, Sears said that the Confederates carried a black flag with a death's head and crossbones.[90] A further account held that five or six Union soldiers, captured at Milliken's Bend, had been hanged. Possibly Confederates did execute Second Lieutenant George L. Conn and Captain Corydon Heath, but when Grant's officers questioned Confederate commanders on this point, the southerners denied any such hangings had ever taken place.[91] On June 9, an Iowa soldier named David West wrote his father that "the Rebs seem to be intent on killing us all." But West added that if the Confederates had persisted in their attack, "we would have had to surrender being over powered." This white eyewitness to the

43

actual fight apparently thought he *could* safely surrender. Confederates captured at least one black soldier at Milliken's Bend who lived to collect his pension. At the same time, the War Department's published *Official Record* of the war includes a report by one Confederate officer with the sentence, "I consider it an unfortunate circumstance that any armed negroes were captured."[92]

While some drew moral strength from alleged Confederate savagery, others used Milliken's Bend to feed doubts about white commitment to black soldiering. James Gordon Bennett's paper, the *New York Herald*, reported that "the negroes . . . fought better than their white officers, many of whom, it is said, skulked." Bennett also credited the gunboats, more than the infantry, with winning the fight. Union troops fought with "energy and desperation," he said, but added that they could only hold the attackers at bay until rescued by the navy.[93]

White officers' flight seemed to prove that the North lacked real commitment to emancipation. These white men had so little confidence in their own soldiers that they ran when the first guns blazed, according to this view. The Confederate commander reported that the black troops fought "with considerable obstinacy, while the white or true Yankee portion ran like whipped curs almost as soon as the charge was ordered."[94] Cornwell later wrote that this referred to the 10th Cavalry, who slunk away rather than join the battle. It could also be a gratuitous swipe at the 23rd Iowa, a racist jibe at whites willing to fight alongside blacks. Or, perhaps, the Iowans really did desert their black comrades. Herman Lieb wrote that "the 23rd Iowa Infty left the field soon after the enemy got possession of the levee, headed by their Colonel, and was seen no more."[95]

Probably not. Samuel Glasgow, himself a member of the 23rd, was in the hospital during the fight but heard it said that "the Old 23 [had] to fight against 3000 of the Enemy," but even so retreated only reluctantly; "the Colonel . . . had to order them the third time before they would retreat." Hyperbole, of course. Even

Glasgow added, "I just believe it," which means he recognized the exaggeration. Nonetheless, those veterans of the Vicksburg campaign numbered only about one hundred when they went into the fight and lost sixty-two killed and wounded at Milliken's Bend. Those casualties seem too high to say that the 23rd "ran like whipped curs."[96]

The conduct of the black units' white officers continued as an object of controversy long after the fight. Many years later, Cornwell argued that a regimental historian named J. H. Morgan charged that Herman Lieb had run from the battle, jumping into the river to save himself. "This same Gen. Lieb is now a prominent politician in Chicago," Morgan added. If any such regimental history ever existed, it is apparently no longer extant. In any case, while David Cornwell had few positive memories of senior officers, he claimed he steadfastly supported Lieb and demanded space in the *Springfield Monitor* to defend Lieb's honor after Morgan's allegations appeared in that paper. Cornwell believed that Morgan's story came from 10th Illinois veterans still harboring a grudge against the black soldiers. According to Cornwell, Morgan privately confessed that one of the Illinois soldiers had gone into the blacks' camp and had "frankly gave them his opinion of them as a race and as soldiers, and that he got pretty roughly handled." This may be based on truth. Before the battle, the *Chicago Tribune* reported that two drunken 10th Cavalrymen had beaten two black soldiers. White commanders of the black unit then ordered the two cavalrymen whipped by black soldiers. The 10th Cavalry nearly rioted when it got the news, stopped only by its own officers.[97] Thus, the Illinois soldiers may have taken their revenge twenty years later by spreading false stories about the blacks' commander, or so claimed Cornwell.[98]

While Lieb apparently showed courage in the battle, some white officers may have actually deserted the field that day. Cornwell regarded Lieutenant Colonel Cyrus Sears as a "faking, self glorifying" author of contradictory accounts of the battle. According to Cornwell, Sears and some fellow 11th Louisiana officers disappeared during the battle, each protecting the other afterward with false statements.[99] Both Cornwell and Sears agreed that the most authentic account of the fight came from Herman Lieb. The War Department never published Lieb's battle report, so both Sears and Cornwell included differing versions of it in their memoirs. Lieb leveled no criticism against Sears but commented that Colonel Edwin W. Chamberlain, 11th Louisiana commander, "was nowhere to be seen on the field."[100]

Positive comments about the black soldiers' courage circulated widely both in and out of the army. On June 11, one Iowa soldier wrote his wife that "where the Negroes were posted they stood and Fought bravely." The Union commander said, "It is impossible for men to show greater gallantry than the negro troops in this fight." Grant wrote later that the "very raw" black soldiers "behaved well." The *Chicago Tribune* said the black soldiers "fought like tigers—better, in fact, than their white officers."[101] Another Illinois newspaper exulted that "the niggers have whipped the chivalry," taking prisoners and making the rest run. The *Daily Illinois State Journal* may have paid the black troops its ultimate compliment when it printed a letter saying that they fought "just like Illinois soldiers." Such comments seemed to point toward a dramatic change of heart. Charles Dana wrote later that the battle "revolutionized" sentiment in the Union army, making white northerners more sympathetic to the plight of black southerners. "Prominent officers," Dana wrote Stanton, "who used in private to sneer at the idea" of the blacks fighting "are now heartily in favor of it."[102]

The Milliken's Bend fight held newspapers' attention only briefly. News of Robert E. Lee's movement into Pennsylvania hit the northern newspapers as they still digested reports from Milliken's Bend, struggling to extract its meaning. On June 16, all hell had broken loose on the New York newspapers' front pages. "Invasion!" the *New York Times* trumpeted, publishing a front-page map detailing "The Rebel Movement" into the North. Its continuing column on "The War in Mississippi" went to page 8 and stayed on the inside pages as Lee moved deeper into Pennsylvania. When this happened, the *Times* was still reporting that the navy gunboat *Choctaw* rather than the infantry deserved most of the credit for winning Milliken's Bend. The *New York Tribune* and the *New York Herald* printed their first detailed dispatches written by their own Vicksburg correspondents on June 19. The newspapers were still trying to make sense out of what had happened at Milliken's Bend when Robert E. Lee began moving his army northward. Gettysburg swamped any further efforts to find the truth.[103]

The newspapers did not have the last word, of course. Within a year of the fight, quickie histories appeared, providing contradictory assessments of black soldiers' valor. Horace Greeley's book emphasized the role played by Union gunboats. With cries of "No quarter!" attacking Confederates drove the "green, awkward Blacks" from their positions. Greeley related how the Union commander hailed a passing steamer, calling for help. The Rebels retreated when bombarded by the *Choctaw*. Greeley made the gunboats so central to the story that he even attributed the heavy casualties among the black troops to friendly fire from the gunboats. An alternative view appeared in *The Rebellion Record*, a compilation of military reports and firsthand battle accounts edited by Frank Moore. Moore's *Record* included three accounts of the Milliken's Bend fight. The first came from G. G. Edwards, who wrote that he had been on the battlefield throughout the fight and watched the black soldiers "with interest." Like Dana, Edwards thought the battle marked a turning point in whites' attitudes. "Tauntingly it has been said," he wrote, "that negroes won't fight." Instead, when the Confederates charged with bayonets, the black troops "met the shock like heroes." After Milliken's Bend, Edwards declared, only "a dastard and a brute" would dare accuse blacks of cowardice. Another correspondent described the new black soldiers as efficient and capable fighters. When the Confederates attacked, a black soldier promptly told his colonel, "Massa, the seccesh are in camp." When the colonel ordered the men to load their guns, the black soldier coolly replied, "We have done did dat now, massa." The soldiers lined up for battle before their colonel could get himself ready and on duty. This author agreed that Milliken's Bend marked a significant turning point in the war. By this account, a captured Confederate plaintively begged that "his own negroes" not be placed over him as a guard. "His request was *not* granted."[104]

In his 1866 Civil War history, John S. C. Abbott added his purple prose to those hailing black heroism. The black soldiers, Abbott wrote, attacked "with a war-cry which from their resonant throats rose above the clangor of the battle." They counterattacked "like heaven's black tornado, plunged headlong with fixed bayonets into the thickest of the rebel ranks." The Confederates fought back "with frenzied energy" because "to be whipped by negroes was to drink the last dregs of the cup of humiliation." Abbott celebrated the drinking. Black soldiers forced that chalice to their masters' lips and the Confederate attackers "bit the dust."[105]

According to Vicksburg's diarists, a week after the Confederates' failed Milliken's Bend attack, Confederate discipline broke inside Vicksburg. Confederate deserters reaching the Union lines described the garrison as desperately short of food and ammunition. These deserters, hungry and worn out themselves, predicted the town could not hold out for more than another thirty days. On June 19, a spy contradicted the deserters, reporting that Vicksburg's defenders had enough food to last until the end of August and remained determined to hold out.[106] Inside Vicksburg, Confederate troops vigorously plundered townspeople's gardens and vegetable patches. There would be no joking about this at the reunions. First individual soldiers and then gangs of starving Confederates deserted their positions at night, scavenging for food. By the end of June, even some Confederate officers had joined the looting parties.[107]

On June 25, the Union army tried to break the Confederate defenses by burrowing under their positions. At 4:00 P.M., Fort

Hill exploded with 1,200 pounds of powder placed under it. Union troops rushed into the crater, the 45th Illinois leading the way. The explosion, however, had failed to breach the fort. The 45th found themselves trapped in a blasted canyon roughly fifty yards in diameter. Despite horrendous Confederate gunfire, the Union infantry held the crater through the night. Stephen Beck remembered crawling up to the crater's lip and firing his gun without aim. Other soldiers reloaded guns and passed them up to the soldiers at the top. Beck fired and rotated guns so fast that the hot gun barrels blistered his hands. The next day, Confederates hurled grenades made from six-pound shells that landed among the Yankee troops acting as gun loaders. Beck saw the first grenade land right in Robert Vance's lap and explode. This first blast mangled Vance; a second bomb shredded his body. "It was too much for mortal men to stand such destruction," Beck wrote. The gun loaders fled and the shooters hastened to follow. Soldiers began calling the crater "The Slaughter Pen." Beck remembered this killing as very personal, "for [the Rebels] could hear our men holler and groan when struck." Only a few feet separated the two sides.[108]

By the end of June, Confederate deserters told Union interrogators that the garrison had exhausted its supplies and could not hold out much longer.[109] Grant met with his commanders to determine if a new assault should be made. The officers decided to wait, trusting that the deserters were right and the garrison would soon surrender.[110] On July 3, a white flag appeared on the Confederate works. One southern soldier remembered later seeing a Confederate in full uniform mounted on a gray horse and followed by a courier galloping from the lines. He unfurled his white flag while under fire. Then, for the first time since May 25, firing halted. Hours passed, and the soldiers speculated about what was going on. Some feared the truce was only another break to bury more dead. One Texan recalled "a peculiar deathlike stillness reigning around the lines." A Mississippian claimed later that from his position he could see Grant and Pemberton negotiate.

Colonel J. H. Jones watched Grant, remembering later his beard as iron gray and close cropped, sitting impassively while Pemberton nervously pulled on his whiskers. When dawn broke gloriously on Saturday, the Fourth of July, the soldiers still wondered what had happened and what was happening. The Texan J. E. Gaskell heard loud huzzas and saw Union soldiers approaching. Finally, a report came that the city would be surrendered at ten o'clock. Gaskell recalled later that word of surrender "pierced our hearts." Brave men wept, according to Gaskell. Another veteran recalled the starved defenders as staggering like drunken men. At ten, the Union soldiers fell in, and their band played "Hail Columbia." Then they marched into Vicksburg.[111]

Notes

1. Roy P. Basler, ed., *Walt Whitman's Memoranda during the War [&] Death of Abraham Lincoln* (Bloomington: Indiana University Press, 1962), 5.

2. James P. Boyd diary, August 21, 1861, Illinois State Historical Society, Springfield.

3. James M. McPherson, *For Cause and Comrades: Why Men Fought in the Civil War* (New York: Oxford University Press, 1997), is the best example. See also Larry M. Logue, *To Appomattox and Beyond: The Civil War Soldier in War and Peace* (Chicago: Ivan R. Dee, 1996), 2–17; Michael Barton, *Goodmen: The Character of Civil War Soldiers* (University Park: Pennsylvania State University Press, 1981); Gerald Linderman, *Embattled Courage: The Experience of Combat in the American Civil War* (New York: Collier Macmillan, 1987); and Reid Mitchell, *Civil War Soldiers* (New York: Viking, 1988).

4. Rowland Chambers diary, May 24, 1863, Hill Memorial Library, Louisiana State University, Baton Rouge.

5. Phillip Shaw Paludan, *"A People's Contest": The Union and Civil War, 1861–1865* (New York: Harper & Row, 1988), 3–31.

6. Boyd diary, August 21, September 7, 1861.

7. Boyd diary, September 7, 1861; Charles Royster, *The Destructive War: William Tecumseh Sherman, Stonewall Jackson, and the Americans*

(New York: Knopf, 1991), 79; Gerald Leonard, *The Invention of Party Politics: Federalism, Popular Sovereignty, and Constitutional Development in Jacksonian Illinois* (Chapel Hill: University of North Carolina Press, 2002); Keith E. Whittington, *Constitutional Construction: Divided Powers and Constitutional Meaning* (Cambridge, Mass.: Harvard University Press, 1999), 1–19. What Leonard, relying on Whittington, calls an unwritten constitution Jean Baker calls "a subculture." Jean H. Baker, *Affairs of Party: The Political Culture of Northern Democrats in the Mid-Nineteenth Century* (Ithaca, N.Y.: Cornell University Press, 1983), 22.

8. Samuel H. Glasgow to Emma Glasgow, August 24, 1862, and Henry Glasgow to Emma Glasgow, September 19, 1862, Samuel H. Glasgow Papers, State Historical Society of Iowa, Des Moines.

9. John G. Given to M. E. Morris, September 13, 1862, John G. Given Papers, Illinois State Historical Society, Springfield.

10. McPherson, *For Cause and Comrades*, 3–13.

11. James R. Arnold, *Grant Wins the War: Decision at Vicksburg* (New York: John Wiley & Sons, 1997); Earl Schenck Miers, *The Web of Victory: Grant at Vicksburg* (New York: Knopf, 1955).

12. Albert O. Marshall diary, Illinois State Historical Society, Springfield; Isaac H. Elliott, *History of the Thirty-Third Regiment, Illinois Veteran Volunteer Infantry in the Civil War, 22nd August, 1861, to 7th December, 1865* (Gibson City, Ill.: privately published, 1902), 125–26.

13. Given to Matilda Garrett, October 11, 1862, Given Papers.

14. James M. McPherson, *Battle Cry of Freedom: The Civil War Era* (New York: Oxford University Press, 1988), 392–401; for an excellent discussion of the Mississippi's geographic importance, see Warren E. Grabau, *Ninety-Eight Days: A Geographer's View of the Vicksburg Campaign* (Knoxville: University of Tennessee Press, 2000), 3–13.

15. McPherson, *Battle Cry of Freedom*, 400–402.

16. Arnold, *Grant Wins the War*, 10–11.

17. McPherson, *Battle Cry of Freedom*, 418–20.

18. Rowland Chambers diary, vol. 6, Hill Memorial Library, Louisiana State University, Baton Rouge.

19. Richard L. Howard, *History of the 124th Regiment, Illinois Infantry Volunteers Otherwise Known as the "Hundred and Two Dozen," from August, 1862, to August, 1865* (Springfield, Ill.: Bokker, 1880), 18–19; Given to home, November 13, 1862, Given Papers.

20. Boyd diary, December 5, 1862.

21. Sam Glasgow to Emma Glasgow, January 20, 1863, Glasgow Papers. *Jayhawker* is a term usually associated with Kansas and means a guerilla fighter acting outside the normal rules. Jayhawking implies pillaging.

22. Seneca B. Thrall to wife, December 3, 1862, in Mildred Throne, ed., "An Iowa Doctor in Blue: The Letters of Seneca B. Thrall, 1862–1864," *Iowa Journal of History* 58 (April 1960): 119; Boyd diary, December 6, 1862, Manuscripts Department, Illinois State Historical Society, Springfield.

23. George Read Lee diary, December 8, 1862, Manuscripts Department, Illinois State Historical Society, Springfield.

24. Howard, *History of the 124th Regiment*, 20–21; S. C. Beck, *A True Sketch of His Army Life* (n.p.: [1914]), 2.

25. Howard, *History of the 124th Regiment*, 30–35.

26. Edwin Cole Bearss, *The Campaign for Vicksburg*, 3 vols. (Dayton, Ohio: Morningside, 1985), 1:307–18.

27. Kennedy to wife, December 21, 1862, folder 2, William J. Kennedy Papers, Manuscripts Department, Illinois State Historical Society, Springfield.

28. Adam Badeau, *Military History of Ulysses S. Grant*, 3 vols. (1867; repr., New York: D. Appleton and Co., 1881), 1:140; Arnold, *Grant Wins the War*, 32; David Cornwell, "Dan Caverno: True Tale of American Life on the Farm, in a Country Store, and in the Volunteer Army" [1908], U.S. Army Military History Institute, Carlisle, Pennsylvania; DeWitt Clinton Loudon to Hannah, January 1, 1863, folder 8, DeWitt Clinton Loudon Papers, Ohio Historical Society, Columbus; Howard, *History of the 124th Regiment*, 47–48.

29. Griffin diary, February 11, 1863; Clinton B. Fisk to Ross, commanding Yazoo expedition, March 6, 1863, *The War of the Rebellion: A Compilation of the Official Records of the Union and Confederate Armies*, 129 vols. (Washington, D.C.: U.S. Government Printing Office, 1880–1901), series I, vol. 24, part III, 87. Hereinafter cited as OR. Royster, *Destructive War*, 85.

30. Stephen D. Lee, "Details of Important Work by Two Confederate Telegraph Operators, Christmas Eve, 1862, Which Prevented the Almost Complete Surprise of the Confederate Army at Vicksburg," *Publications of the Mississippi Historical Society* 8 (1904): 51–55.

31. William T. Sherman, *Memoirs of Gen. W. T. Sherman, Written by Himself*, 2 vols. (New York: Charles L. Webster, 1891), 1:313–17.

32. Sherman, *Memoirs of Gen. W. T. Sherman*, 319–20; Bearss, *The Vicksburg Campaign*, 1:194.

33. George W. Morgan, "The Assault on Chickasaw Bluffs," in *Battles and Leaders of the Civil War*, 4 vols. (New York: Century, 1884–1887), 3:463.

34. Henry C. Bear to wife, December 29, 1862, in Wayne C. Temple, ed., *The Civil War Letters of Henry C. Bear: A Soldier in the 116th Illinois Volunteer Infantry* (Harrogate, Tenn.: Lincoln Memorial University Press, 1961), 23.

35. Morgan, "The Assault on Chickasaw Bluffs," 462–63.

36. Morgan, "The Assault on Chickasaw Bluffs," 462–67.

37. Bearss, *The Vicksburg Campaign*, 1:194–201.

38. Sherman, *Memoirs of Gen. W. T. Sherman*, 317–20; Sherman to John A. Rawlins, January 3, 1863, OR, series I, vol. 27, part I, 605–9; Bear to wife, December 29, 1862, in Temple, *The Civil War Letters of Henry C. Bear*, 24.

39. Herman Hattaway, *General Stephen D. Lee* (Jackson: University Press of Mississippi, 1976), 62–77; Stephen D. Lee, report, January 1863, OR,, series I, vol. 27 part I, 680–84.

40. Morgan, "The Assault on Chickasaw Bluffs," 469.

41. Bearss, *The Vicksburg Campaign*, 1:433–45.

42. General L. F. Hubbard, "Minnesota at the Siege of Vicksburg," *Vicksburg Herald*, May 25, 1907; Bearss, *The Vicksburg Campaign*, 1:437–38.

43. Arnold, *Grant Wins the War*, 49–50; Bearss, *The Vicksburg Campaign*, 479–591.

44. Charles A. Dana, *Recollections of the Civil War, with the Leaders at Washington and in the Field in the Sixties* (New York: D. Appleton and Company, 1898), 21–28.

45. Grant to N. P. Banks, March 22, 1862, OR, series I, vol. 24, part III, 125–26.

46. William T. Withers to Stephen D. Lee, January 3, 1863, OR, series I, vol. 27, part I, 686–89; Withers to Lee, January 6, 1863, OR, series I, vol. 27, part I, 689–94.

47. James D. Richardson, comp., *A Compilation of the Messages and Papers of the Presidents* (Washington, D.C.: U.S. Government Printing

Office, 1897), 6:157–59; Halleck to Grant, March 31, 1863, OR, series I, vol. 24, part III, 156–57.

48. Loudon to Hannah, October 28, 1862, folder 8, Loudon Papers.

49. Kennedy to wife, December 18, 1862, folder 2, Kennedy Papers.

50. Julius D. Allen to Hillery, February 22, 1863, in Julius D. Allen, *A Soldier's Letters* (Rushville, Ind.: Republican Co., 1893), 20; Seneca B. Thrall to wife, January 20, 1863, in Throne, "An Iowa Doctor in Blue," 126.

51. John Brunston Pearson to Henry, March 4, 1863, John Brunston Pearson Papers, Special Collections, Leslie F. Malpass Library, Western Illinois University, Macomb.

52. James Pickett Jones, *Black Jack: John A. Logan and Southern Illinois in the Civil War Era* (1967; repr., Carbondale: Southern Illinois University Press, 1995), 16–17, 44, 75–89.

53. Cornwell, "Dan Caverno," 117; Thaddeus B. Packard Civil War journal compiled from letters to his wife, Manuscripts Department, Illinois State Historical Society, Springfield; Griffin diary, John A. Griffin Papers, Manuscripts Department, Illinois State Historical Society, Springfield. Howard paraphrased Logan's speech in *History of the 124th Regiment*, 65–66. For Thomas's speeches as "bad," see Dana to Stanton, April 20, 1863, OR, series I, vol. 24, part 1, 78. Michael T. Meier, "Lorenzo Thomas and the Recruitment of Blacks in the Mississippi Valley, 1863–1865," in John David Smith, ed., *Black Soldiers in Blue: African American Troops in the Civil War Era* (Chapel Hill: University of North Carolina Press, 2002), disputes Dana's negative judgment by claiming that Thomas put an end to doubts about his oratory on May 23, 1863, when he spoke to assembled freed people. It seems likely, however, that Dana meant that Thomas was "bad" in the sense that he did not appeal to white troops, a judgment Howard confirmed.

54. Cornwell, "Dan Caverno," 121; Joseph T. Glatthaar, *Forged in Battle: The Civil War Alliance of Black Soldiers and White Officers* (Baton Rouge: Louisiana State University Press, 1990), 12–19, 35–41.

55. Statement by F. A. Roziene as Relates to His Sickness, etc., March 24, 1898, Frederick Roziene pension application, 1186027, National Archives, Washington, D.C.; Glatthaar, *Forged in Battle*, 44–59.

56. Grant to John A. McClernand, April 12, 1863, OR, series I, vol. 24, part III, 188; Arnold, *Grant Wins the War*, 73–74. For deserters re-

ports, see Dana to Stanton, April 1, 1863, OR, series I, vol. 24, part I, 69; Sherman, *Memoirs of Gen. W. T. Sherman*, 343.

57. Dana, *Recollections of the Civil War*, 28.

58. Dana, *Recollections of the Civil War*, 58, 59, 85.

59. Dana, *Recollections of the Civil War*, 32–33; Terrence J. Winschel, "Fighting Politician: John A. McClernand," in Steven E. Woodworth, ed., *Grant's Lieutenants: From Cairo to Vicksburg* (Lawrence: University Press of Kansas), 129–50.

60. Bearss, *The Vicksburg Campaign*, 2:63–65; Grabau, *Ninety-Eight Days*, 41.

61. Bearss, *The Vicksburg Campaign*, 2:68.

62. Dana to Stanton, April 17, 1863, OR, series I, vol. 24, part I, 76; Arnold, *Grant Wins the War*, 74–78; Bearss, *The Vicksburg Campaign*, 2:73–74.

63. Grabau, *Ninety-Eight Days*, 67–70.

64. Grabau, *Ninety-Eight Days*, 144–45.

65. Grabau, *Ninety-Eight Days*, 186–87.

66. Grant to Stephen A. Hurlbut, May 5, 1863, OR, series I, vol. 24, part III, 274–75; T. S. Bowers to Hurlbut, May 5, 1863, OR, series I, vol. 24, part III, 275–76; Grant to Sherman, May 9, 1863, OR, series I, vol. 24, part III, 285–86.

67. Dana to Stanton, May 4, 1863, OR, series I, vol. 24, part I, 84.

68. Sherman to Mower, May 15, 1863, OR, series I, vol. 24, part III, 315.

69. Frederick Grant, "The Siege of Vicksburg," *Vicksburg Evening Post*, November 8, 1907.

70. *Vicksburg Evening Post*, October 17, 1917.

71. [Mary Webster Loughborough], *My Cave Life in Vicksburg with Letters of Trial and Travel* (1864; repr., Vicksburg, Miss.: Vicksburg and Warren County Historical Society, 1990), 43; Dora Miller, "War Diary of a Union Woman in the South," May 17, 1863; G. W. Cable, ed., typescript, Old Court House Museum, Vicksburg; Halleck's Report, November 15, 1863, OR, series I, vol. 23, part I, 5.

72. Howard, *History of the 124th Regiment*, 104.

73. Bear to wife, May 21, 1863, in Temple, *The Civil War Letters of Henry C. Bear*, 41; J. J. Kellogg, *War Experiences and the Story of the Vicksburg Campaign from "Milliken's Bend" to July 4, 1863* (n.p., 1913), 26–32; Sherman, *Memoirs of Gen. W. T. Sherman*, 353.

74. J. H. Jones, "The Rank and File at Vicksburg," *Publications of the Mississippi Historical Society* 7 (1903): 20–21; *Vicksburg Evening Post*, November 24, 1893.

75. Hubbard, "Minnesota at the Siege of Vicksburg."

76. Kellogg, *War Experiences*, 47–48; Beck, *A True Sketch of His Army Life*, 11.

77. Sherman, *Memoirs of Gen. W. T. Sherman*, 355–56; Winschel, "Fighting Politician," 140–47.

78. W. Maury Darst, ed., "The Vicksburg Diary of Mrs. Alfred Ingraham (May 2–June 13, 1863)," *Journal of Mississippi History* 44 (1982): 148–79. Mrs. Ingraham, though she described herself "a real old cantakerous [*sic*] rebel," was a sister of Union General George Meade.

79. Beck, *A True Sketch of His Army Life*, 12.

80. T. Michael Parrish, *Richard Taylor: Soldier Prince of Dixie* (Chapel Hill: University of North Carolina Press, 1992), 240–67; Bearss, *The Campaign for Vicksburg*, 3:1153–56; Cornwell, "Dan Caverno," 129.

81. John Gordon deposition, July 7, 1905, pension application 1007781, certificate 1122876, and John Howard deposition, December 26, 1908, pension application 584280, certificate 673556, National Archives, Washington, D.C.; Cornwell, "Dan Caverno," 122–23; Civil War pensions, National Archives, Washington, D.C.

82. Cornwell, "Dan Caverno," 129. Kirk Savage argues that the suitability of former slaves for military discipline required that their service be forgotten for fear of undermining white soldiers' new claims to manhood. Kirk Savage, *Standing Soldiers, Kneeling Slaves: Race, War, and Monuments in Nineteenth-Century America* (Princeton, N.J.: Princeton University Press, 1997), esp. 181.

83. Cornwell, "Dan Caverno," 130–31.

84. Cornwell, "Dan Caverno," 132.

85. Benjamin Quarles, *The Negro in the Civil War* (Boston: Little, Brown, 1953), 220–24; Dudley Taylor Cornish, *The Sable Arm: Negro Troops in the Union Army, 1861–1865* (New York: Longmans, Green, 1956), 144–45.

86. David Cornwell, "The Battle of Milliken's Bend," *Washington National Tribune*, February 13, 1908; Examining Surgeon's Certificate, January 18, 1881, John Brown pension application 299910, certificate 280188;

Surgeon's Certificate, November 25, 1903, John Howard pension application 584280, certificate 673556; Surgeon's Certificate, June 27, 1906, Mike Caston pension application 600789, certificate 509638; general affidavit, June 29, 1889, William Marshall pension application 325535, certificate 551258; and claim for invalid pension, February 25, 1874, Samuel Morris pension application 190310, certificate 134012, National Archives, Washington, D.C.; Elias S. Dennis, report of attack on Milliken's Bend, June 12, 1863, OR, series I, vol. 24, part II, 446–48; Cyrus Sears, *Paper of Cyrus Sears* (Columbus, Ohio: F. J. Heer Printing Co., 1909), 15.

87. Sylvester Laning deposition, September 3, 1886, Susan Easton pension application 250747, and Sylvester Laning deposition, March 26, 1884, Alexander Murphy pension application 454411, certificate 285815, National Archives, Washington, D.C. Two other doctors claimed to be present, Orasmus Easton and William M. Glenny. William M. Glenny deposition, September 17, 1886, Susan Easton pension application 250747, and W. J. Guild deposition, National Archives, Washington, D.C.

88. *New York Times*, June 12, 1863.

89. *Chicago Tribune*, June 12, 1863; *New York Tribune*, June 13, 1863.

90. David West to father, June 9, 1863, folder 20, box 4, Civil War Papers, State Historical Society of Iowa, Des Moines; *Springfield Daily Illinois State Journal*, August 4, 1863; G. G. Edwards, "Fight at Milliken's Bend, Miss.," in Frank Moore, ed., *The Rebellion Record* (1864), 7:13; "Another Account" in Moore, *The Rebellion Record*, 15; Sears, *Paper of Cyrus Sears*, 14. Ironically, in 2003 at least one U.S. unit went into battle against Iraq with a black flag that included the skull-and-crossbones insignia.

91. E. K. Owen to David D. Porter, June 16, 1873, OR, series I, vol. 24, part III, 425; Grant to R. Taylor, June 22, 1863, OR, series I, vol. 24, part III, 425–26; R. Taylor to Grant, June 27, 1863, OR, series I, vol. 24, part III, 443–44; Richard Lowe, "Battle on the Levee: The Fight at Milliken's Bend," in Smith, *Black Soldiers in Blue*, 125–26; Bearss, *The Campaign for Vicksburg*, 3:1180–81.

92. War Department return, Pleasant Barnett pension application 790480, certificate 925096; J. G. Walker, report on operations, July 10, 1863, OR, series I, vol. 24, part II, 466.

93. *New York Herald*, June 13, 1863.

57

94. Sam Glasgow to Emma Glasgow, June 11, 1863, Glasgow Papers; J. G. Walker, report of attack on Milliken's Bend, OR, series I, vol. 24, part II, 467; U. S. Grant, *Personal Memoirs of U. S. Grant*, E. B. Long, ed. (1885; repr., Cleveland, Ohio: World Publishing Co., 1952), 285.

95. Cornwell, "Dan Caverno," 138.

96. Sam Glasgow to wife, June 11, 1863, Glasgow Papers.

97. *Chicago Tribune*, June 9, 1863.

98. Cornwell, "Dan Caverno," 143–44.

99. Cornwell, "Dan Caverno," 139–40.

100. Sears, *Paper of Cyrus Sears*, 8–11, 16; Cornwell, "Dan Caverno," 136–38.

101. *Chicago Tribune*, June 13, 1863.

102. *Springfield Daily Illinois State Journal*, July 6, 1863; Horace Greeley, *The American Conflict: A History of the Great Rebellion in the United States of America, 1860–65*, 2 vols. (Hartford, Conn.: O. D. Case & Co., 1866), 2:319. William A. Crafts, in *The Southern Rebellion, Being a History of the United States*, 2 vols. (Boston: Samuel Walker & Co., 1862–1867), 2:385, also credits the gunboats with winning the battle: the Confederates "would undoubtedly have overwhelmed the colored troops had it not been for the gunboats." John William Draper, in *History of the American Civil War*, 3 vols. (London: Longmans, Green, 1871), 3:54, passed over Milliken's Bend almost dismissively, also saying that the black troops would have been defeated but for the gunboats.

103. *New York Tribune*, June 16, 1863; *New York Herald*, June 16, 1863; *New York Times*, June 12, 15, 16, 1863.

104. Edwards, "Fight at Milliken's Bend," 12–13; "Another Account," 15. The *Springfield Daily Illinois State Journal*, July 6, 1863, account includes the anecdote about the slave guarding his former master.

105. John S. C. Abbott, *The History of the Civil War in America*, 2 vols. (New York: Henry Bill, 1862, 1866), 2:291.

106. Dana to Stanton, May 26, 1863, OR, series I, vol. 24, part I, 89; Dana to Stanton, June 14, 1863, OR, series I, vol. 24, part I, 98; Dana to Stanton, June 20, 1863, OR, series I, vol. 24, part I, 104.

107. Rowland Chambers diary, June 8, 9, 10, 11, 13, 14, 16, 17, 23, 30, 1863.

108. Howard, *History of the 124th Regiment*, 117–19; Beck, *A True Sketch of His Army Life*, 14–15.

109. Dana to Stanton, June 29, 1863, OR, series I, vol. 24, part I, 112.

110. Dana to Stanton, June 30, 1863, OR, series I, vol. 24, part I, 112–13.

111. J. E. Gaskell, "Surrendered at Vicksburg," *Confederate Veteran* 33 (August 1925): 286; Jones, "The Rank and File at Vicksburg," 29; Howard, *History of the 124th Regiment*, 121–23; *Vicksburg Evening Post*, July 15, 1890.

The Meaning of the Civil War in Reconstruction

O
N July 4, Grant's soldiers entered Vicksburg, looking under porches and in outhouses for Confederate soldiers trying to avoid surrender. This searching, prying into private spaces—an invasion by the national authority—could have been a metaphor for the dramatic change that the Civil War seemed to promise. Before the war, despite their city's many commercial connections around the world, ordinary Vicksburgers had enjoyed a fairly insular life. Certainly in the years before secession, the notion that a powerful national government would establish lasting institutional enclaves in their midst seemed not just foreign but impossible.[1] So it was natural that as the blue-clad soldiers marched into their town, Vicksburgers wondered how long and in what form the national authority would stay. Would the northern victory permanently bring the national government into the lives of ordinary citizens? In the deepest sense, those Union soldiers, peering into Vicksburg's outhouses, searched not only for elusive Confederate soldiers but for the meaning of their victory as well.

Though it actually began while war continued, historians define Reconstruction as "the violent, dramatic, and still controversial era that followed the Civil War." Between 1863 and 1877, the national government sought to reconstruct the seceded states by making former slaves into citizens and voters. Since this effort brought the national government into direct contact with ordinary citizens, it challenged traditional federalism, which used a theory of divided sovereignty or dual federalism to shield the states' autonomy from Washington's "interference." Historians once called Reconstruction a failure, a misdirected and perhaps insincere effort by vengeful northerners more interested in punishing the South than elevating the African American victims of slavery. The civil rights revolution upset such thinking. The foremost historian of Reconstruction now calls it "unfinished," holding out the hope that its promise of racial justice can yet be achieved.[2] Reconstruction tested the federal government's commitment not only to remaking the South but also to making itself a permanent presence in the lives of all Americans.

People in Vicksburg usually remember Reconstruction for the tensions between invading white soldiers, white citizens, black civilians, and black soldiers over the North's commitment to equal rights and the white South's resistance. Seen this way, reformers' aspirations for black rights, tied to black soldiering, failed miserably. But Reconstruction cannot be understood only through such thwarted ambitions. The Civil War and Reconstruction really did change Vicksburg's social, constitutional, and physical landscape, creating the raw material for future interpretations of the Civil War's meaning.

Some of the white Union soldiers understood Vicksburg's fall as an opportunity to punish white southerners further and, at the same time, extend a measure of justice to the former slaves. Yankees turned some local whites out of their homes, allowing freed slaves to take the property. "One of the yankee officers told Dukie," Lavinia Shannon wrote, "that if he would take the oath he would be allowed to remain in our house." Lavinia's brother, Marmaduke or "Dukie," would do no such thing. "Of course he refused," Lavinia Shannon continued, "and the officer went and sent up a lot of negroes to live in the house." Northern whites and local blacks partied in the house. Union soldiers then distributed whites' clothing among the freed slaves.[3]

Whites in Vicksburg saw Reconstruction as expected Yankee vandalism, an entirely illegitimate expression of national power. In 1861, the *Vicksburg Citizen* had reported that New York robbers had joined the Union army "for the open and avowed purpose of pillaging the Southern cities and towns."[4] White southerners told and retold their stories of thieving invaders and made the most of such memories. One civilian woman remembered later that she confessed her worries that her house would be pillaged to a Union officer. As she told the story later, the officer replied, "Why, madam, we come to protect you, our soldiers are gentlemen." This officer even challenged the woman, "Where have they pillaged?" Nonetheless, the woman continued her story, Union soldiers looted the house, taking dresses, quilts, and blankets. "All were crazy for plunder," this white citizen wrote, "and when officers were opposed to such wholesale thieving, they were unable to control their men." This story has a rehearsed quality, as if told many times for effect. A more genuine reflection of whites' contemporary fears comes from their letters written at the time. From these records, a picture emerges of civilians cowering in their homes through that first night, hearing shouted voices, shooting, and soldiers crashing through fences.[5]

For Vicksburg's black population, the arrival of Union troops brought with it the promise of nationally protected emancipation. Many freed slaves would always remember July 4 as the day they finally tasted freedom. And liberty definitely differed from bondage in the most fundamental ways possible. Whites, for example, no longer had the right to shoot black people. Charlie Brick learned this lesson the hard way when he encountered black women rummaging through a house, taking whites' property. When Brick told them to stop, his command inspired an unexpected storm of curses. They were free, the women cried, and had all the rights he had. Unconvinced, Brick did what whites had always done when confronted with impudent "runaways": he shot one in the leg. Brick had acted "normally" and within his rights under the slavery regime, but times had changed. A crowd of black men appeared, cursing him. When he tried to shoot at them, they grabbed him and cowhided him. One black man held Brick's own gun to the white man's head and ordered him to call the former slave "master." For a moment, at least, things really had changed.[6]

Abraham Lincoln included a provision for arming freedmen as soldiers in his Emancipation Proclamation because he recognized that soldiering earned emancipation. Black soldiers dressed in blue uniforms on the streets of Vicksburg amounted to a national challenge to local white autonomy. Whites viewed armed black men in uniform as the most alarming consequence of their defeat. Black men with guns had been their worst nightmare through slavery, suggesting servile insurrection or, at least, manly independence. Now, every Sunday evening, black troops marched about town in their blue uniforms, commanded by white officers with swords and scarlet sashes, "making a fine show," Alice Shannon wrote disgustedly. For Shannon, black soldiers amounted to the greatest affront of all. "I am getting to hate all the negroes," she wrote her sister.[7]

The North's commitment to black soldiering raised questions in white minds about whether African Americans could be soldiers, whether they really deserved citizenship. The stories whites circulated about black soldiers' conduct revealed their doubts. Using army discipline to turn enslaved men into free citizens carried with it ironies and contradictions not lost on even the illiterate. Colonel Herman Lieb began training recruits by reminding them that "you have with uplifted hands voluntarily taken a sacred oath to respect your officers and obey their orders." Lieb worried that the men "may as yet not fully understand the benefits which will result for your down-trodden race by standing firmly on your sacred oath and proving yourselves obedient, orderly, and clean soldiers." Deserters would be shot, Lieb warned, adding that there was no greater crime in the army. You must defend the liberty purchased for you with the lives of thousands of white soldiers, Lieb said. Just in case this concept might be too abstract, Lieb added that this liberty would "enable you to make homes for your families and defend them while they are cultivating the soil which the government will assign them."[8]

Despite the best efforts of Lieb and other white commanders of black regiments, some soldiers simply wandered away from duty, searching for their families. Edmund Turner's regiment left him with his father after he came down with measles. "I had only been enlisted a few days and did not know much about the rules of the army," he pleaded later. He did not even have a uniform yet. Once he got over the measles, Turner simply joined another regiment, thinking one was as good as the next. White soldiers deserted too, of course, but white officers thought their black recruits especially prone to desertion. One army doctor said that "the black race" suffered from homesickness more readily than white soldiers, "becoming from this cause so debilitated in mind and body as to fall easy victims to any disease and many deaths accredited to other causes might more properly be classed under the head of nostalgia."[9]

More seriously, one company in the 49th U.S. Colored Infantry mutinied. Captain James P. Hall, getting a complaint that the black soldiers' quarters smelled bad, investigated, finding that several of the men had boxes filled with spoiled meat, rotten bread, and green apples, "all in a very filthy condition." Hall ordered the boxes and their contents burned. On June 13, 1864, when the men found their property had been destroyed, they grumbled among themselves and then marched to the captain's tent to protest. They stacked their weapons and announced they would do no further army duties until Hall promised to treat them better. Confronted with a similar situation with white troops, John A. Logan had roared, "I'll give them enough of stacking arms," and made the malcontents stack and unstack their arms for twelve hours straight. That was sufficient punishment. Commanding black troops, Hall reacted differently. He promptly had twenty-two protesters arrested, including two corporals and a sergeant. Twelve of the arrested men had fought at Milliken's Bend. A very quick court-martial followed, with no defense counsel provided for the defendants. One man went free, but a firing squad executed two, and the rest went to prison for life. Both of the condemned men, Giles Simms and Washington Fountaine, not only had fought at Milliken's Bend but also had been wounded in that bloody battle. It took a year, but eventually someone in the chain of command decided life in prison was an overly harsh punishment for the soldiers' protest. In 1865, authorities decided to forgive the imprisoned soldiers and return them to their unit. This came too late for Simms and Fountaine.[10]

The inability of white military authorities to control their black enlisted soldiers completely created a memory useful for Mississippi whites determined to resist the permanent expansion of national power. In April 1865, a group of soldiers of the 52nd U.S. Colored Infantry slipped out of their camp, making their way to Jared Reese Cook's plantation. Pushing into Cook's house, they demanded of Mrs. Cook, "Old woman, where's your silver?" One soldier knocked Minerva Cook in the head with the butt of his musket. Then others fired their weapons, killing Minerva and injuring Jared. Authorities arrested twelve and hanged eight.[11]

That story whites would tell for a long time. When a white newspaper repeated the story in 1909, it recalled that the Union commander marched the entire 52nd Regiment out to Flood's Bottom, where the hangings occurred. The commander, Morgan L. Smith, allowed the soldiers to take their guns but without cartridges, making them watch the executions "before their very eyes." According to this 1909 newspaper, older citizens still talked about the 1865 episode "frequently."[12] In 1993, Gordon Cotton, curator of the Old Court House Museum, retold the story in a booklet titled *Horrible Outrage!* Cotton interviewed Patricia Brown Young, a descendant of Minerva Cook. "Mother often told me the story of my great-grandmother's death and would show where one of the bullets had struck the headboard of the bed," Young said. According to Young, William Faulkner had been a friend of the Cook family and knew all about the story. Young quoted the great writer as saying, "This is the reason the South will never forget."[13]

Despite such setbacks army law enforcement actually offered the Republican North its best opportunity to remake southern society. Here, too, the North's commitment proved limited. The Union army only policed Vicksburg from its surrender on July 4, 1863, until July 1865. Whatever the permanent consequences of the war might be, they could not come from the point of those bayonets. In two years, the army arrested 1,586 civilians for such crimes as theft, drunkenness, disloyalty, insulting an officer, and "secret charges." During this time of army occupation, freed slaves from the countryside flocked to Vicksburg, building an immense refugee camp around and in the city. Disease ravaged the filthy hovels, as did crime and gunfire. Perhaps understandably, Grant had little interest in continuing such a system. He wanted to demobilize the army as quickly as possible, returning the task of governing the defeated South to the southerners themselves. Just months after Appomattox, Vicksburg selected two ex-Confederates as mayor and judge.[14]

The end of military occupation seemed to promise a return to life before the Civil War, with the old white hierarchy restored. President Andrew Johnson's great failure came in his inability to inspire or nurture a new leadership class in the defeated South. He simply could not imagine the southern states run by anyone other than the same white elites that had been in charge before secession.[15] In Vicksburg, the North's experiment with black soldiers ended abruptly on March 22, 1866. On that day, the army mustered out all its black soldiers as part of Andrew Johnson's campaign of concessions to the white South. During Johnson's term, Vicksburg's government came to resemble the city's antebellum administration. It disciplined black people through highly discriminatory laws designed to return them to a slavelike status. Under these statutes, blacks could not travel about the state without written evidence of their employment. "Masters" could still inflict "moderate corporeal chastisement" on their "apprentices." Blacks could testify against whites in court, but only "when a party or parties to the suit, either plaintiff or plaintiffs, defendant or defendants." These laws made interracial marriage a crime. They charged justices of the peace with rounding up vagrants and hiring out their labor, with the county collecting any wages earned. The statute defined vagrants as "idle and dissipated persons" but also included jugglers and "persons who neglect their calling or employment, misspend what they earn." Thieves could be hung by their thumbs, a punishment designed for people who could not be spared from the fields to serve a jail sentence.[16] Lawmakers meant to restore local authority, taking the job of crime control from the army and putting it back in the hands of state sheriffs, constables, county courts, and grand juries.

White Mississippians enacted these laws out of fear—they expected blacks, unchained from slavery, to rage out of control. Whites also tendered these statutes to set in law their interpretation of the Civil War. The Civil War, Mississippi lawmakers proclaimed, did not mean they could no longer whip blacks. Emancipation did not mean that whites could not force their former slaves to work. The Civil War ended slavery, but the pass system, compulsory labor, and the whip continued.

The most radical Republicans, expecting that the national authority would protect citizens' civil rights, erupted in outrage.[17] "Not to put too fine a point on it," the *Chicago Tribune* said, but "we tell the white men of Mississippi that the men of the North will convert the State of Mississippi into a frogpond before they will allow any such law to disgrace one foot of soil in which the bones of our soldiers sleep and over which the flag of freedom waves."[18]

Conservative whites also complained about the laws, refusing to believe that the Civil War meant that whites' tax money had to support an extensive network of courts to control black criminality. Some white Mississippians considered absurd and unworkable the idea of using law to compel good order and discipline from animal-like African Americans. Under slavery, after all, whites had controlled blacks informally, on the spot, and with hardly any tax monies at all.[19]

To counter the Black Codes, Congress defined citizenship and delineated citizens' rights for the first time on April 9, 1866. This response argued that the war meant that U.S. citizens had rights that could be protected by federal authority in federal court.[20] In 1867, Congress went further, wresting Reconstruction from Andrew Johnson with a law dividing the South into military districts, each governed by an army general. Johnson tried to thwart these assaults on his power. As commander in chief, he picked the generals and chose conservative men generally hostile to black rights. Edward O. C. Ord, commander of Mississippi and Arkansas, military district 4, had made statements against black voting. As it turned out, however, Ord's strong sense of duty led him to enforce congressional acts in his district.[21] His sincerity, though, could hardly overcome the fact that by 1867 he had few soldiers left to apply pressure against racial violence. By now, fewer than 300 Union soldiers remained on duty in Vicksburg. Despite the small number of troops, there is little doubt that the ordinary Vicksburger felt the new surge of national power. Ord wielded real force, replacing the sheriff and other members of local government with Republicans. Charles Furlong, a former Union army officer, became head of the Republicans' Vicksburg "ring." Furlong shrewdly played a careful political game, extending enough low-level offices to black Republicans to keep the rank and file content but not so many as to upset white Republicans.[22] Furlong ran Vicksburg until 1873. That year, at the Republican county convention, black Republicans demanded control of the party. And they got it, banishing Furlong, who had been sheriff, to the state legislature and making Peter Crosby, a former slave and Union army veteran, sheriff instead. In Mississippi, sheriffs traditionally headed local government. And since they collected taxes and fees, sheriffs could make a lot of money. Furlong had kept whites quiescent by limiting black voters' access to real power; a black man collecting the taxes galvanized white opposition. In 1874, an ad hoc white militia ousted Crosby. Crosby counterattacked, marching rural blacks toward town, mobilizing a sort of grassroots militia across the Civil War battleground to reclaim his job. When whites bloodily repelled Crosby's followers, local whites constructed their narrative of the "riot" around a theme of reunification and reconciliation: a former Union army soldier improbably named Peoria Hog perched atop the courthouse cupola sounded the alarm when he spotted Crosby's men approaching. Then, as whites tell the story, "the streets began to fill with armed men, ready to meet the mobs. Only a few years before some had worn the gray, others the blue, but now they were united in a common cause."[23] Though the U.S. Army returned Crosby to office and he formally continued as sheriff until October 28, 1875, white opposition rendered him ineffective.[24]

White conservatives had effectively erased much of what the Union army had accomplished a decade earlier. In the election campaign of 1875, whites so thoroughly dominated the field that blacks did not even nominate a candidate. White vigilantes patrolled the county day and night. When blacks tried to celebrate the Fourth of July with a reading of the Declaration of Independence, whites stormed the courthouse. Blacks could hold even their most innocuous political meetings only in secret, in the swamps outside of town. Whites proudly proclaimed themselves "unreconstructed," and white Union army veterans put race ahead of region. Those who served in the force that put down Crosby talked about what happened only among themselves. Service in that effort became a shared secret among whites. It is hard to imagine any other event that did more to forge white citizens into a unified racial coalition. Whatever racial advances had been achieved in war had been eradicated.[25]

Under the Fourteenth Amendment, Congress had (or thought it had) authority to overcome such local intransigence. The freed people demanded that they do so. "We are animated," James Lynch wrote in 1868, "by a controlling desire to secure for ourselves equality before the law, and at the ballot box." Another black man wrote that he desired equal rights with whites, "formed and created, as we are, by the same Creator! Endowed with the same intellect!!" For a moment, Republicans thought such demands could be met. In 1869, the *Philadelphia Press* reported that "the South is accepting the laws on it as a finality." The *Press* predicted that white southerners "will make not further opposition to the complete enfranchisement of blacks." In 1870, Congress passed the Enforcement Act, designed to protect ordinary citizens' federal voting rights.[26] A year later, on April 20, 1871, Congress passed another Enforcement Act, this one aimed at Ku Klux Klan violence. The 1871 law made it a crime for "any person . . . under color of any law, statute, ordinance, regulation, custom, or usage of any state" to deprive any person of "any rights, privileges, or immunities secured by the Constitution."[27] In theory, these laws gave federal prosecutors sweeping new opportunities to attack whites' racial violence.

In some places, the U.S. attorneys boldly and creatively used these laws to indict violent white racists. In Tennessee, William W. Murray, seeing black citizens brutalized nearly every day, ordered nine men arrested. This effort failed when defense counsel tore down prosecution witnesses' testimony through cross-examination. Murray tried again in 1876, reading the Fourteenth Amendment language (which forbade the states from "enforc[ing]" biased laws) as applying to the states' executive branches, including the sheriffs so often complicitous in mob action. Murray indicted a sheriff and three of his deputies for conspiring with a mob. The case went to the U.S. Supreme Court, where the justices threw it out. The Fourteenth Amendment did not cover individual wrongs, only wrongs committed by the state, the justices ruled, ignoring Murray's argument that misconduct by a sheriff and his deputies surely constituted a state action covered by the Fourteenth Amendment.[28]

In Mississippi, the U.S. attorneys achieved dramatic successes in 1872, winning a 73 percent conviction rate against white vigilantes and accounting for nearly three quarters of all Enforcement Act convictions won by the entire Justice Department. Prosecutors faced long odds in bringing such cases. The lawyers had to work virtually around the clock. Urged on by his superiors in Washington, the U.S. attorney stationed in Vicksburg, Tennessee-born Luke Lea, expended many hours on the illegal logging of federal lands, trying to track down and identify missing timber. This distracted Lea from civil rights, sending the prosecutor on a fruitless mission to identify logs as stolen federal property. Federal authorities also had to overcome determined local resistance. In northern Mississippi, when the U.S. attorney ordered Enforcement Act violators arrested, his marshal believed intense and local opposition made "the experiment . . . a dangerous one." Congressional Republicans crafted such laws "to be an engine of torture for the South and her people, and never through any love for the negro," white southerners alleged. The *Vicksburg Herald* thought the authors of the civil rights laws "a class of men who had never been in the army . . . men who skulked behind civil position and 'bumb proofs' of various kinds until the enemy was manacled." Thus, the laws came from a "miserable, cowardly hatred of the South."[29]

The political grumblings of small-caliber southern politicians would hardly have derailed federal civil rights enforcement without the Supreme Court's help. Defendants challenged the constitutionality of the laws against them. One historian has written that the Court "eliminated" national jurisdiction over civil rights. That goes too far. In the 1880s, the Justice Department still brought as many as 200 criminal prosecutions under the Enforcement Acts, a far cry from the 1,304 cases processed in 1873, but not zero, either. Even as late as the 1890s, Justice Department lawyers brought between 83 and 306 prosecutions per year. But these small numbers—there were just 17 in the entire South in 1893—indicate that the Justice Department no longer vigorously policed civil rights. At the end of the nineteenth century, the Court barely left the Justice Department a constitutional toehold for enforcement.[30] Radical Republicans' utopian dream of a potent national force defending the civil rights of ordinary citizens against all aggressions lay in tatters.

If the Reconstruction effort is to be judged by northern Republicans' willingness to "convert the State of Mississippi into a frogpond," then it must be counted a failure. In 1870, the army closed its Vicksburg camp. This does not mean that the national government withdrew from local life in Mississippi. Vicksburg would forever be remembered as the site of a great Civil War battle; Civil War and Reconstruction memories, however contested, became a permanent part of Vicksburg life. The national government's most powerful and lasting contribution to Vicksburg's Civil War memory came on its physical landscape. In 1866, the federal government built a national cemetery behind an old Confederate gun emplacement. This memorial to fallen Union soldiers, almost all buried anonymously in nameless graves, would become a monument to valor so lasting that even white southerners came to respect it.

In war, soldiers kill their enemies and then disrespect their bodies. One Indiana soldier wrote, "Our ded was generally buryed totealy desent" but not "the rebs." Those, this soldier said, "was gethered up in piles and heaved in to holes any way to get them out of sight."[31] Southerners took much the same view of their fallen foes. Alice Crutcher told her sister that there was a dead Yankee buried in the strawberry bed under the peach trees. His comrades had thrown him in a bomb crater. "I would not care," Crutcher snarled, "if they were all over the garden, it would only make the soil richer."[32] After its Vicksburg victory, the North neglected its dead. In 1866, the U.S. government built its Vicksburg National Cemetery not out of some great or noble idealism but because the stench of death still hung over the farms around Vicksburg three years after the battle ended and three years after Lincoln had dedicated Gettysburg's National Cemetery. The government did not allow its dead to rot in Pennsylvania for three years after the battle; it did, though, in Mississippi.[33]

If politics is simply war by other means, after Vicksburg's surrender Union and Confederate sympathizers continued the war through their treatment of the dead. John A. Logan, as commander of the Grand Army of the Republic (GAR), called on Union veterans to decorate the graves of fallen comrades with flowers starting May 30, 1868. The *Vicksburg Weekly Republican* charged that former Confederates converted soldiers' graves into "cabbage gardens." Such allegations were true. Farmers plowed up the skeletons of Union soldiers, destroying headboards, sometimes deliberately insulting the remains. In 1868, a federal agent named George Macy reported that Adam Lynd, after claiming he had no Union army corpses on his property, had "wantonly Plowed over our Union dead, scattering the bones in every direction." Blacks picked up the scattered remains and placed them on stumps. One black man told Macy that Lynd had ordered his laborers to deny the existence of any Union dead to "any damd Yankees . . . enquiring for Graves." Macy reported that he had disinterred thirty-seven Union dead on the Lynd plantation, including one with an ambrotype showing a mother and child. The dead soldier with the ambrotype had gotten within fifteen yards of the Confederate breastworks, Macy noted. "Certainly his grave should have been respected," Macy wrote angrily, "*but it was not.*"[34]

One federal officer complained that another farmer had delivered the bones of Union soldiers "*in bulk*" to the city cemetery. Soldiers who were hastily buried after Grant's failed May assaults proved especially vulnerable. In February 1866, Colonel James F. Rushing inspected the Vicksburg battlefield. What he found sickened him. The condition of the dead, Rushing wrote in his report, "is more deplorable than any post I have visited." Wild animals feasted on Union corpses, half buried in shallow graves. Rushing estimated 8,000 dead lay on the Mississippi side of the river and another 2,000 on the Louisiana side. Rushing urged the national government to take charge rather then leaving the rotting remains of Union soldiers to the mercies of their enemies. He proposed construction of a national military cemetery in Vicksburg. Later that year, Congress authorized purchase of land for a national cemetery. On August 27, 1866, the government purchased forty rugged acres for $9,000.[35]

As the U.S. Army moved to recover the Union dead, white southerners made the recovery of their dead a project for their women. The Vicksburg Confederate Cemetery Association organized on May 15, 1866, with Mrs. E. T. Eggleston as president. She soon resigned, to be replaced by Mrs. John Willis. Mrs. E. D. Wright then headed the organization, continuing to do so until 1891. In June 1866, the Confederate Cemetery Association thanked Colonel G. T. Parker, U.S. Army, for marking and numbering the Confederate dead he came across while locating the Union fallen. Parker turned over to the Confederate Association a ledger book with 3,000 Confederate graves recorded. The Confederates acquired land for a Confederate cemetery in the same meeting in which they received Parker's book.[36] That white southern women stepped forward to commemorate the southern dead became an important element in the white South's Civil War memory. "To the women of the South has fallen most of this duty of keeping alive the memory of the heroes who wore the gray," the *Vicksburg Evening Post* reported in 1902. This narrative transformed the Civil War into a struggle to protect women—from northern invaders and, especially, from dangerous, violent black men.[37]

White southerners so thoroughly associated white women with Civil War commemorations that, in the twentieth century, Mississippi veterans agitated for a monument specifically dedicated to Confederate women. Southern white women, closely identified with the South's Lost Cause movement, honored Confederate leaders, especially Jefferson Davis. They promoted what they saw as womanly virtues, such as moral purity. They collected money and built monuments. On September 10, 1894, white southern women rendezvoused in Nashville to organize the United Daughters of the Confederacy.[38]

74

Mrs. E. T. Eggleston, first president, Vicksburg Cemetery Association. Author's collection.

Mrs. E. D. Wright, longtime president of the Vicksburg Cemetery Association. Author's collection.

Women apparently had no trouble winning over white southern men with their Lost Cause rhetoric. Twelve years after the Nashville meeting, in 1906, Mississippi's state veterans' organization debated a proposal to build a monument to Confederate women. Proponents reminded their fellows that while monuments had been built for various leaders, "to date nothing has been done to perpetuate the women who sacrificed more than all others on behalf of the South." Newspapers reported that the question sparked a heated controversy, but after debate, the proposal carried by an overwhelming majority. Mississippi dedicated its monument to Confederate women in 1912; across the South, other states built similar monuments.[39]

While the white South used women and sentimental appeals to celebrate its sacrifice and the need for white racial solidarity, the North did not ignore its women. Iowa built a Civil War monument on its capitol grounds before Mississippi in the 1890s. But while Mississippi's monument shows strong but chaste women giving succor to a soldier, Iowa's monument includes a half-naked woman, an allegorical figure of Iowa, surrounded by whooping Union soldiers and guarded by mounted Iowa generals. Iowa's *Handbook for Iowa Soldiers' and Sailors' Monument* describes the female Iowa figure as "vigorously modeled" with "splendid physical development." While the Mississippi women gaze sternly ahead, Mrs. Iowa looks dreamily heavenward while thrusting her awesome breasts at the viewer who, again according to the *Handbook*, is held "spellbound." A massive phallic-like column rises behind her, topped by another female figure, representing victory.[40]

Little trace of such triumphalism reached Vicksburg. The federal government turned graves registration into a bureaucratic bookkeeping operation. As late as October 1866, Union dead hastily buried in levees remained in their wartime graves, their bodies washing away almost daily.[41] Army commanders instructed their officers to keep careful records of recovered remains, using printed forms to document, "*at the grave*," any identifying marks.[42] The army placed Captain James W. Scully in

Mississippi's Civil War Monument, outside the state capitol building, recognizes the role of white southern women. Author's photograph.

charge of establishing the cemetery. Scully, an army quartermaster, needed coffins and, at the end of 1866, complained that no one had yet sent him any. He had dug 1,000 remains out of the levees but had no way to rebury them.[43]

Scully's operation to recover the dead sparked cynical rumors around Vicksburg. Congressmen received letters complaining that Scully treated the remains he recovered "barbarously." Stories of dogs and hogs eating the dead made the rounds; some gossiped that Scully paid a bounty for skulls. While a preliminary investigation cleared Scully of profiting from his work, it did document defilement of the dead. In the summer of 1867, Captain Charles W. Folsom made his way to Vicksburg to investigate persistent complaints against Scully. His report described Scully as too busy to personally supervise the recovery and reinterment of remains. In fact, Folsom could not find anyone really in charge. He soon recommended that all of Scully's foremen be discharged. Shortly after Folsom's visit, the army relieved Scully of his duties and charged him with corruption, finding it suspicious that he contracted with Julius J. Casparo for the manufacture of 1,800 coffins when Casparo had no skills in carpentry and no means of hiring carpenters. A court-martial found Casparo had bribed Scully, but President Andrew Johnson disapproved the findings, thus overturning the verdict and returning Scully to duty. The army assigned Scully away from Vicksburg.[44]

Conceived in sin, the National Cemetery nonetheless became the national government's most permanent contribution to Vicksburg's landscape. The government buried 17,077 Union dead at the Vicksburg cemetery; 12,909 of them could not be identified. Only Union dead rested in its forty terraced acres. Some local whites said later they felt no connection to the site. For the freed people, though, the National Cemetery became freedom's artifact, a tangible remnant of the nation's commitment to their emancipation. Aged black soldiers living in Vicksburg formed their own veterans' organization, a chapter of the Grand Army of the Republic, which had begun in Illinois as a political machine

Iowa's Civil War Monument also uses a female motif, though differently than Mississippi. Author's photographs.

and evolved into a lobbying organization on behalf of Union veterans. It admitted black members but confined them primarily to all-black chapters. Vicksburg organized its first GAR post in 1889. Within a year, a "colored" GAR post had formed as well. Some Mississippi GAR leaders tried to ban black posts, wanting to oust African American veterans from their organization. Their efforts failed.[45] In Vicksburg, often desperately poor black veterans contributed small sums to their GAR post so that, as they died, they could be buried with dignity. When one old soldier expired, a comrade remembered simply, "We boys buried him out at the National Cemetery, Vicksburg." Though segregated, interments did represent the one privilege that postbellum black Mississippians enjoyed that Confederates did not. Blacks made the most of it. At the end of May, every year, thousands of blacks from miles around gathered at the National Cemetery. In 1887, 1,500 African Americans marched to the site, forming a large procession. Four decades later, the numbers of blacks attending services on Memorial Day numbered 10,000, and they enjoyed appropriate GAR rituals, singing, and prayer.[46]

When African Americans gathered for Memorial Day, they read aloud Lincoln's Gettysburg Address. Though written for the Pennsylvania cemetery, Lincoln's short speech applied to Mississippi as well. Lincoln had said, "We are met on a great battlefield. . . . We have come to dedicate a portion of that field." Such generalized language worked in Vicksburg as well as in Gettysburg. More important, the iconic status of the address disguised its subversive nature. Garry Wills wrote that Lincoln's speech changed America, "correcting the Constitution itself without overthrowing it."[47] Oppressed people, living in a segregated society, marched to Vicksburg's battlefield and said that "our fathers brought forth on this continent a new nation, conceived in liberty." They told how the dead buried around them had died not in vain but to give "this nation, under God . . . a new birth of freedom." In essence, Lincoln invented language proclaiming it the business of the national government, "government of the people, by the people, for the people," to guard freedom. American citizenship, Lincoln had orated, began before the Constitution, in 1776. The ideals Lincoln proclaimed at Gettysburg reflected his thinking in 1863. At the end of the nineteenth century, Vicksburg's white population still scorned Lincoln's nationalism even as advertisers used his image to sell their products, a long-dead talisman abstracted from the pulsing blood of his times. To read aloud his old words and understand their original meaning challenged prevailing state-sanctioned segregation and state-sanctioned racial animus.[48]

The African Americans who rallied at the Vicksburg National Cemetery for Memorial Day never allowed themselves to be relegated to outsider status. Gettysburg was a different story. Baltimore's black GAR posts sent black tourists to Gettysburg, where they encountered white prejudice and animosity. According to Jim Weeks, the leading authority on Gettysburg tourism, Pennsylvania whites perceived black excursionists to Gettysburg as degenerated curiosities. Even black leaders thought Gettysburg's black tourists "cut up all kinds of shines" and disgraced their race. "Their archaic form of celebrating did not measure up to the modern standard of commercial culture," Weeks writes.[49]

In this modern commercial culture, the federal government chose to leave African Americans' civil rights in the hands of the states. It also made itself the dispenser of benefits to supplicants. Government clerks, investigators, and accountants became a more profound presence in American life. One way this happened involved quarrels over property army officers expropriated during the war. In contrast to the enlisted men, Union officers taking civilian property often promised compensation. In some cases, those officers even scribbled out a receipt, reassuring property holders that an official transaction had occurred as their men made off with livestock, lumber, and other valuables. After Appomattox, the victims of these confiscations wrote their congressmen, demanding the promised compensation.[50]

In 1871, after six years of petitions and two years of debate, Congress created the Southern Claims Commission to review southern civilians' compensation demands. Congress wanted to pay the claims only of loyal southerners and instructed the three commissioners to require that claimants prove their loyalty as well as the value of the property lost to the army. Asa Owen Aldis of Vermont, James B. Howell of Iowa, and Orange Ferris of New York, all radical Republicans, served as commissioners. These determined Republicans granted few claims: of 22,298 submitted, they approved less than a third, only 7,092. And winning a claim rarely led to full recovery of the property. Very few of the successful claimants recovered all their losses.[51]

The commissioners listened to the statements of aggrieved claimants, asked probing questions, reviewed documents, and encouraged claimants to produce witnesses. And they went further. The commissioners dispatched investigators across the South to probe into the details of ordinary citizens' lives. As they interviewed witnesses, transcribing their testimony, the investigators made a surprising discovery. The slaves said they had owned property. Some enslaved people from Vicksburg insisted they had their own homes and operated their own businesses.[52] Enslaved artisans had negotiated their own contracts with employers.[53] The army had seized their property too, and they also wanted compensation. The commissioners opened a door to a secret world normally denied white people. Black property holders shared thoughts with the commissioners that they had not dared reveal to slavery-era white southerners.[54]

These revelations provoked skepticism, prompting more inquiries, more investigations, and more questions. Some northerners so doubted that slaves could really own anything that they could not imagine that the claims process might involve blacks. Forgetting that black as well as white people populated the South, Illinois Senator Lyman Trumbull protested that before 1871, all legislation assumed that the rebel region of the country—"over which the rebels had absolute control"—was all enemy country "and that everybody within those limits was to be regarded as an enemy." Trumbull conceded that southern unionists suffered when the army passed through, but, Trumbull pointed out, the army suffered too. Moreover, Trumbull just did not trust white southerners. "We know," Trumbull asserted, that southerners, meaning whites, would prove bogus claims "in a region of country where one testified for the other." Trumbull predicted that all southerners would have claims, giving every claimant an interest in covering for his or her fellows.[55]

The commissioners' skeptical and stern review of claims generated an archive of evidence as government investigators looked into marriage, family life, work habits, wealth accumulation, and the South's black–white dynamic, all topics previously closed to federal scrutiny before the war.[56] The Southern Claims Commission collected evidence of African American property holding so unbelievable to white America that scholars began to explore it only as the twentieth century closed.[57]

The Southern Claims Commission collected detailed data on the lives of ordinary people, but it really amounted to only a timid intrusion into society. In 1880, the Committee on War Claims recalled the theory behind the law as "exceedingly questionable" to begin with.[58] A far more extensive effort came from the Civil War pension system, the national government's most vigorous and searching invasion of southerners' lives. The federal law that was passed on July 22, 1861, allowing Lincoln to accept 500,000 volunteer soldiers, also promised that disabled or wounded soldiers would receive the same benefits as disabled U.S. Army veterans. An 1862 law expanded on this promise, guaranteeing pensions to all disabled veterans who enlisted after March 4, 1861, and to their mothers, widows, and orphan sisters.[59] Additional laws further expanded benefits. The 1879 Arrears Act tried to lure more veterans into the federal welfare system by offering back pay to those making new applications. The most sweeping law, however, came in 1890, when Congress offered pensions to all disabled veterans regardless of whether their disability came from their Civil War service.[60]

85

This federal intervention into ordinary citizens' lives proved both enduring and expansive. Between 1880 and 1910, a quarter of the national budget went to paying Civil War pensions. After 1887, the Pension Bureau operated the biggest brick building in the world. By 1910, more than a quarter of all American men older than age sixty-five received federal welfare benefits. A corps of investigators, surgeons, clerks, and lawyers administered this massive system of payments.[61]

The language of the pension laws did not discriminate on the basis of race. Nonetheless, black Civil War veterans found it harder to collect their pensions than did their white counterparts. Ninety-two percent of white veterans made at least one successful application; 75 percent of blacks had comparable success. Part of this disparity can be explained by the black soldiers' lack of resources. Many simply did not have the money to pay for a trip to the nearest surgical board. Claim agents sometimes misrepresented the claims of their black clients, forging evidence even when representing genuine veterans. Black soldiers changed their names more often than white veterans, making proof of identity more difficult. Pension Bureau officers scrutinized black applications with more suspicion than they did white claims, trusting white witnesses over black ones. All veterans had to prove themselves morally worthy to win pension benefits, and white bureaucrats defined proper behavior by middle-class white standards.[62] This, at least, is what one scholar has written. It seems entirely plausible, but, after all, it still remains just one historian's story. To find how Vicksburg's veterans actually fared requires a new look at their pension experiences.

The basic application procedure did not change much through Civil War soldiers' lifetimes. Veterans (or their widows or minor children) first filled out a declaration, often called a Declaration for Disability Pension. These sworn affidavits required the veteran to spell out the details of his service and his physical ailments. The bureau required that applications be accompanied by affidavits from others able to verify the essential facts claimed by the veteran. Government bureaucrats checked the veterans' statements against Civil War records, looking over old rosters to see if the alleged soldier really served in the army.

In questionable cases, the Pension Bureau called on special examiners to investigate the alleged facts. Across the country, some 300 (in 1895) special examiners maintained offices in larger towns and cities. These pension detectives searched marriage records, combed through cemeteries, scrutinized city directories, and questioned witnesses, locating lost relatives and army buddies for interviews.[63] In some cases, Pension Bureau sleuths displayed photographs of putative veterans to other old soldiers to verify identity. Special examiners often worked on widows' claims, and their investigations have a prying moral dimension that could either amuse or outrage a modern reader. Detectives tried to determine if a "ceremonial marriage" between veterans and female claimants had occurred. When critics charge that the Pension Bureau imposed white Victorian morality on former slaves, these special examiner investigations stand as the prime evidence.

The examiners looking into the Milliken's Bend veterans seemed more respectful of African American marriage customs than one might expect from nineteenth-century racists. When special examiner D. W. Harper found that Martha Anderson had been married, as a slave, to Salam Davis before her "legal" marriage to army veteran Peter Anderson, he reported that the earlier marriage did not void her second union. Thus, she got her pension. Does this mean that Harper disrespected slave marriages? Martha Anderson called herself "married" to Davis. She lived with him for seven or eight years and had a child by him. "We separated four years before the war," she told Harper, but her first husband still lived when she married Anderson. None of these facts troubled Harper.[64]

Delilah Fatherie did not fare so well. Special examiner Alexander J. Rurke wanted to know if Fatherie knew or heard that her husband, Willis, had been married before. "Yes sir," Fatherie answered, "I never knew or heard of any former marriage

Pension Bureau agents displayed photographs of Civil War veterans to verify their identity. This photograph shows John Gordon, Milliken's Bend veteran. National Archives.

by him to any other woman." Rurke knew she was lying and confronted her with depositions from the first wife and other neighbors showing that, in fact, Fatherie had married a man still wed to Mahala Johnson. Confronted with this evidence, Fatherie broke down: "Yes sir," she finally admitted, "I knew of it; that is, I heard of it." Rurke recommended that Fatherie not be pensioned, and she was not. Did he impose middle-class white values on a former slave? Perhaps. But Fatherie admitted that "my mother . . . and my step father . . . both told me before I married Willis Fatherie that he had a wife around somewhere and they did think I ought to be careful letting a married man court me." Once she started confessing, Fatherie piled detail on detail. She had met and talked to Mahala before her marriage. The community regarded Willis as married to Mahala—"She was then known by the community as Willis Fatherie's wife." She violated working-class black values.[65]

Examiners had little sympathy for "marriages" when the parties knew they had nondivorced spouses still alive. In another case, the examiner found a woman with a nondivorced husband still alive and sniffed, "This is very different from a marriage where the contracting parties supposed a former spouse dead."[66] But examiners took cohabitation very seriously. Elsie Hunter married Robert Hunter when both were slaves. This union ended involuntarily when whites sold Robert Hunter away. In 1864, Elsie Hunter married William Brooks, but she shortly deserted Brooks. Two years later, Elsie reunited with her slave husband and married him, though she remained legally married to Brooks, not divorcing him until 1867. In 1905, the chief of the Pension Bureau's Law Division rendered judgment on all of Elsie's marriages. The slave marriage had no legal force, he declared, and served as no impediment to her marriage to Brooks. Her marriage to Brooks was still valid when she married Hunter, and that "marriage" had no legal force. But she then stayed with Hunter for thirty-six years and bore him several children. The chief of the Law Division judged them truly married.[67] It is hard to see a lot of "middle=class" bias at work here. The Pension Bureau decided Elsie and Robert merely cohabited and had never had a valid "ceremonial marriage." Despite this, the bureau judged they had a marriage worthy of respect and, more concretely, a pension.

In another case, Nettie Martin could not prove her marriage to Milliken's Bend veteran John Martin. Yellow fever had killed the witnesses, the church where the marriage had been performed no longer existed, and no documentation of the Martins' marriage survived. "This case will have to be adjudicated by implication solely," the special examiner reported. "The mere fact of negroes living together cannot be accepted as presumptive evidence of marriage for some negroes change husbands and wives with a change of the seasons." Nonetheless, testimony by neighbors proved to the examiner's satisfaction that a real marriage existed and had for thirty years.[68] The head of the law division stated the rule: "It is a principle of law of almost universal application that a ceremony regarded by the parties as a valid one is sufficient to constitute a binding marriage even though there may have been some irregularity in the issuance of a license."[69]

The Pension Bureau traded in memory. And this may be why illiterate black applicants found themselves at such a disadvantage compared to white veterans, though it is striking how articulate claimants before the Southern Claims Commission seem when compared with the veterans appearing before pension examiners. While the Southern Claims Commissioners recovered a wealth of detail, which they preserved in first-person narratives, pension investigators, often working many years later, confronted people who had a hard time remembering much of anything. In 1899, Mary Palmer impressed special examiner Bedford Mackey as having an "exceptionally good reputation." She struck Mackey as "an honest, truthful, self-respecting old woman." It is fortunate for Palmer that she made such a good impression, for the text of her testimony seems less than compelling. She could not remember the date of her marriage. She admitted having a slave husband "who went off with the soldiers during the war and I have not seen or heard of him since." Though she admitted the possibility of a living husband in addition to her soldier, she got her pension.[70] In a fairly typical case, soldier William Caston could not remember the date of his enlistment or the date of his discharge and said that a fire had destroyed his army discharge paper.[71] Susan Rodgers told a special examiner that "I reckon I must have told the preacher what my name was but I done forgot what I told him."[72] By the time a special examiner got to Milliken's Bend veteran Gabriel Bell, nineteen years after he became eligible for a pension and nine years after his initial application, he languished in the St. Louis poorhouse insane ward, almost blind, hard of hearing, emaciated, and "mentally so confused that I could get little from him." He had no shoes because another inmate had stolen them. The examiner called on a "stentorian-voiced attendant" to shout questions at the old man but found the answers unreliable. "I did not feel that he was mentally competent to accept notice of special examination and I did not obtain his mark on one." The examiner closed his report with a plea that the aging former slave be moved out of the insane ward—"a place which taxes even a strong mind"—and into a soldiers' retirement home.[73]

Often the soldiers' bodies served as the best record of their service, the surest validation of fading and uncertain memories. Here, too, the new federal willingness to examine ordinary citizens' affairs is evident. Government doctors examined the bodies of applicants, reading the scar tissue to find every gunshot wound and bayonet thrust. Doctors studied the veterans' urine, observing its color and measuring its sugar and acid. War Department records only imperfectly recorded the injuries Civil War soldiers suffered at Milliken's Bend; the surgeons pored over veterans' flesh inch by inch to pinpoint old wounds more exactly. And while doctors examined veterans' genitalia, other investigators documented their sexual relationships.

The pension system became most prominent in American life in the 1880s and 1890s, a time when realism developed in American letters. If realism really represented a "culture of surveillance," a "cultural practice," and not just a literary style, then pension investigators can be called "realists" just as surely as William Dean Howells, Theodore Dreiser, or even Stephen Crane. They sought the real and avoided, for the most part, any sentimental attachment to their subjects. And they tried to represent social groups formerly neglected—ordinary soldiers, including African Americans.[74]

The scholarship about this amazing federal intrusion into individual Americans' most private spaces has evolved from condemnation to approval, reflecting increasing comfort with a powerful federal state. In 1918, William H. Glasson thought the 1890 veterans' pension law was the Republican Party's "high bid for the political support" of Union veterans. Furthermore, Glasson charged, the 1890 act cost a billion dollars collected by customs and internal revenue taxation, money paid out to a "favored" class. This redistributed wealth on a colossal and unconscionable scale, Glasson charged. Taxation took money from the poor, and the pension system distributed it to persons who lived better than most taxpayers[75]—or so Glasson wrote, seemingly unaware of the many black pension seekers, some so poor they could get no medical attention for Civil War wounds still oozing pus decades after the war.

Few other writers have been so skeptical as Glasson, though Heywood T. Sanders, writing in 1980, saw the pension system as increasingly political, especially after 1880. In 1886, Democratic President Grover Cleveland vetoed a dependent pension bill, a product of the Republican Party's alliance with the GAR. When the 1888 election put Republicans in control of both Congress and the White House, "the party was not long in attempting to repay its electoral debt to the old soldiers," Sanders wrote. The result was the June 27, 1890, law that opened up the pension system to so many new beneficiaries. In one year, 655,000 applications for new or increased pensions reached the Pension Bureau. By 1890, the same year Congress very nearly but not quite voted to protect black voting rights, the Pension Bureau could boast itself as "the largest executive bureau in the world." Under Republican presidents, the Pension Bureau approved applications far more freely than under Democrats. Democrats sought out and charged fraud. Sanders concluded that the pension system at least contributed to the Republicans' electoral success if it did not guarantee it.[76]

More recently, scholars have remembered the Civil War pension experience for expanding central state authority to benefit the needy. Theda Skocpol concludes that the pension system amounted to "one of the politically most successful social policies ever devised and sustained in the United States." The Civil War pensions were "America's first system of federal social security for the disabled and the elderly . . . a harbinger of things to come in American democracy."[77]

Reconstruction failed to establish a national system for the protection of civil rights. In Vicksburg it built a landscape where veterans and others could commemorate the war, namely, the National Cemetery. The national government also established bureaucracies to collect and analyze Civil War memories. By attaching money to the memories of Union sympathizers and Union veterans, the national government gave value to those memories. Skocpol calls this a "harbinger of things to come." Perhaps. If so, it would be because the Civil War pension system created a memory later generations could draw on when making their own pension and welfare systems. Unquestionably, the Civil War pensions formed a monument to the valor of black and white Union soldiers who fought and died at Vicksburg and on other Civil War battlefields. It may have been an inadequate remembrance, but it was not nothing.

After the Civil War, national efforts to throw protections around former slaves' civil liberties faded in the face of stubborn white opposition. But as the army shrank its presence on southern soil, it planted mines on the battlefield it left behind. The National Cemetery became a place where African Americans could gather and remember the Civil War promise of freedom Lincoln had articulated in his Gettysburg Address. The Southern Claims Commission collected and archived the testimony of former slaves, testimony that documented slaves as articulate, autonomous individuals, more capable capitalists than victims. Those documents recorded African Americans as thinking, independent-minded individuals. Finally, the Pension Bureau documented the military service of Civil War soldiers, including black veterans. Perhaps most important, pension bureaucrats created a model for federal social security for the disabled and the elderly. In the aftermath of war, the national bureaucracy proved more capable of providing social security through pension payments than in aggressively promoting equal rights and defending the freed people's civil liberties with legal action. This preference for welfare over equal rights proved the lasting legacy of Reconstruction.

Notes

1. For antebellum Vicksburg, see Christopher Morris, *Becoming Southern: The Evolution of a Way of Life, Warren County and Vicksburg, Mississippi, 1770–1860* (New York: Oxford University Press, 1995), 114–81; and Christopher Waldrep, *Roots of Disorder: Race and Criminal Justice in the American South, 1817–80* (Urbana: University of Illinois Press, 1998), 7–58.

2. Eric Foner, *Reconstruction: America's Unfinished Revolution, 1863–1877* (New York: Harper & Row, 1988), xix (definition), 602–12.

3. Lavinia to Emmie, July 13, 1863, folder 5, Crutcher-Shannon Papers, Natchez Trace Collection, Barker Texas History Center, University of Texas, Austin.

4. *Vicksburg Citizen*, May 13, 1861.

5. Anne Shannon, finished by Grace or Alice Shannon, to Emma Crutcher, June, July 1863, file 55, Crutcher-Shannon Papers, Mississippi Department of Archives and History, Jackson.

6. Anne to Emma, June, July 1863, file 55, Crutcher-Shannon Papers, Mississippi Department of Archives and History, Jackson.

7. Alice to Emma, November 19, 1863, file 55, Crutcher-Shannon Papers, Mississippi Department of Archives and History, Jackson.

8. H. Lieb, commanded 5th USCT, August 8, 1863, Order Book vol. 6, 5th USCT Heavy Arty Regimental Records, National Archives, Washington, D.C.

9. Mose Germain court-martial, LL1734, box 623, James Brown court-martial, LL1565, box 598; Augustus Harrison court-martial, box 598; Henry Johnson court-martial, box 598; James Johnson court-martial, box 598; Taylor Williams court-martial, box 598; Edmund Turner court-martial, OO108, box 1937; and Johnson Richards court-martial, box 1937, Records of the Office of the Judge Advocate General (Army), court-martial case files, RG 153, National Archives, Washington, D.C.; Henry H. Penneman to B. B. Neal, February 9, 1864, Order Book vol. 6, Fifth USCT Heavy Arty Regimental Records, National Archives, Washington, D.C.

10. James Pickett Jones, *Black Jack: John A. Logan and Southern Illinois in the Civil War Era* (1967; repr., Carbondale: Southern Illinois University Press, 1995), 106; Giles Simms et al., court-martial, LL2492, roll 7, M5023 microfilm, National Archives, Washington, D.C.; 49th USCT Infantry, vol. 2, Descriptive Book, book records of Volunteer Union Organizations RG 94, National Archives, Washington, D.C.

11. Court-martial of Thomas Fore and others, Records of the Judge Advocate General (Army), court-martial case files, RG 153, National Archives, Washington, D.C.

12. *Vicksburg Evening Post*, January 29, 1909.

13. Gordon A. Cotton, *Horrible Outrage! The Murder of Minerva Cook* (Vicksburg, Miss.: privately printed, 1993).

14. Waldrep, *Roots of Disorder*, 86–97.

15. Foner, *Reconstruction*, 176–227.

16. 1865 *Laws of Mississippi*, 82–93.

17. Foner, *Reconstruction*, 230–31.

18. *Chicago Tribune*, December 1, 1865.

19. Waldrep, *Roots of Disorder*, 108–9.

20. Waldrep, *Roots of Disorder*, 105–16.

21. William C. Harris, *The Day of the Carpetbagger: Republican Reconstruction in Mississippi* (Baton Rouge: Louisiana State University Press, 1979), 2–3.

22. Waldrep, *Roots of Disorder*, 122–23; Michael W. Fitzgerald, *The Union League Movement in the Deep South: Politics and Agricultural Change During Reconstruction* (Baton Rouge: Louisiana State University Press, 1989), 64, 90, 97–98.

23. Gordon A. Cotton, *The Old Court House* (Raymond, Miss.: Keith Printing Co., 1982), 27.

24. Waldrep, *Roots of Disorder*, 163–66.

25. Waldrep, *Roots of Disorder*, 167–69.

26. Act of May 31, 1870, 16 Stat. 140; *Vicksburg Republican*, May 20, October 29, 1868; *Philadelphia Press* quoted in *Vicksburg Republican*, January 5, 1869.

27. Act of April 20, 1871, 17 Stat. 13.

28. William W. Murray to George H. Williams, September 5, 1874, and William W. Murray to Alphonso Taft, September 25, 1876, box 998, Western Tennessee, letters received, Source Chronological Files, RG 60, General Records of the Department of Justice, National Archives, College Park, Md.; *United States v. Harris*, 106 U.S. 629 (1882). The printed record identifies the defendants as "R. G. Harris and nineteen others." For the names of all the defendants, see criminal docket, book 220, U.S. Circuit Court, Western Division Tennessee, National Archives, Atlanta, Ga.; *United States v. R. G. Harris*, et al., case 8497, box 1187, RG 367, Supreme Court records, National Archives, Washington, D.C. To identify the defendants serving as state officers, see State Docket A, Circuit Clerk's Office, Crockett County, Tennessee, Alamo, Tenn.

29. For the logging cases, see Luke Lea to Attorney General, December 13, 1878, Southern Mississippi, letters received, Source Chronological Files, RG 60, General Records of the Department of Justice, roll 4, M970, and J. H. Pierce to A. T. Ackerman, May 23, 1871, Northern Mississippi, letters received, Source Chronological Files, RG 60, General Records of the Department of Justice, roll 1, M970, National Archives, Washington, D.C. (microfilm); *Vicksburg Daily Herald*, February 5, 1870.

30. Robert J. Kaczorowski, *The Politics of Judicial Interpretation: The Federal Courts, Department of Justice and Civil Rights, 1866–1876* (New York: Oceana, 1985), 135–72; Xi Wang, *The Trial of Democracy: Black Suffrage and Northern Republicans, 1860–1910* (Athens: University of Georgia Press, 1997), 93–252; Charles Fairman, *Reconstruction and Re-*

union, 1864–88, 2 vols. (New York: Macmillan, 1971–1987), 2:221–289, 436–97.

31. W. F. Hollingworth, "Memorandum of 1863," May 18, 1863, Mississippi Department of Archives and History, Jackson.

32. Alice Shannon to Emma Shannon, November 19, 1863, folder 56, Crutcher-Shannon Papers.

33. Isaac Shoemaker diary, February 11, 1864, Duke University Library, Durham, North Carolina.

34. *Vicksburg Republican,* May 24, 1868; *Vicksburg Weekly Republican,* March 24, 1868; George Macy to Col. Chandler, March 17, 1868, Old Court House Museum, Vicksburg, Mississippi.

35. Richard Meyers, *The Vicksburg National Cemetery: Vicksburg National Military Park, An Administrative History* (Division of History: Office of Archeology and Historic Preservation, March 31, 1968, National Park Service), 1–3.

36. *Commercial Herald Souvenir Edition* (n.d.), Old Court House Museum collection.

37. *Vicksburg Evening Post,* May 23, 1902.

38. Karen Lynne Cox, "Women, the Lost Cause, and the New South: The United Daughters of the Confederacy and the Transmission of Confederate Culture, 1894–1919" (Ph.D. diss., University of Southern Mississippi, 1997), 8, 12–13, 20–83.

39. *Vicksburg Evening Post,* September 14, 1906, June 3, 1912; *Confederate Veteran,* March, April 1915, January 1919.

40. Cora Chaplin Weed, *Handbook for Iowa Soldiers' and Sailors' Monument* (1898; repr., Ottumwa, Iowa: Press of the Camp Pope Bookshop, 1994), 105; Louis Rosenfield Noun, "The Iowa Soldiers' and Sailors' Monument," *Palimpsest* 67 (May/June 1986): 80–93.

41. J. L. Donaldson to J. W. Scully, October 12, 1866, box 3, letters received, U.S. Army Continental Commands, Department of Mississippi, RG 393, National Archives, Washington, D.C.

42. J. L. Donaldson, General Orders No. 8., August 9, 1866, box 3, letters received, U.S. Army Continental Commands, Department of Mississippi, RG 393, National Archives, Washington, D.C.

43. Meyers, *The Vicksburg National Cemetery,* 11–18.

44. General court-martial convened in Vicksburg, June 28, 1867, OO 2333, box 1412, Office of the Judge Advocate General, RG 153,

National Archives, Washington, D.C.; Meyers, *The Vicksburg National Cemetery*, 16–28.

45. *Vicksburg Evening Post*, May 30, 1889, August 20, 1890; Stuart McConnell, *Glorious Contentment: The Grand Army of the Republic, 1865–1900* (Chapel Hill: University of North Carolina Press, 1992), 213–18; Cecilia Elizabeth O'Leary, *To Die for: The Paradox of American Patriotism* (Princeton, N.J.: Princeton University Press, 1999), 65–67; Larry M. Logue, *To Appomattox and Beyond: The Civil War Soldier in War and Peace* (Chicago: Ivan R. Dee, 1996), 94–102.

46. Charles Mitchell affidavit, June 13, 1914, Randall Davis pension application 1133588, certificate 1150251, National Archives, Washington, D.C.; *Vicksburg Evening Post*, May 31, 1887, October 16, 1917.

47. Garry Wills, *Lincoln at Gettysburg: The Words That Remade America* (New York: Simon & Schuster, 1992), 147.

48. Wills, *Lincoln at Gettysburg*, 125–47.

49. Jim Weeks, *Gettysburg: Memory, Market, and an American Shrine* (Princeton, N.J.: Princeton University Press, 2003), 92–98.

50. *Diary and Correspondence of Salmon P. Chase*, in *Annual Report of the American Historical Association 1902*, 2 vols. (Washington, D.C.: U.S. Government Printing Office, 1889–1903), 2:45–46.

51. Sarah Larson, "Records of the Southern Claims Commission," *Prologue* 12 (winter 1980): 207–18.

52. Matilda Anderson deposition in Matilda Anderson file 6935, box 207, Settled Case Files for Claims Approved by the Southern Claims Commission, 1871–1880, Records of the Lands, Files, and Miscellaneous Division, Records of the Accounting Officers of the Department of the Treasury, RG 217, National Archives, Washington, D.C. (hereinafter cited as SCC records).

53. M. Steigelman deposition, Matilda Anderson file 6935, box 207, SCC records.

54. Henry Banks deposition, Henry Banks file 14443, box 207, SCC records; Albert Deval deposition, November 1871, Albert Deval claim 6954, box 208, SCC records.

55. Lyman Trumbull, speaking on "Military Supplies in Rebel States," March 4, 1870, *Congressional Globe*, 41st Cong., 2nd sess., 1685.

56. Noel G. Harrison, "Atop an Anvil: The Civilians' War in Fairfax and Alexandria Counties, April 1861–April 1862," *Virginia Magazine of History and Biography* 106 (1998): 133–66; James Penn, "The Geographical Variation of Unionism in Louisiana: A Study of the Southern Claims Data," *Louisiana History* 30 (1989): 399–418; Michael K. Honey, "The War within the Confederacy: White Unionists of North Carolina," *Prologue* 18 (summer 1986): 75–93; John Hammond Moore, "In Sherman's Wake: Atlanta and the Southern Claims Commission, 1871–1880," *Atlanta Historical Journal* 29 (summer 1985): 5–18; Eugene A. Hatfield, "Stephen Green Dorsey and the Southern Claims Commission: A Question of Loyalty," *Atlanta Historical Journal* 29 (summer 1985): 19–29; John Hammond Moore, "Sherman's 'Fifth Column': A Guide to Unionist Activity in Georgia," *Georgia Historical Quarterly* 68 (fall 1984): 383–409; John Hammond Moore, "Richmond Area Residents and the Southern Claims Commission, 1871–1880," *Virginia Magazine of History and Biography* 93 (July 1983): 285–95; John Hammond Moore, "Getting Uncle Sam's Dollars: South Carolinians and the Southern Claims Commission, 1871–1880," *South Carolina Historical Magazine* 82 (July 1981): 248–62.

57. Edna Greene Medford, "'I Was Always a Union Man': The Dilemma of Free Blacks in Confederate Virginia," *Slavery and Abolition* 15 (1994): 1–16; Dylan Penningroth, "Slavery, Freedom and Social Claims to Property among African Americans in Liberty County, Georgia, 1850–1880," *Journal of American History* 84 (1997): 405–35.

58. *Relief of Certain Citizens Claiming to Be Loyal*, House of Representatives Report No. 1467, 46th Cong., 2nd sess., May 21, 1880.

59. William H. Glasson, *Federal Military Pensions in the United States* (New York: Oxford University Press, 1918), 124–25.

60. Glasson, *Federal Military Pensions in the United States*, 164–238; John William Oliver, "History of Civil War Military Pensions, 1861–1885," *Bulletin of the University of Wisconsin* 844 (1917): 55–111.

61. Theda Skocpol, "America's First Social Security System: The Expansion of Benefits for Civil War Veterans," *Political Science Quarterly* 108 (1993): 85–86; O'Leary, *To Die For*, 45.

62. Donald R. Shaffer, "'I Do Not Suppose That Uncle Sam Looks at the Skin': African Americans and the Civil War Pension System, 1865–1934," *Civil War History* 46 (June 2000): 132–47.

63. H. A. Kingsley to William Boyd Allison, June 22, 1894, box 294, William Boyd Allison Papers, State Historical Society of Iowa, Des Moines.

64. D. W. Harper, special examiner's report, December 30, 1893, Martha Anderson application 517012, National Archives, Washington, D.C.

65. Alexander J. Rurke, special examiner's report, June 9, 1906, Delilah Fatherie pension application 8818161, National Archives, Washington, D.C.

66. M. Whitehead, special examiner's report, March 30, 1899, Mary Lacy pension application 663314, National Archives, Washington, D.C.

67. Chief Law Division, memorandum, February 18, 1905, Elsie Hunter pension application 761695, certificate 588271, National Archives, Washington, D.C.

68. Charles Whitehead, special examiner's report, March 18, 1904, Nettie Martin pension application 759623, certificate 570674, National Archives, Washington, D.C.

69. Chief, Law Division, memorandum, April 1, 1904, National Archives, Washington, D.C.

70. Bedford Mackey, special examiner's report, February 28, 1899, Mary Palmer pension application 571684, certificate 476029, National Archives, Washington, D.C.

71. Cadure Caston, alias William Caston, claimant's affidavit, June 22, 1899, William Caston pension application 1126425, National Archives, Washington, D.C.

72. Susan Rodgers deposition, June 25, 1885 Susan Rodgers application 147472, certificate 111645, National Archives, Washington, D.C.

73. James L. Davenport, special examiner's report, December 13, 1909, Gabriel Bell pension application 271834, National Archives, Washington, D.C.

74. Amy Kaplan, *The Social Construction of American Realism* (Chicago: University of Chicago Press, 1988), 7–9, 21; Giorgio Mariani, *Spectacular Narratives: Representations of Class and War in Stephen Crane and the American 1890s* (New York: Peter Lang, 1992).

75. Glasson, *Federal Military Pensions in the United States*, 238–39.

76. Heywood T. Sanders, "Paying for the 'Bloody Shirt': The Politics of Civil War Pensions," in Barry S. Rundquest, ed., *Political Benefits: Empirical Studies of American Public Programs* (Lexington, Mass.: D C Heath, 1980), 137–49.

77. Skocpol, "America's First Social Security System," 116.

The Generals' War

Of many a score—aye, thousands, North and South, of un-
writ heroes, unknown heroisms, incredible, impromptu,
first-class desperations—who tells? No history, ever—No
poem sings, nor music sounds, those bravest men of all—
those deeds. No formal General's report, nor print, nor
book in the library, no column in the paper, embalms the
bravest.

—Walt Whitman[1]

IN the summer of 1865, Ulysses Grant traveled across the
North, meeting large crowds. He could already tell from his
reception how Americans wanted to remember the Civil War.
Everywhere he went, Grant later recalled, he encountered
people with opinions about various generals and theories about
their strategies and tactics. As journalists hungrily reported—or
misreported—the exchanges, Grant found himself defending his
subordinates from criticism and offering opinions about various
opponents.[2]

For anyone hoping that America might produce a national
Civil War narrative not only focusing on military adventure but
also taking into account emancipation and black aspirations for
freedom and justice, the memoirs of the great generals, especially
Grant, posed a formidable obstacle. The nation was awash in
books and articles, yet the memoirs of Grant and the other gener-

102

als seemed to suck all the oxygen out of any alternative war narrative. As Grant himself realized that summer of 1865, Americans could not get enough inside information about high-command decisions.

There were other voices. Americans made choices about which Civil War narratives would dominate. Even before the Civil War, Americans had begun to democratize their commemorations of war. Veterans of the War of 1812 organized to petition for better benefits, insisting that ordinary soldiers deserved recognition. The federal government built an obelisk over the graves of Mexican War soldiers, one of the first federal efforts to commemorate ordinary soldiers.[3] In part because of photography and increased literacy, the Civil War engendered a sense that every soldier had a story to tell and that every individual's story had value. The Civil War also mobilized far more Americans than any previous war. After Appomattox, Americans memorialized ordinary soldiers more than ever before.[4] Dramatists and novelists offered sentimental reunion romances, often using emotional and passionate women as a metaphor for all white southerners.[5] In 1879, Albion Tourgée offered a dissenting view when he published *A Fool's Errand*, a Republican view of Reconstruction.[6]

Many ordinary soldiers wrote their own Civil War histories, either as autobiographies or as regimental histories. Some regimental historians began writing or planning to write their books before the war ended. More often, regiments elected committees or appointed regimental historians at postwar reunions. Some contracted with commercial publishers, while others simply went to their hometown printer.[7] Those regimental histories certainly offered an alternative to the generals' stories. They could be downright insubordinate. The three comrades detailed to write *The Story of the Fifty-Fifth Illinois Volunteer Infantry in the Civil War* frankly told their readers they had little interest in "indiscriminate and turgid eulogy of those in high position." Instead, they demanded "simple justice for the patriotic rank and file."[8]

Regimental histories sometimes expressed sympathy for the slaves. By 1862, northern popular war literature delighted in depicting slaves overcoming their erstwhile owners' authority. As the war progressed, *Frank Leslie's Illustrated Newspaper* and *Harper's Weekly* moved away from crudely caricatured depictions of blacks to more positive illustrations.[9] In 1873, the U.S. Supreme Court continued the same sentiment when it paid tribute to "the poor victims whose enforced servitude was the foundation of the quarrel" between the sections. The Court remembered that black men "(for they proved themselves men in that terrible crisis) offered their services and were accepted by thousands." Justice Samuel Miller admired black masculinity. But that gendered perspective did not prevent him from writing a decision that left those southern black men (and their women) without federal protection against violent white racists.[10]

Another alternative to high-ranking memoirists came from blacks themselves. African Americans, speaking through sympathetic white writers and as authors themselves, put their views on the record. *The Nation*, founded by a group of forty that included abolitionists, dispatched John Richard Dennett to Dixie. Dennett's reports delivered telling insights into American race relations.[11] Another sympathetic white writer, Edward Howland, likened slavery to a bandage "tied tight about the body politic, preventing the free circulation of ideas." The South's "foolish," "reckless," and "criminal" attack on Fort Sumter stripped that bandage aside, and the loyal population arose "like a giant roused from a drugged sleep."[12] Other writers agreed that the "Sumter cowardice" had led even proslavery northerners to cast aside their sympathy for the peculiar institution in favor of the Union.[13]

Horace Greeley's 1866 history of the war included a chapter devoted to "Negro Soldiery." Greeley narrated black service in the American Revolution and the War of 1812. In the Civil War, whites turned to black volunteers only after George McClellan's campaign against Richmond failed, leading to new calls for 600,000 new soldiers. As Greeley saw it, ambition overcame prejudice. The policy of commissioning white enlisted men willing to serve as officers in black regiments went a long way toward skewering their prejudices. "There were few, if any, instances of a white sergeant or corporal whose dignity or whose nose revolted at the proximity of Blacks as private soldiers, if he might secure a lieutenancy by deeming them not unsavory." In the end, Greeley concluded, "It is no longer fairly disputable that they played a very important and useful part in the overthrow of the Rebellion." Some black regiments performed better than whites, Greeley said, and man for man they proved equal to white troops.[14]

In 1867, William A. Crafts called the Milliken's Bend battle crucial in his book *The Southern Rebellion*. Militarily, Crafts conceded, the skirmish meant little. The battle mattered because blacks proved they could fight. "The rebels professed to believe," Crafts wrote, that a degraded people "possessed no quality essential to the soldier." Even some northerners, Crafts added, had their doubts, as did Union army officers. Black valor at Milliken's Bend dispelled such prejudice. After the battle, Union officers "more freely sought command of such men."[15]

Thomas Wentworth Higginson had commanded a South Carolina black regiment that never went near Vicksburg, but his popular account of black soldiers' Civil War service shows that whites could still appreciate black valor five years after Appomattox. He based his 1870 book *Army Life in a Black Regiment* on his wartime diary. An experienced author, Higginson wrote a sensible account, finding black soldiers to be "very much like other men." He recalled that one staff officer had described black soldiers as "intensely human." Higginson thought this quite apt, "a striking and comprehensive description."[16]

Black authors also spoke for their race. The first black account appeared in 1867, when William Wells Brown published *The Negro in the American Rebellion*. Although his history appeared just two years after Appomattox, Brown claimed he acted only after waiting patiently for someone else who was more competent to do the work. Brown's twentieth-century editor complained that he sounded "petulant," but perhaps Brown's remark should be interpreted as evidence that he could already see white America beginning to forget black Civil War service.[17] In 1886, George W. Williams, a veteran himself, produced another history of black soldiering,[18] and another black war veteran, Joseph T. Wilson, published his account three years after that.[19]

All three of these black authors presented books quite different from Higginson's first-person journalistic approach. Brown, Williams, and Wilson all sought to redeem their race by writing epochal histories, more or less along the lines pioneered by Greeley in 1866. Brown started his story in 1620, proceeding through the Denmark Vesey and Nat Turner rebellions before reaching the Civil War.[20] George W. Williams went even deeper in the past, beginning his story in the Egyptian Sixth Dynasty before advancing to the Revolution and then the Civil War. Williams wanted to combat negative stereotypes with his own more positive generalizations. In a chapter titled "Negro Idiosyncracies," Williams insisted that slavery actually strengthened its victims physically, making them more resistant to disease than were their oppressors. A less sophisticated writer than Higginson, Williams indulged in stereotypes: describing blacks as gentle, teachable, and happy-go-lucky. But Williams meant these as positive characterizations. Not cowardly at all, African Americans were instead "thoroughly unselfish," patient, and poetic.[21] Though he did not go back to ancient Egypt, Wilson also dug deep to find a long history of black military valor, including black soldiering in the Revolution, the War of 1812, and then the Civil War. In his preface, Wilson described his book as a labor of love, rousing proud feelings for his race, and "awakening an intense love of country" at the same time.[22]

All three authors described Milliken's Bend as the most brutal battle in the war, a place where black troops proved themselves against a savage Confederate attack. Brown framed Milliken's Bend as a defeat for the planters' idea that their slaves would not dare fight them. All three authors emphasized Confederate ruth-

106

lessness. Brown called this battle "the most desperate of this war" and inaccurately claimed the southern attackers took no prisoners, killing any blacks they captured. In Williams's and Wilson's accounts, attacking Confederate troops yelled, "No quarter!" Williams described the inexperienced Confederates as veterans to emphasize the accomplishment of the raw black soldiers who stood firm. And Williams wanted his readers to know that the Confederate attackers outnumbered the black defenders, pushing them back against the levee through sheer force of numbers. In hand-to-hand combat, bayonets flashed, and soldiers used their muskets as clubs. Brown relied on an anonymous article from *The Rebellion Record* to describe dead white and black soldiers lying side by side, in some cases having bayoneted each other. Even when not quoting them verbatim, these narratives closely followed journalists' articles published shortly after the battle: heroic men fighting well in the face of overwhelming odds against a murderous enemy.[23]

All three writers agreed that the battle proved black courage. The three relied extensively on a letter by Captain Matthew M. Miller. Proclaiming the bravery of his men, this white officer declared, "I never more wish to hear the expression, 'The Niggers won't fight.'" Miller's account appears in all three books because this white officer made the point all three authors wanted remembered. Black courage at least upset the old racial hierarchy, if it did not turn it upside down. Brown repeated the story that when the former slave captured a slave owner, the prisoner pleaded that "*his own* negroes" not be made his guards. "This battle," Brown concluded, "satisfied the slave-masters of the South that their charm was gone; and that the negro, as a slave was lost forever."[24] Williams declared that black troops at Milliken's Bend won "a priceless heritage of the race for whose freedom they nobly contended." Williams emphasized that while the troops had only recently escaped slavery, they knew the value of freedom: "Those who fell in conflict with their old enemy did not grudge the price they paid."[25]

These authors understood that not only did they record black heroism as white racism intensified, but they also did so at a time when most readers favored a Civil War narrative based on generals' accounts. Joseph Wilson said he wrote his book as a corrective for popular histories "which ascribe to the generals and colonels who commanded, instead of the soldiers who did the fighting, victory or defeat." Wilson insisted that while he had no desire to detract from the commanders, "My aim is to credit the soldiers with whatever heroism they may have displayed."[26] Though books describing ordinary black soldiers' courage circulated, the most widely read and eagerly devoured writings came, directly or indirectly, from the generals remembering their strategic and tactical decisions, not from the privates or the journalists. Many of the books about black soldiering met the fate of *The Negro in the American Revolution*, which (according to its 1971 editor) did not attract the attention it deserved.[27]

Ordinary soldiers had to compete with generals for attention. For several years after Appomattox, at least one new biography of Grant appeared annually.[28] These biographers so focused their attention on generals that they sometimes showed remarkable ignorance about facts known to every private in the army, as when Adam Badeau (a former colonel himself) claimed Grant's army "learned" to forage only after the Holly Springs debacle.[29] *Century* magazine sought the highest-ranking officers for its Civil War series published between 1884 and 1887. To tell its Vicksburg story, *Century* recruited General Joseph Johnston, General Ulysses Grant, and S. H. Lockett, "chief engineer of the defenses."[30] *Century* relied so heavily on generals as to make itself the subject of ridicule. George Peck wrote *How Private George W. Peck Put Down the Rebellion* as a satire on the *Century* series. Peck, a politician and newspaper humorist, wrote that so many generals had claimed that the war turned on their particular efforts as to present "a kind of history that is going to mix up generations yet unborn in the most hopeless manner." To set the record straight, Peck decided to describe "*the* decisive battle of the war." Peck explained that he had discussed the matter with other veterans, and they had urged him to submit his manuscript to *Century*. As "a plain, unvarnished private soldier," Peck wrote that he hesitated to go against all the *Century* generals. "I am something of a liar myself," Peck wrote, "and can do fairly well in my own class." But on the pages of *Century*, Peck feared, "I was entered in too fast a class of liars."[31]

Peck had a point. The nation understood Vicksburg—and the Civil War generally—largely as a contest between competing generals. The army with the superior generals won, not the side with the better cause. For the South, this worked well. In 1866, Edward A. Pollard's *The Lost Cause* explained that the South lost the Civil War only through bad generaling.[32] Unlike Richardson, Higginson, and Williams, Pollard passionately believed in slavery and stressed that the South's cause did not lead to its downfall. In 1866, Pollard, a Richmond journalist, still expected and hoped the war would resume, and he believed, as he had all through the war, that the South would ultimately prevail with slavery restored in some form.[33] Pollard's view of Vicksburg followed the thinking of another Confederate writer, A. S. Abrams, who in 1863 had argued that with better and more capable generals, the South could have defeated the North at Vicksburg.[34] Pollard agreed, denigrating the Confederate commander at Vicksburg, John C. Pemberton, and chastising Jefferson Davis generally for his "grotesque" selections of generals, including Pemberton. Pemberton was so incompetent, according to Pollard, that even Grant, a man "without any marked ability, certainly without genius, without fortune, without influence . . . no spark of military genius," could prevail. Pollard's single concession to Pemberton came when he asserted that Grant won only because he had the larger army. The South should have won—and someday would win—because it had the superior cause: slavery.[35]

Northern writers did not entirely dissent from Pollard's assessment of the top generals at Vicksburg. In his 1866 biography of Grant, Henry Coppee wrote that "notwithstanding the bitter rebel spirit which pervades Pollard's work, I desire to say that it is, in many cases, very fair and just." Coppee agreed with Pollard's negative assessment of Pemberton. "The enemy," Coppee wrote about the Bruinsburg landing, "should have resisted the advance . . . but they did not." Coppee rapidly sketched Pemberton's failings: he "should" have fought at Port Gibson but did not; he "should not have fought at Raymond" but did; he moved so "irresolutely" and weakly at Champion's Hill as to demoralize his troops. But while sharing Pollard's appraisal of Pemberton, Coppee, of course, rejected Pollard's view of Grant. According to Coppee, Grant "was active, versatile, tenacious of purpose, Napoleonic in his judgment and use of men."[36]

William Swinton's 1867 *Twelve Decisive Battles of the War* also seconded Pollard on key points. Swinton, born in Scotland and educated in Canada, had been a *New York Times* war correspondent through the Civil War. His articles criticized Union generals so sharply and his methods proved so unsavory that the army finally banned him from the lines. Nevertheless, in his 1867 narrative of the Vicksburg siege, Swinton directed most of his critical comments not at Grant but at Pemberton. He did not doubt Pemberton's courage or his commitment to the Confederate cause despite his northern birth. Swinton did reiterate the view that once Union gunboats had passed Vicksburg's batteries, defending that particular place became pointless. After Vicksburg's river batteries had been proven ineffective, Pemberton's duty changed: he now had to watch out for his army, not Vicksburg, according to Swinton. Instead of obeying the sensible orders of his commander, Joseph Johnston, Pemberton "by his ill-judged motions" entangled "himself in toil from which at length there was no escape." "Deluded still by his one fixed idea of defending Vicksburg," he "threw away" chances to save his army. Johnston's commands were "prescient"—and ignored by Pemberton. Swinton did not criticize Grant in his Vicksburg chapter, but his condemnation of Pemberton was so thorough as to leave little reason to praise Grant's strategic thinking. Swinton applauded Grant's bravery, saying he acted "unmoved by all the perils of the operation." But on this point, Swinton again anticipated future writers: all the generals exhibited courage, including Pemberton. It was an American trait.[37] Black soldiers do not appear in Swinton's book.

Seven years later, Johnston himself continued this critical appraisal of Pemberton in a memoir titled *Narrative of Military Operations during the Civil War*. This was the first major entry in the generals' battle of reminiscences. Johnston packed his book with documents not generally available, as Congress would not authorize publication of the government's archive of Civil War communications for another six years. Unfortunately, Johnston also loaded his narrative with venom and bile; he had a few scores to settle, particularly with Jefferson Davis.

Johnston began his *Narrative* in 1861. In two quick sentences on his first page, he dispensed with the causes of the Civil War. Virginians, Johnston reported, did not think Lincoln's election justified secession; his call for troops did. Johnston himself believed secession a revolution justified by traditional American maxims: "free government is founded on the consent of the governed." Johnston wrote that he had been "educated in such opinions" and "naturally determined to return to the State of which I was a native . . . and, if necessary, fight in [its] defense."[38] Later, he called the Confederate effort a "war against subjugation."[39]

Historians have pointed out that Johnston's favorite military strategy involved concentrating his forces at one point and then rolling the dice on one all-or-nothing attack. In the Peninsular campaign, Johnston had proposed delivering a knockout punch to the Union by massing Confederate forces, uniting various commands. "Such a victory would have decided not only the campaign, but the war," he believed.[40] Both Johnston and his biographers placed enormous confidence in the importance of such strategic decision making.

A musket shot to the shoulder forced Johnston to give up command of the Confederacy's eastern front. Returning to duty in November 1862, Johnston learned that Davis had decided to make him theater commander of the South's western armies. That fall, Davis had created a new department, covering Mississippi and eastern Louisiana, under Pemberton's command. General Theophilus Hunter Holmes commanded Confederates west of the Mississippi River. Braxton Bragg led an army in Tennessee. Ulysses S. Grant commanded the Union forces confronting these commands. Once again, Johnston favored a mass attack, urging that Pemberton's and Holmes's troops (and perhaps Bragg's) be joined into a unified force against Grant. "This suggestion," Johnston wrote, "was not adopted, nor noticed."[41]

Johnston complained to Davis that he disliked commanding these disparate armies spread far apart, with different goals and fighting different adversaries. Johnston wrote that Davis "reflected" on his complaint and then explained that Richmond was too far from the western theater to allow proper presidential supervision of the armies. Davis wanted an officer stationed in the West, "with authority to transfer troops from one army to the other in an emergency." Johnston wrote that clearly he was not the proper officer to exercise such responsibility since he was already on record believing that such transfers ought not be attempted.[42]

Johnston related that on April 11, 1863, Pemberton reported that Grant had halted his planned attack on Vicksburg and offered to send 8,000 troops to Bragg in Tennessee. Within a week, though, when Union gunboats and transports ran past Vicksburg's river batteries, Pemberton realized that Grant had not given up on Vicksburg. When Grant landed his forces below Vicksburg, crossing over to the east side of the river, Pemberton telegraphed that his forces had fought furiously and now needed reinforcements. On May 12, he informed Johnston that Grant was driving toward Edwards's depot. Pemberton again pleaded for more troops.[43] Johnston urged Pemberton to "unite your whole force" and confront the attackers. Johnston conceded that Sherman maintained his corps at Milliken's Bend, above Vicksburg, ready to pounce, if Pemberton massed his army against the eastern threat.[44]

The next day, General John Gregg briefed Johnston on the situation around Vicksburg. Pemberton had his headquarters at Bovina. McPherson had marched from Raymond to Clinton, placing his army between Johnston and Pemberton. Pemberton calculated that McPherson had been detached from Grant's army to block any effort to reinforce the Confederates defending Vicksburg. Johnston again instructed Pemberton to mass his forces, saying, "If practicable come up on his rear at once."[45]

On May 14, Johnston learned that not one but two Union army corps, Sherman's as well as McPherson's, had advanced on Jackson. At this time, Johnston wrote, Pemberton had 32,000 men. Johnston again urged Pemberton to mass his entire force against Grant's army. And again, Johnston evinced great confidence in his favorite strategy. "It would decide the campaign," he wrote Pemberton.[46]

Eleven hours after he got his orders from Johnston, Pemberton wrote that he did not plan to attack Grant but rather hoped to maneuver federal troops into an attack on his own dug-in troops. Johnston wrote that Pemberton's message demoralized him. Johnston directed Pemberton to march to Clinton so the two commanders could join forces. Johnston related that Pemberton assembled his officers in a council of war to decide whether to obey his superior's order. Most of the officers wanted to follow orders and go to Clinton. Only a minority wanted to attack Grant's supply lines "by placing the army on the road from Jackson and Raymond to Port Gibson," forcing Grant to attack a defended position. Johnston wrote that though he had little faith in the minority's proposal, Pemberton nonetheless adopted it. Johnston pictured Pemberton as almost irrational: "General Pemberton . . . determined to execute a measure which he disapproved, which his council of war opposed, and which was in violation of the orders of his commander."[47]

Unaware that his subordinate was not following orders, Johnston wrote that he innocently marched two brigades to effect a rendezvous. Only after he had moved his troops into position did Johnston learn that Pemberton would not be following orders. Pemberton reported that he was defending the Big Black bridge behind Vicksburg, but by the time Johnston received the message, Union forces had already overwhelmed Pemberton's forces and crossed the Big Black. With that information in hand, Johnston issued his fourth order to Pemberton. "If it is not too late," he wrote, "evacuate Vicksburg and its dependencies and march to the northeast." Johnston reasoned that Vicksburg could no longer be held. "If . . . you are invested in Vicksburg, you must ultimately surrender." Better to save the troops than defend a hopeless position. At this point in the narrative, Johnston paused to answer charges that he should have personally gone to Vicksburg and taken command. "If at anytime after my arrival in Jackson I had been strong enough to attempt such a ride," he would have done so.[48]

On May 19, Johnston received a new message from Pemberton, reporting that the general had again assembled a council of war to debate the merits of superior orders. Pemberton told Johnston that all his officers agreed to disobey the order. He also opined that Vicksburg remained "the most important point in the Confederacy." Johnston begged to differ. Pemberton, Johnston pointed out, wrote this judgment after Union gunboats had proved themselves entirely capable of running past Vicksburg's batteries. Echoing Swinton, Johnston reasoned that since the batteries did not work, Vicksburg had no military value.[49] At this point, Johnston still assured Pemberton that he was assembling a force to rescue the Vicksburg Confederates. "Hold out," he instructed.[50]

Johnston's narrative of the siege also recounted his correspondence with Jefferson Davis. After the war, Lost Cause mythologists would argue vigorously that the North won only because it had larger armies than the South.[51] Anticipating these later historical quarrels, Davis and Johnston themselves disagreed over the number of Confederate troops they had available. On May 27, Johnston telegraphed Davis that Pemberton had estimated Grant's forces at no less than 60,000. When reinforced, Johnston informed his president, he would have only 23,000. In his reply, Davis disagreed: "The reinforcements sent you exceed, by say seven thousand, the estimate of your dispatch." The Confederate secretary of war, Davis said, estimated Johnston's number at 34,000. The secretary of war, Johnston snapped back, "is greatly mistaken." On June 4, Johnston bluntly told Richmond that he could not help Pemberton because he lacked sufficient troops for the task. Eleven days later, Johnston called Vicksburg "hopeless." Less than a week later, the secretary of war, James A. Seddon, wrote Johnston that he could "rely upon it, the eyes and hopes of the whole Confederacy are upon you, with the full confidence that you will act." Seddon even said that it would be better to try to break the siege around Vicksburg and fail than to do nothing. Seddon thought "noble daring" superior to "prudence."[52]

Johnston particularly disliked Seddon's attack on his "prudence." Prudence had much to recommend to Johnston, for he feared that a "wild spirit" dictated Seddon's thinking. Considering the secretary of war simply irresponsible, Johnston wrote that he refused "to waste the lives and blood of his soldiers" on a hopeless cause.[53] In this judgment submitted to history, Johnston would find a powerful ally in Ulysses S. Grant.

The same year Johnston published his *Narrative*, Congress authorized organizing the government's archive of Civil War military reports and orders for publication. Work progressed slowly; not until 1880 did Congress authorize the actual printing of the first volumes of the *Official Record of the War of the Rebellion*. By then, former Union army officers edited the volumes alongside ex-Confederates. Both sides insisted the *Official Record* be strictly neutral. In the words of one Michigan Republican, the publication would appear "without any opinion, without any coloring, without any shadowing of anybody." A former Confederate colonel agreed: the editors were not to write history but merely preserve the material from which history would one day be written. Preservation, not editorial judgment, was the mission. Without the books, one supporter of the project warned, the entire Civil War archive could disappear in a fire at any moment.[54]

However, plenty of editorial judgments became available outside the *Official Record of the War of the Rebellion*. In 1879, the Confederate commander at Milliken's Bend, Richard Taylor, published his Civil War memoir *Destruction and Reconstruction*. Taylor used his book to sketch officers and political leaders candidly. Robert E. Lee "was without ambition, and . . . kept duty as his guide." Lincoln's secretary of war lusted after power. McClellan thought his army "too precious for gunpowder."[55] After his Virginia successes led to promotion and transfer to Louisiana, Taylor met with Pemberton to coordinate their operations. Taylor remembered meeting with the Pennsylvania-born Confederate in 1843 or 1844 and being impressed by Pemberton's states' rights convictions. Not many in the military held such views so strongly, Taylor said later. Yet while Taylor did not doubt Pemberton's loyalty, he did question his abilities. "Davis could have known nothing of Pemberton except that his military record was good," Taylor explained, absolving his brother-in-law of all blame, "and it is difficult to foresee that a distinguished subordinate will prove incompetent in command." Pemberton could not competently lead troops on his own, Taylor concluded.[56]

Taylor led the Confederate attackers at Milliken's Bend. His biographer devoted two full pages to a detailed description of the battle; Taylor himself passed over the fight in half a paragraph. His men attacked at dawn, Taylor wrote, and "the negroes were driven over the levee to the protection of gunboats in the river." Still convinced the Confederacy should retake New Orleans, Taylor regarded the whole Milliken's Bend exercise as a waste of time. "As foreseen," he wrote, "our movement resulted, and could result, in nothing." It is possible to read Taylor's memoir and conclude that Taylor himself contributed to the Milliken's Bend failure. He had divided his forces to attack not only Milliken's Bend but also another Union camp at the same time. His biographer grumbled that Taylor should have kept his forces together for greater punch, attacking the two objectives one after the other rather than at the same time.[57] When Taylor's book appeared, northerners writing in *The Nation* and the *New York Herald* approved. William T. Sherman expressed irritation, but his complaints focused on Taylor's sharply drawn portraits, which he thought "stigmatize[d] good men." Taylor had compared Sherman to Grant unfavorably, saying that Grant respected noncombatants "in the true spirit of a soldier," while Sherman did not. Despite his reservations and despite Taylor's criticism, Sherman ultimately regarded Taylor's text as "honest, fair, and just."[58]

In 1881, Jefferson Davis published his own memoir of the Civil War, *The Rise and Fall of the Confederate Government*. Coming in at more than 1,500 pages in two volumes, Davis's book was nothing if not more comprehensive than Johnston's and Taylor's. Just like Johnston, Davis wanted to answer critics.

Davis began his section covering the Vicksburg campaign by praising Earl Van Dorn as gallant, daring, gentle, and generous. According to Davis, Van Dorn "possessed . . . both the confidence and the affection of his men." Although Van Dorn lost at Corinth, Davis hastily excused that defeat, writing that he had deployed his soldiers skillfully.[59] Of course, Van Dorn's greatest contribution to the Confederate effort came the night of December 15, 1862, with his strike at Grant's supply depot. Davis recounted Grant's push through Mississippi, describing his construction of "an immense depot of supplies at Holly Springs." He credited Van Dorn with forcing Grant out of Mississippi.[60]

While Davis singled out Van Dorn for special praise, he did not always remember subordinates. As Grant retreated after his Holly Springs debacle, Sherman pushed down the Mississippi River to be bloodily repulsed just above Vicksburg at Chickasaw Bayou. The Confederate commander at Chickasaw Bayou, Stephen D. Lee, got no mention from Davis.[61]

Like every other narrator of the Vicksburg campaign, Davis next described Grant's various efforts through the spring of 1863. Grant then moved his troops down the Mississippi on the Louisiana side, landing below Vicksburg. Since Davis instructed Pemberton to defend Vicksburg, it is no surprise that Davis vindicated Pemberton's decision to hold that city rather than take to the field and engage Grant, as Johnston had advised. Davis pointed out that Grant maintained a corps above Vicksburg. "This demonstration was merely a feint," Davis conceded, "but, had Pemberton withdrawn his troops, that feint could have been converted into a real attack."[62] Davis also accepted and reiterated Pemberton's complaint that he lacked adequate cavalry.[63]

Davis wrote that he ordered Johnston "to repair in person to any part of his command, whenever his presence might be for the time necessary or desirable." But instead of going to Vicksburg himself, Johnston went to Jackson, where he began corresponding with Pemberton. Why Johnston kept his distance is not so hard to understand. He considered his authority over two armies "nominal" and did not want to encroach on the authority of the true commanders ostensibly under his control. Davis charged that Johnston's failure to go personally to Vicksburg resulted in "confusion" and a "want of co-intelligence" with Pemberton.[64]

In his *Narrative*, Johnston claimed that once Union gunboats demonstrated that they could pass the Confederate batteries at Vicksburg, the fortress lost its strategic importance. Davis did not agree. In his book, Davis insisted that Grant's relentless determination to capture Vicksburg demonstrated the town's continued strategic significance.[65]

In his account of the siege, Davis accused Union forces of abusing white southern women. In his raid through Mississippi, Union cavalry commander Benjamin Grierson outraged defenseless women and children, "constituting a record alike unworthy a soldier and a gentleman." Davis also castigated the Union navy for shelling Vicksburg, gunfire that did more damage to civilian property than to the army. Davis thought Vicksburg's female population stood up well to the affront. These "gentlewomen" heroically faced incessant shelling, nursed the sick, and soothed the dying. They never departed from the "softer character of their sex," Davis carefully noted, but "they seemed as indifferent to danger as any of the soldiers who lined the trenches."[66]

Johnston and Pemberton, Davis reminded his readers, had quite different ideas about how to engage Grant's army. Davis wrote that he made every effort to reinforce Johnston's army to a level that would encourage the reluctant general to break the siege. Pemberton surrendered, according to Davis, when he "despair[ed] of aid from the exterior." Davis proved far more restrained in his criticism of Johnston than Johnston had been of him. The Mississippian leveled his most serious verbal assault on the general by citing Grant's authority: "It was always a matter of surprise to Grant . . . that Johnston failed to make the attempt to break up the siege of Vicksburg."[67]

More than virtually any other memoirist, the former Confederate president considered slavery at great length in his memoir. Davis pointed out that all the states sponsored slavery at the time the framers of the Constitution finished their work. Fewer slaves populated the North than the South, but, Davis emphasized repeatedly, this resulted from economic and not moral considerations. The Confederate president regretted that the war had been characterized as a struggle between freedom and slavery. Such powerful rhetoric crippled the southern cause, Davis thought, faulting southern politicians for failing to counteract such rhetoric. Davis reviewed the history of sectional conflict, going over the Northwest Ordinance, the Missouri Compromise, the 1850 Compromise, California's admission into the Union as a free state, and the Fugitive Slave Law. At no point in the quarrel, Davis maintained, did the North genuinely agitate for an end to slavery or honestly champion freedom.[68]

In Davis's view, slavery was not the cause but merely the occasion for the Civil War.[69] The South left the Union not to protect slavery but because northerners waged a "systematic and persistent struggle to deprive the Southern States of equality in the Union." The North, Davis charged, wanted to "generally . . . discriminate in legislation against the interests of" the South. This campaign culminated in northerners' demand that southern slave owners be excluded from the western territories.[70] The Civil War, in short, was all about constitutional principles, not slavery and certainly not any sentimental concern for the plight of slaves.

While Johnston and Davis each wrote their memoirs to settle scores, giving their tomes a poisonous flavor, Johnston's northern counterpart at Vicksburg has usually been depicted as trading his memories for quintessentially American motives: Grant wanted to make money. His book stands "as a great personal achievement of a dying man trying to retrieve his family's well-being."[71] The project began after Grant discovered he had throat cancer (February 1885), a time when he had little money. As Grant suffered, he labored over his story, finishing the last words just before he breathed his last on July 23, 1885.[72]

Grant did write for his family's well-being, but he had decided to shape the portrait he knew history would paint of his war service well before he ever discovered that lump in his throat. In 1867, Adam Badeau based his authoritative *Military History of Ulysses S. Grant* on interviews with Grant. In broad outlines, Badeau captured Grant's story as the general wanted it told. Beginning with Grant's humble but quintessentially American origins, Badeau then emphasized the obstacles Grant overcame, including criticism on the eve of his Vicksburg campaign. He concluded with a tribute to the American character, as articulated by Grant's life.[73] In 1868, Charles Dana and J. H. Wilson told Grant's story in a campaign biography. Dana and Wilson rejected "the rebel writers'" efforts to "palliate the soreness of their defeat" by claiming Grant won only through superior numbers. Grant's generalship allowed him to concentrate his forces for victory, Dana and Wilson countered. Pemberton, on the other hand, appears in Dana and Wilson's book as a bit dense, unable to understand the principles of warfare that guided Johnston. On this point, they reflected Grant's thinking. In casual conversation, Grant described Pemberton as "a fool" for "shut[ting] up thirty thousand troops" in Vicksburg "for me to capture." In their version, Dana and Wilson described Pemberton as collecting his forces behind fortifications "which had already shown their inutility." However, Dana and Wilson, writing in the midst of Grant's campaign for the White House, emphasized Grant's genius more than Pemberton's incompetence. "There is nothing in history since Hannibal invaded Italy to compare with" Grant's achievement, they concluded in one hyperbolic passage.[74]

The outlines of Grant's version of history appeared more fully after he left the presidency, when he toured Europe, Asia, and Africa with journalist John Russell Young. Young's book narrating the journey was no mere travel account. Grant talked extensively about his life, and Young published these recollections in his volume titled *Around the World with General Grant*. In his conversations with Young, Grant defended his Vicksburg campaign as the most perfect in the war. Grant spoke after southern writers such as General Dabney Maury had written that the "glare" of Grant's great results had "dazzled" historians into overestimating his military skills, which consisted chiefly of a commitment to an inhumane war of attrition.[75] By Grant's contrary account, his Vicksburg strategy seemed all the more bold for violating "all the principles of the art of war" as well as contravening his instructions from Washington. Grant emphasized the riskiness of his gamble: if he failed, "the politicians in Washington" would "root me up and throw me away as a useless weed."[76]

Grant also outlined for Young the limits of his commitment to black rights. In an 1866 book Grant had "sanctioned," Henry Coppee presented the general as a professional, a "manly soldier" rather than a politician. Before the war, Grant had been a Democrat with no sympathy for slaves, willing to concede the South all its rights, "perhaps more." As a soldier, though, Grant followed orders when commanded to recruit black regiments.[77] With Young, Grant expanded on this view, saying that the national government had made a mistake in extending suffrage to blacks after the war. "It was unjust to the negro to throw upon him the responsibilities of citizenship." Black voting also cheated the North, Grant insisted. "We have given the old slave-holders forty votes in the electoral college." White elites kept the electoral votes and disfranchised blacks. Giving blacks the vote in the first place led to this, "one of the gravest mistakes in the policy of reconstruction."[78]

In his 1868 biography of Grant, Albert D. Richardson depicted the great general as sympathetic to black southerners. While he recognized Lorenzo Thomas's 1863 recruiting mission, Richardson staked out claims for his own man, insisting that "Grant had already paved the way for this." According to Richardson, Grant helped remove whites' prejudices against armed blacks by using them as laborers. He paid them ten dollars a month and issued them the same rations and clothing as enlisted white soldiers. "The plan had worked to a charm," Richardson wrote. "The blacks proved unexpectedly faithful, zealous, and tractable," and whites, "already quite willing to arm them with the spade," began to consider giving them muskets. The idea that using freed slaves as laborers somehow "paved the way" for converting them into combat soldiers suggests that Richardson interpreted the facts in a way most favorable to his subject. What is significant is that in 1868, Richardson still *wanted* to "spin" Grant as a promoter of black military service. Richardson structured his narrative as a story of northern white patriotism overcoming racism. In one telling anecdote, Richardson described an Indiana colonel, famous for his "violent" bigotry, confronted with a freed African American woman shouting, "Bress de Lord!" Richardson has the woman's genuine enthusiasm for the Union winning over the colonel, and his troops cheered their colonel's embarrassed conversion. Richardson wrote that after the colonel's exchange with the freed woman, he never again heard the officer denounce black people. The Civil War, Richardson still thought in 1868, had changed the hearts of northern whites.[79]

Grant did not rely only on journalists like Coppee and Young to put out his version of history. Returning from his travels, he wrote three articles for *Century*, receiving $3,000 for his efforts. The magazine then proposed publishing Grant's memoirs. At this juncture, Samuel L. Clemens (Mark Twain) intervened, convincing Grant that he should get more money than *Century* planned to pay. Grant finished the work at a health resort above Saratoga, New York, wrapped in blankets on his porch. Grant died one week after he finished the last chapter. Clemens published the memoirs, paying Grant's family $450,000.[80]

Far better written than Johnston's narrative, Grant's book proved more influential as well. Not only northerners but white southerners as well hailed Grant as "one of the greatest soldiers of a war that decided so much." "Full of human sympathy and animated by an unflagging sense of duty," the *Memphis Ledger* wrote, Grant had "a plain, blunt, direct way of dealing with all affairs" that made his writing especially reliable.[81] Grant had the advantage of publishing his memoir just as Joel T. Headley released *The Life of Ulysses S. Grant*, arguing that Grant's superior character explained his accomplishments.[82] Grant's book confirmed Headley's assessment. Historians writing about the Vicksburg campaign still depend largely on Grant's account. A modern writer's judgment of Grant's personality and writing style, "unmarred by pompous excesses,"[83] repeats Headley's 1885 assessment of Grant: "simple, unpretending, unsuspicious."[84]

From the first page of his reminiscences, Grant painted himself as thoroughly American, humble, and plain. "My family," he began, "is American, and has been for generations."[85] His recounting of the Grant genealogy revealed an ordinary American family. His own early life took him from "indifferent" schools to an "uneventful" life in Georgetown, Ohio, to nearby Ripley.[86] Grant seduced his reader with revelations that he disliked hard work as a youth and that military life "had no charms for me."[87]

Grant's story of the Civil War revealed his own conviction that by 1885, at least, reconciliation had become the dominant theme of the war. This came across most clearly in the section where he briefly discusses his own politics and the role of race and slavery in secession. Grant told how he voted for the first time in 1856 and cast his ballot for James Buchanan. Grant sounded defensive about this. The Republican Party, he explained, not only opposed the extension of slavery but went too far as well, favoring compulsory abolition. Grant exaggerated. Before the war, the Republican Party had championed free labor and had opposed extending slavery into the territories but did not favor immediate emancipation. Grant's 1885 prose still recorded whites' antebellum indignation at emancipation—without even compensating the slave owners for their losses. And such worries, merely abstract concerns for white northerners, had not plumbed the bottom of their racism. In 1865, the Republican program frightened whites on an even deeper, more visceral level. Educated people should have known better, Grant wrote in retrospect, but in 1856 the Republican Party even threatened social equality between the races. Looking back from his reconciliationist perspective, Grant could see the foolishness of such fears. The election of Lincoln, secession, and emancipation, Grant wrote, did not lead to "the most horrible visions" whites feared before the war. "The nation still lives, and the people are just as free to avoid social intimacy with the blacks as ever they were, or as they are with white people."[88] Whatever else the Civil War might mean, in 1885, the leader of Union troops did not think it meant social equality of the races. In his biography, Headley explained that Grant went to war simply because the South had insulted the flag by firing on it at Fort Sumter.[89]

Grant's story was also one of his own rise from obscurity, another theme repeated by historians. Grant began with few ambitions. "I had the vanity to think that as a cavalry officer I might succeed very well in the command of a brigade," he wrote. After he captured Fort Donelson, Grant wrote, "The way was opened to the National forces all over the South-west without much resistance." But no one in the Union high command would authorize Grant's plan along such lines.[90] Until Vicksburg, Grant presented himself as laboring, often ignored, under the plodding, uninspired H. W. Halleck.[91] When Grant finally did gain a measure of fame, the results were not immediately positive. When he seemed stalled outside Vicksburg, the northern newspapers "clamored for my removal." All through the siege, he and his men had to suffer journalists' "gibes."[92]

Grant emphasized the bold nature of his Vicksburg gambit. He decided, he wrote, to cut loose from his base, knowing that Halleck would not approve and knowing further that Sherman counseled against such a course. Grant, according to his memoirs, calculated that by the time Washington could interfere with his plans, he would have either succeeded or failed and his superiors' opinion would not matter either way.[93] At times, Grant wrote that he "cut loose altogether" from his supply line, and other times he remembered that he made the country supply bacon and molasses but maintained a supply line for ammunition, bread, and coffee.[94]

Sherman went to his grave convinced that Grant unwisely chose his Vicksburg strategy for political rather than military reasons. Grant did not want to be criticized in the North for another retreat; Sherman wanted to return to Memphis and start over again, moving across land to the back of Vicksburg.[95] In fact, by Grant's own account, the decision was political. The North already felt disheartened, he wrote, and the last election had gone badly for the Republicans. The zeal for enlisting had collapsed, leading to conscription. Another retreat to Memphis, Grant decided, would be useless. Public support for the war would dry up, and there would be no men or materials for a new march from Memphis.[96]

Though Grant always praised the valor of ordinary Confederate soldiers, his negative appraisal of his adversaries in the Vicksburg campaign proved enduring. Grant the memoirist was not so kind to Johnston as he had been in the *Herald* interviews, and his critical judgment of Johnston and Pemberton doomed any effort to revive the reputations of those officers. Johnston, Grant wrote, was "vacillating and undecided." He had been overrated.[97] At the same time, Grant shared at least one element of Johnston's appraisal of Pemberton. When Johnston instructed Pemberton to abandon Vicksburg and march northeast to Clinton, Grant maneuvered his army in anticipation of the attack. It surprised him when Pemberton disobeyed his orders. Grant denounced as foolishness Pemberton's feeble effort to cut his supply line. There was no supply line to cut, Grant claimed: "I . . . had no base, having abandoned it more than a week before." Perhaps Grant's eagerness to disparage Pemberton led him into this hyperbole or outright falsehood. As recent historians have shown, Grant certainly did maintain connections to his base all through the campaign. He could hardly depend on the countryside to furnish his soldiers with their ammunition.[98] Though he does not mount a legalistic indictment of Pemberton as did Johnston, Grant sharply censured the Confederate general in a few short sentences. Pemberton should have followed Johnston's orders and abandoned Vicksburg. It would have been proper, Grant wrote, and it would have conformed to his orders.[99]

Grant supported Johnston's account on another key point. Johnston hesitated to attack Grant's forces as the Union general besieged Vicksburg after Richmond urged him to attack even at the risk of failure. Grant thought Johnston's reluctance to attack wise. The Confederates had dug themselves in around Vicksburg, but so had his men. The Union army would have "rejoiced at the opportunity of defending ourselves" against such an ill-advised assault.[100]

Grant the memoirist praised, albeit briefly, the black troops' heroism at Milliken's Bend. In his biography of the great general, Headley gave a somewhat longer account of Grant's experience with black soldiers. According to Headley, some thought Grant's "anti-abolition principles" meant he would refuse to allow black men into the army. "But they were mistaken," Headley added. According to Headley, this willingness to use black soldiers signaled no particular empathy across racial lines. Grant understood that using blacks for garrison duty freed up white troops for real fighting. Shortly after Vicksburg's fall, Grant went to work organizing black regiments—for occupation duty. Lincoln had exaggerated expectations for the black recruits, Headley explained, actually thinking that enlisting black men into combat would "close this contest." According to Headley, Grant did not share such fanciful thinking and saw no special significance to adding blacks to his army. They were just soldiers. As soldiers, though, Grant believed they were entitled to be treated as such. When he heard that Confederate authorities had hanged captured black soldiers, Grant let it be known that he would treat captured Confederates the same way if the practice continued. Determined to present Grant to his readers as a plain man, Headley wrote that Grant made the threat without "windy threats" or "pompous declamation," just a "quiet, calm utterance of his duty."[101]

In 1898, Charles A. Dana's memoir appeared, offering a civilian's view of the Vicksburg siege from inside Grant's headquarters. Far more than the generals, the Dana memoir promised to restore emancipation and race to Civil War memory. Unlike Grant, Dana had a strong antislavery reputation. Before the war, Dana had served as an editor of Horace Greeley's *New York Tribune* and championed antislavery, pushing Greeley toward abolitionism. According to Dana's biographer, Greeley "threw his whole soul" into the fight against slavery, and his heart overflowed with sympathy for the slaves, but Dana was "the stronger and more aggressive character" of the two. Ida M. Tarbell wrote that Dana and James S. Pike had "held to an aggressive anti-slavery policy" even when Greeley's courage fell short, "as often happened."[102] Greeley's *Tribune* argued that while slavery should not be allowed in the territories, it should be left alone in the states.[103] Dana became Secretary of War Edwin M. Stanton's observer in Grant's high command after Greeley forced him out of his *Tribune* job. Dana's "memoir" of his experiences, written by Ida M. Tarbell from interviews with the putative author, suggested that actual experience with slavery and black troops could moderate white northerners' racism. "I had seen slavery in Maryland, Kentucky, Virginia, and Missouri," Dana said, "but it was not until I saw these great Louisiana plantations with all their apparatus for living and working that I really felt the aristocratic nature of the institution." Louisiana's aristocratic slavery intensified Dana's determination to preserve "the territorial and political integrity of the nation . . . at all costs."[104]

Dana, the abolitionist, used what happened at Milliken's Bend on June 7, 1863, to make the emancipationist argument. Dana's source was General E. S. Dennis, who based his narrative on Herman Lieb's unpublished report. Dana quoted Dennis as saying, "It is impossible for men to show greater gallantry than the negro troops in that fight." In his 1868 biography of Grant, Dana, writing with Wilson, had barely mentioned the episode, but now, Dana told Tarbell, the Milliken's Bend fight "completely revolutionized the sentiment of the army." Opposition to enlisting black troops faded. At the same time, reports reached the Union officers that the Confederates found the prospect of armed blacks horrifying.[105]

Yet Dana's insights into slavery and black soldiering were brief and buried in his longer and more detailed analyses of Union generals. Dana's assessments could be acerbic and blunt. General M. K. Lawler, Dana said, was "as brave as a lion, and has about as much brains." General A. J. Smith's "head is clear though rather thick."[106] While Dana detailed his observation of Grant's generals down to the level of brigadier, his most important critiques praised the capabilities of Grant and Sherman.

Dana arrived at Grant's headquarters on April 6. Grant unhesitatingly took the former journalist into his confidence, explaining his "new project." This new project, of course, was the plan to pass Vicksburg on the Mississippi's Louisiana side and then cross the river at Grand Gulf and come at Vicksburg from the east and south. Dana talked at length with Sherman, who preferred to attack through the Yazoo Pass or Lake Providence. But gradually, Dana thought he could see Sherman slowly warming to Grant's plan.[107]

Many observers thought Grant common looking, someone whose physical appearance belied a hidden greatness. Dana saw Grant as modest, disinterested, honest, and judicial; not great, "except morally"; and not brilliant, but "sincere, thoughtful, deep and gifted with courage that never faltered." Dana saw Grant more positively than did the author of the *Lost Cause*, but not so differently. Dana and Pollard agreed that Grant was a plain man, less than brilliant.[108]

Dana became most enthused when talking about Sherman. He seemed particularly drawn to Sherman, "a genius" with the "widest intellectual acquisitions." As the siege progressed, Sherman's brilliance continued to impress the journalist. Curiously, though slavery's aristocracy hardened Dana against the institution, the "brilliant" Sherman saw the same thing to no effect.[109]

Dana shared Grant's negative appraisal of Pemberton. The Confederate troops fought well, Dana said, but Pemberton misused them. His dispositions throughout the campaign were "weak" and "easily overcome." Dana cited Johnston's *Narrative* as giving a true picture of Pemberton: he simply did not understand Grant's strategy.[110] Like all the other major memoirists, Dana's narrative ultimately pictured the Civil War as a clash between generals, strategic genius matched against strategic blunder. The war hardly seemed a clash of great ideas or rival social traditions by this account.

Taken together, all these memoirs generated a metanarrative about the Civil War, one that rendered the war as a series of strategic decisions by generals. Perhaps the reaction against this narrative makes clear how it glorified command decision. Henry Van Ness Boynton, writing in 1875, and Donn Piatt, writing in 1893, sharply criticized Sherman and other generals for their bloody blunders. Humorist and politician George W. Peck ridiculed the generals'-eye view in 1887 with *How Private*

Geo. W. Peck Put Down the Rebellion or the Funny Experiences of a Raw Recruit. The best-known critique, however, came from Stephen Crane in *The Red Badge of Courage.* Published in 1895, Crane's novel tells the Civil War story from a private's perspective. Crane's realism—and his character's resentment of generals and inability to avoid their martial spirit—criticized Gilded Age views of the Civil War. In Crane's vision, the soldiers abandoned a black character to focus on military minutiae.[111]

Some veterans agreed with Crane. On October 7, 1908, Cyrus Sears made a speech to the Ohio Department of the Loyal Legion of the United States. Sears had been a lieutenant colonel, commanding black troops at Milliken's Bend. Military historians have recently discovered Sears's text but have sometimes belittled it for claiming the Confederates charged into battle under a skull-and-crossbones flag.[112] Sears's speech was significant for more important reasons than that. Sears enthusiastically praised the heroism of the black soldiers at Milliken's Bend, even claiming that they fought better than the white troops also present at the battle. According to Sears, after he spoke, he received compliments, and "according to custom," the old soldiers routinely agreed to publish his address. Several days later, Sears learned that one veteran present objected to publication of his paean to black valor. After talking the matter over, the Legion refused to print Sears's speech. This repudiation stung Sears, and he quit the Legion. "Without spectacles," Sears wrote, "it seemed easy to read between the lines of the discussion that the kick was largely, if not mainly, on account of lingering prejudice against giving the negro a 'square deal.'"[113]

Not many white people wanted to read between those lines. By the twentieth century, the story of Grant's genius and Pemberton's failure had been solidly established. This was true in the South just as in the North. In 1939, Colonel A. G. Paxton delivered a narrative of the siege to the assembled Descendants of the Participants of the Campaign, Siege, and Defense of Vicksburg. Newspapers described Paxton as "unreconstructed," white Mississippians' favorite appellation for themselves. Paxton described Robert E. Lee as brilliant, "Christ-like," and a master of strategy and tactics. Ulysses S. Grant, by contrast, was not brilliant, graduating fifth from the bottom of his West Point class, Paxton said. But, Paxton continued, he had a retentive mind, disciplined his army, and fought ruthlessly. Grant treated his enemies viciously, Paxton said, yet extended charity to those same foes once defeated. Paxton faulted Davis for failing to delegate, trying to supervise his military forces personally. As a result, the defender of Vicksburg, Pemberton, found himself serving two masters: Davis and his military commander, Joseph Johnston. The results, Paxton hardly needed to remind his audience, proved disastrous.[114]

Paxton closed his address by saying he did not intend to eulogize Grant or reflect on the "fine characters" of the Confederates, but Paxton nonetheless sharply criticized Davis and Pemberton. Paxton described Pemberton as sending only small forces against Grant after Johnston ordered him to mass his forces for a general attack. Pemberton decided to obey Davis and hold Vicksburg at all costs, even though he knew that doing so meant the loss of stores and ammunition collected in the city, the loss of Port Hudson, the surrender of the Mississippi, and the bisection of the Confederacy. Paxton closed by looking at the lessons learned, chiefly that tenacity guarantees success "if one's opponent is 'serving two masters.'"[115] This was what decided the Civil War: inferior generals on one side and more capable ones on the other.

Notes

1. Roy P. Basler, ed., *Walt Whitman's Memoranda during the War [&] Death of Abraham Lincoln* (Bloomington: Indiana University Press, 1962), 16.

2. E. B. Long, ed., *Personal Memoirs of U. S. Grant* (Cleveland: World, 1952), 186.

3. G. Kurt Piehler, *Remembering War the American Way* (Washington, D.C.: Smithsonian Institution Press, 1995), 10–46.

4. Alice Fahs, *The Imagined Civil War: Popular Literature of the North & South, 1861–1865* (Chapel Hill: University of North Carolina Press, 2001), esp. 93–119; Kirk Savage, *Standing Soldiers, Kneeling Slaves: Race, War, and Monuments in Nineteenth-Century America* (Princeton, N.J.: Princeton University Press, 1997), 167–81.

5. Nina Silber, *The Romance of Reunion: Northerners and the South, 1865–1900* (Chapel Hill: University of North Carolina Press, 1993), 93–158; David W. Blight, *Race and Reunion: The Civil War in American Memory* (Cambridge, Mass.: Harvard University Press, 2001), 211–54.

6. Albion Tourgee, *A Fool's Errand: A Novel of the South during Reconstruction* (New York: Ford, Howard & Hurlbert, 1879).

7. J. R. Kinnear, *History of the Eighty-Sixth Regiment Illinois Volunteer Infantry* (Chicago: Tribune Co., 1866); L. G. Bennett and William H. Haigh, *History of the Thirty-Sixth Regiment Illinois Volunteers, during the War of the Rebellion* (Aurora, Ill.: Knickerbocker & Hodder, 1876); W. H. Bentley, *History of the 77th Illinois Volunteer Infantry, Sept. 2, 1862–July 10, 1865* (Peoria, Ill.: Edward Hine, printer, 1883); Committee of the Regiment, *The Story of the Fifty-Fifth Regiment Illinois Volunteer Infantry in the Civil War* (Clinton, Mass.: W. J. Coulter, 1887); *A History of the Seventy-Third Regiment Illinois Infantry Volunteers* (n.p.: Regimental Reunion of Survivors of the 73d Illinois Infantry Volunteers, 1890); H. H. Orendorff et al., *Reminiscences of the Civil War from Diaries of Members of the 103d Illinois Volunteer Infantry 1904* (Chicago: J. F. Leaming & Co., 1904).

8. Committee of the Regiment, *The Story of the Fifty-Fifth Regiment Illinois Volunteer Infantry in the Civil War*, 6.

9. Fahs, *The Imagined Civil War*, 150–94; Committee of the Regiment, *The Story of the Fifty-Fifth Regiment Illinois Volunteer Infantry in the Civil War*, 153; Bentley, *History of the 77th Illinois Volunteer Infantry*, 103.

10. Slaughterhouse Cases, 16 Wall. 36 (1873); Robert J. Kaczorowski, *The Politics of Judicial Interpretation: The Federal Courts, Department of Justice and Civil Rights, 1866–1876* (New York: Oceana, 1985), 143–66; Pamela Brandwein, *Reconstructing Reconstruction: The Supreme Court and the Production of Historical Truth* (Durham, N.C.: Duke University Press, 1999), 61–95.

11. John Richard Dennett, *The South as It Is, 1865–1866*, ed. Henry M. Christman (Baton Rouge: Louisiana State University Press, 1965).

12. Edward Howland, *Grant as a Soldier and Statesman: Being a Succinct History of His Military and Civil Career* (Hartford, Conn.: J. B. Burr & Co., 1868), 13–15.

13. Henry Coppee, *Grant and His Campaigns: A Military Biography* (New York: Charles B. Richardson, 1866), 14.

14. Horace Greeley, *The American Conflict: A History of the Great Rebellion in the United States of America, 1860–65*, 2 vols. (Hartford, Conn.: O. D. Case & Co., 1864–1866), 2:511–28, 527 (first quotation), 528 (second quotation).

15. W. A. Crafts, *The Southern Rebellion, Being a History of the United States*, 2 vols. (Boston: Samuel Walker & Co., 1862–1867), 2:385.

16. Thomas Wentworth Higginson, *Army Life in a Black Regiment*, ed. Howard Mumford Jones (1870; repr., East Lansing: Michigan State University Press, 1960), 190–203. See also Christopher Looby, ed., *The Complete Civil War Journal and Selected Letters of Thomas Wentworth Higginson* (Chicago: University of Chicago Press, 2000).

17. William Wells Brown, *The Negro in the American Revolution*, ed. William Edward Farrison (1867; repr., New York: Citadel Press, 1971), vi, 137–41.

18. George W. Williams, *A History of the Negro Troops in the War of the Rebellion, 1861–1865* (1886; repr., New York: Negro Universities Press, 1969).

19. Joseph T. Wilson, *The Black Phalanx* (1890; repr., New York: Arno, 1968).

20. Brown, *The Negro in the American Revolution*, 1–36.

21. Williams, *A History of the Negro Troops in the War of the Rebellion*, 167–69.

22. Wilson, *The Black Phalanx*, preface (unpaginated).

23. Brown, *The Negro in the American Revolution*, 137–41; Williams, *A History of the Negro Troops in the War of the Rebellion*, 228–30; Wilson, *Black Phalanx*, 203–7; G. G. Edwards, "Fight at Milliken's Bend," in Frank Moore, ed., *The Rebellion Record: A Diary of American Events*, 11 vols. (New York: G. P. Putnam, D. Van Nostrand, 1861–1868), 7:12–13; "Another Account," in Moore, *The Rebellion Record*, 13–15.

24. Brown, *The Negro in the American Revolution*, vi, 137–41.

25. Williams, *A History of the Negro Troops in the War of the Rebellion*, 228.

26. Wilson, *The Black Phalanx*, preface (unpaginated).

27. Brown, *The Negro in the American Revolution*, introduction (unpaginated).

28. Amy Kaplan, *The Social Construction of American Realism* (Chicago: University of Chicago Press, 1988); Coppee, *Grant and His Campaigns*; Adam Badeau, *Military History of Ulysses S. Grant*, 3 vols. (1867; repr., New York: D. Appleton and Co., 1881); Howland, *Grant as a Soldier and Statesman*.

29. Badeau, *Military History of Ulysses S. Grant*, 1:140–41.

30. S. H. Lockett, "The Defense of Vicksburg," in Robert Underwood Johnson and Clarence Clough Buel, eds., *Battles and Leaders of the Civil War*, 4 vols. (New York: Century, 1884–1887), 3:482–92; General Joseph E. Johnston, "Jefferson Davis and the Mississippi Campaign," in *Battles and Leaders of the Civil War*, 472–81; General George W. Morgan, "The Assault on Chickasaw Bluffs," in *Battles and Leaders of the Civil War*, 467–70; General Ulysses S. Grant, "The Vicksburg Campaign," in *Battles and Leaders of the Civil War*, 493–538; General Andrew Hickenlooper, "The Vicksburg Mine," in *Battles and Leaders of the Civil War*, 539–42; Blight, *Race and Reunion*, 50–51, 160–79. Reid Mitchell has recently observed that Bell Irvin Wiley opened and closed the field of scholarly inquiry into ordinary soldiers—in 1943 and 1952. Mitchell's essay is an excellent review of the historiography of ordinary soldiers. Reid Mitchell, "'Not the General but the Soldier': The Study of Civil War Soldiers," in James M. McPherson and William J. Cooper, Jr., *Writing the Civil War: The Quest to Understand* (Columbia: University of South Carolina Press, 1998), 81–95.

31. *How Private George W. Peck Put Down the Rebellion* (Chicago: Belford, Clarke & Co., 1887), 11–12.

32. Brooks D. Simpson, "Continuous Hammering and Mere Attrition: Lost Cause Critics and the Military Reputation of Ulysses S. Grant," in Gary W. Gallagher and Alan T. Nolan, eds., *The Myth of the Lost Cause and Civil War History* (Bloomington: Indiana University Press, 2000), 147–50; Emory M. Thomas, "Rebellion and Conventional

Warfare: Confederate Strategy and Military Policy," in Mcpherson and Cooper, *Writing the Civil War*, 37–38.

33. Jack P. Maddex, Jr., *The Reconstruction of Edward A. Pollard: A Rebel's Conversion to Postbellum Unionism* (Chapel Hill: University of North Carolina Press, 1974), 24–42.

34. But certainly not all. Many, perhaps most, scholars agree that cultural factors determined the outcome of the conflict. Nonetheless, it hardly seems controversial to recognize that many Civil War books have placed great weight on generalship. See, for example, Steven E. Woodworth, *Jefferson Davis and His Generals: The Failure of Confederate Command in the West* (Lawrence: University Press of Kansas, 1990).

35. Simpson, "Continuous Hammering and Mere Attrition," 147–50.

36. Coppee, *Grant and His Campaigns*, 72, 161, 169, 192.

37. William Swinton, *The Twelve Decisive Battles of the War: A History of the Eastern and Western Campaigns in Relations to the Actions That Decided Their Issue* (New York: Dick and Fitzgerald, 1867), 290, 294–95, 299–300, 285.

38. Joseph E. Johnston, *Narrative of Military Operations Directed during the Late War between the States* (New York: D. Appleton & Co., 1874), 10.

39. Johnston, *Narrative of Military Operations*, 13.

40. Johnston, *Narrative of Military Operations*, 113.

41. Johnston, *Narrative of Military Operations*, 147–50.

42. Johnston, *Narrative of Military Operations*, 155.

43. Johnston, *Narrative of Military Operations*, 174–75.

44. Johnston, *Narrative of Military Operations*, 170; Long, *Personal Memoirs of U. S. Grant*, 251.

45. Johnston, *Narrative of Military Operations*, 176.

46. Johnston, *Narrative of Military Operations*, 178.

47. Johnston, *Narrative of Military Operations*, 181.

48. Johnston, *Narrative of Military Operations*, 186–87.

49. Johnston, *Narrative of Military Operations*, 188.

50. Johnston, *Narrative of Military Operations*, 189.

51. Simpson, "Continuous Hammering and Mere Attrition," 147–69.

52. Johnston, *Narrative of Military Operations*, 197–201.

53. Johnston, *Narrative of Military Operations*, 202.

54. *Congressional Record*, 46th Cong., 2nd sess., vol. 10, May 27, 1880, 3872–78.

55. Richard B. Harwell, introduction, in Richard Taylor, *Destruction and Reconstruction: Personal Experiences of the Late War* (New York: Longmans, Green and Co., 1955), xxiii.

56. Taylor, *Destruction and Reconstruction*, 137–38.

57. Taylor, *Destruction and Reconstruction*, 166–67; T. Michael Parrish, *Richard Taylor: Soldier Prince of Dixie* (Chapel Hill: University of North Carolina Press, 1992), 288–90.

58. Parrish, *Richard Taylor*, 492–94; Taylor, *Destruction and Reconstruction*, 179.

59. Jefferson Davis, *The Rise and Fall of the Confederate Government*, 2 vols. (New York: D. Appleton, 1881), 1:388–89.

60. Davis, *The Rise and Fall of the Confederate Government*, 1:391.

61. Davis, *The Rise and Fall of the Confederate Government*, 1:392–93.

62. Davis, *The Rise and Fall of the Confederate Government*, 1:400.

63. Davis, *The Rise and Fall of the Confederate Government*, 1:402–3.

64. Johnston, *Narrative of Military Operations*, 154; Davis, *The Rise and Fall of the Confederate Government*, 1:405.

65. Davis, *The Rise and Fall of the Confederate Government*, 1:400.

66. Davis, *The Rise and Fall of the Confederate Government*, 1:399, 414.

67. Davis, *The Rise and Fall of the Confederate Government*, 1:422–24.

68. Davis, *The Rise and Fall of the Confederate Government*, 1:3–17.

69. Davis, *The Rise and Fall of the Confederate Government*, 78.

70. Davis, *The Rise and Fall of the Confederate Government*, 1:83.

71. Blight, *Race and Reunion*, 212.

72. Simpson, "Continuous Hammering and Mere Attrition," 161–62.

73. Badeau, *Military History of Ulysses S. Grant*, 1:7–21, 180, 404–5.

74. Charles A. Dana and J. H. Wilson, *The Life of Ulysses S. Grant* (Springfield, Mass.: Gurdon Bill & Company, 1868), 117–19, 126; John Y. Simon, ed., *The Papers of Ulysses S. Grant*, 26 vols. (Carbondale: Southern Illinois University Press, 1867–), 16:257n1.

75. Dabney H. Maury, "Grant as a Soldier and Civilian," *Southern Historical Society Papers* 5 (May 1878): 227–39.

76. John Russell Young, *Around the World with General Grant*, 2 vols. (New York: American News Company, 1879), 2:615–16.

77. Coppee, *Grant and His Campaigns*, 152.

78. Young, *Around the World with General Grant*, 2:361–62.

79. Albert D. Richardson, *Personal History of Ulysses S. Grant* (1866; repr., Hartford, Conn.: American Publishing Co., 1885), 291, 300–303.

80. Edmund Wilson, *Patriotic Gore: Studies in the Literature of the American Civil War* (New York: Oxford University Press, 1962), 131–73.

81. *Memphis Ledger*, reprinted in the *Vicksburg Evening Post*, July 1, 1886.

82. J. T. Headley, *The Life of Ulysses S. Grant* (New York: Perkins Book Co., 1885). For Grant's character, see passim, esp. 581–90.

83. Blight, *Race and Reunion*, 212.

84. Headley, *The Life of Ulysses S. Grant*, 88.

85. Long, *Personal Memoirs of U. S. Grant*, 3.

86. Long, *Personal Memoirs of U. S. Grant*, 7, 11.

87. Long, *Personal Memoirs of U. S. Grant*, 10, 14.

88. Long, *Personal Memoirs of U. S. Grant*, 108; Eric Foner, *Free Soil, Free Labor, Free Men: The Ideology of the Republican Party before the Civil War* (New York: Oxford University Press, 1970).

89. Headley, *The Life of Ulysses S. Grant*, 36, 41.

90. Long, *Personal Memoirs of U. S. Grant*, 239, 163.

91. Long, *Personal Memoirs of U. S. Grant*, 192.

92. Long, *Personal Memoirs of U. S. Grant*, 238, 291. Headley makes the same argument in *The Life of Ulysses S. Grant*, 117–47.

93. Long, *Personal Memoirs of U. S. Grant*, 258.

94. Long, *Personal Memoirs of U. S. Grant*, 256, 258, 259, 262.

95. W. T. Sherman, *Memoirs of Gen. W. T. Sherman, Written by Himself*, 2 vols. (1875; repr., New York: Charles L. Webster & Co., 1891), 1:343–45.

96. Long, *Personal Memoirs of U. S. Grant*, 283.

97. Long, *Personal Memoirs of U. S. Grant*, 187–88.

98. Long, *Personal Memoirs of U. S. Grant*, 268; Warren E. Grabau, *Ninety-Eight Days: A Geographer's View of the Vicksburg Campaign* (Knoxville: University of Tennessee Press, 2000), 29–38; Edwin Cole Bearss, *Grant Strikes a Fatal Blow: The Campaign for Vicksburg* (Dayton, Ohio: Morningside, 1986), 435–36.

99. Long, *Personal Memoirs of U. S. Grant*, 273.

100. Long, *Personal Memoirs of U. S. Grant*, 287.

101. Headley, *The Life of Ulysses S. Grant*, 227–30. Joseph T. Glatthaar has argued that Lincoln's expectations were not so exaggerated. Black troops helped make the difference between victory and defeat. Joseph T. Glatthaar, "Black Glory: The African-American Role in Union Victory," in Gabor S. Boritt and James M. Mcpherson, eds., *Why the Confederacy Lost* (New York: Oxford University Press, 1992), 133–62.

102. James Harrison Wilson, *The Life of Charles A. Dana* (New York: Harper and Brothers, 1907), 61, 94–102, 110–24; Ida M. Tarbell, "Charles A. Dana in the Civil War," *McClure's Magazine* 9 (October 1897): 1087–89.

103. Wilson, *The Life of Charles A. Dana*, 160.

104. Ida M. Tarbell, *All in the Day's Work: An Autobiography* (New York: Macmillan, 1939), 174–77; Charles A. Dana, *Recollections of the Civil War* (1898; repr., Lincoln: University of Nebraska Press, 1996), 29.

105. Dana and Wilson, *The Life of Ulysses S. Grant*, 135; Dana, *Recollections of the Civil War*, 86. In 1907, Wilson repeated this assessment in *The Life of Charles A. Dana*, 235.

106. Dana, *Recollections of the Civil War*, 64–65.

107. Dana, *Recollections of the Civil War*, 31–32.

108. Dana, *Recollections of the Civil War*, 61.

109. Dana, *Recollections of the Civil War*, 29, 57.

110. Dana, *Recollections of the Civil War*, 96–97.

111. Charles Royster, *The Destructive War: William Tecumseh Sherman, Stonewall Jackson, and the Americans* (New York: Knopf, 1991), 287–89; George W. Peck, *How Private Geo. W. Peck Put Down the Rebellion or the Funny Experiences of a Raw Recruit* (Chicago: Belford, Clarke & Co., 1887); Marilyn Grant, "One More Civil War Memoir," *Wisconsin Magazine of History* 65 (winter 1981–1982): 122–29; Stephen Crane, *The Red Badge of Courage* (New York: D. Appleton, 1895); Eric J. Gislason, "*The Red Badge of Courage*: An Episode of the American Civil War," http://xroads.virginia.edu/~HYPER/CRANE/reviews/section1.html; George Mariani, *Spectacular Narratives: Representations of Class and War in Stephen Crane and the American 1890s* (New York: Peter Lang, 1992), 139–71.

112. Richard Lowe, "Battle on the Levee: The Fight at Milliken's Bend," in John David Smith, ed., *Black Soldiers in Blue: African American Troops in the Civil War Era* (Chapel Hill: University of North Carolina Press, 2002), 125.

113. Cyrus Sears, *Paper of Cyrus Sears* (Columbus, Ohio: F. J. Heer Printing Co., 1909), 3.

114. *Vicksburg Evening Post*, May 8, 1939.

115. *Vicksburg Evening Post*, May 8, 1939.

The Boys from Iowa

Future years will never know the seething hell and the black infernal background of countless minor scenes and interiors, (not the few great battles) of the Secession War; and it is best they should not. In the mushy influences of current times the fervid atmosphere and typical events of those years are in danger of being totally forgotten.

—Walt Whitman[1]

I
N 1887, summer had settled on Vicksburg by June 11. Just two days before, the scorching sun had taken its first casualty when heat prostration felled a young plumber. Albert Wiliby recovered after a night of feverish delirium.[2]

In this heat, crowds thronged the streets to dedicate the city's first Civil War monument. Celebrants sought shelter under merchants' awnings and inside the shops along the main street. Parading militia soldiers could not avoid the sun. In the steaming temperatures, they marched past red, white, and blue decorated buildings and streets draped with patriotic bunting, streamers, and the Stars and Stripes. Some younger men dressed as American Revolutionaries, "their muscular legs . . . well displayed in buff breeches and high boots," according to the *Vicksburg Commercial Herald*. An excursion train disgorged Louisiana vets after a long and uncomfortable journey in tightly packed cars. Young men in gilt buttons and "bright" uniforms mingled with aging Civil War veterans.[3]

Speakers celebrated the Lost Cause, the Confederates' heroic endurance, a valor so great as to be admired even by their enemies. As they spoke, thunder roared and a cooling breeze swept through the stifling town. Rain poured, soaking soldiers and civilians alike, but the orators continued their speech making. "Let others tell of the new South," one man called to the crowd, "'tis the old South that has my love." But speakers also acknowledged "the stain of slavery," exulting that "the victors proved themselves worthy of victory!" and pronounced themselves "proud of our starry banner."[4]

When the crowds dispersed and the trains returned soldiers and visitors to their homes far from Vicksburg, they left behind the Louisiana monument on Monroe Street. Dedicated to that state's soldiers who fell in the siege, the shaft looked much like a large cemetery marker.[5] For years, Confederate veterans rallied around the Louisiana monument on Confederate Memorial Day, *their* monument to the battle, not the North's. Years later, the heat and rain in that Mississippi delirium would be forgotten.

Accounts of their meeting became the stuff of legend in Vicksburg. "It was in 1895," John Festus Merry remembered later, "when the idea of having a national park in Vicksburg first came to me." There were parks in Gettysburg, Chickamauga, and Shiloh. Merry thought the battle for Vicksburg had been at least as important as any of those other battles and deserved its own park.[6] It is possible that the ex-Confederate editor of the *Vicksburg Evening Post* had something to do with Merry's park idea. In 1908, John G. Cashman, the *Post*'s editor, claimed to have written in February 1895 a petition calling for a park. In an article accompanying the petition, the *Post* said that "Captain Merry got his thought from the petition written by Mr. Cashman, and amplified and enlarged it."[7]

The Louisiana Monument, the South's first Civil War monument in the city of Vicksburg. It celebrated the South's Lost Cause. Author's photograph.

John Festus Merry, "father" of Vicksburg National Military Park. He lobbied Congress for a bill creating the park. Courtesy State Historical Society of Iowa.

Wherever the original idea came from, Merry understood that Congress would more likely authorize a park if both southerners and northerners petitioned for it. Merry, a former officer in the Union army, wrote a letter to Confederate General Stephen D. Lee, suggesting a meeting; he would bring eight Union veterans, and Lee would bring a like number of former Confederates. Lee agreed, and Merry and his party journeyed to Vicksburg to meet the former Confederates in the Hotel Piazza's basement. Years later, Merry would remember Lee as skeptical, doubting that Congress would appropriate money for such a venture. Nonetheless, Lee promised to do all he could to help.[8]

Merry became so closely identified with commemorating the battle over Vicksburg that it might seem his wartime experiences defined his whole life. In a disturbingly plausible theory, veteran war correspondent Chris Hedges writes that war "can give us purpose, meaning, a reason for living." A shallow and vapid ordinary life, by comparison, seems trivial. War "gives us resolve, a cause. It allows us to be noble."[9] And so, perhaps, it was for Merry. He joined the 21st Iowa in 1862 but left a year later for health reasons. He recovered and served as a second lieutenant in the 46th Iowa Infantry, a regiment that saw only one hundred days of service in 1864, mostly guarding a railroad far from Vicksburg. After the war, he joined the Grand Army of the Republic, an organization of Union army veterans, and near the end of his life, in 1915, he became the "commander" of all Iowa veterans.[10]

It may matter more that in 1880 Merry had joined the Illinois Central Railroad. As Merry told the story later, he had arranged with the Illinois Central Railway Company for a special excursion train to carry his fellow Methodists to a camp meeting. Merry sold tickets so enthusiastically that he caught the attention of Illinois Central officials. They invited him to join the company, and he worked his way up through the ranks to assistant general passenger agent. He later served as Illinois Central general immigration commissioner, promoting railroad travel up and down the Mississippi valley. In 1911, when Merry retired, one newspaper credited him with attracting thousands of farmers to the South "by means of the literature he circulated, the addresses he delivered and the excursions he conducted." Merry believed building a shrine to Civil War soldiers' heroism would draw northern tourists down the Illinois Central tracks that ran from Chicago through Vicksburg to New Orleans. In 1895, tourists traveling from the North to Vicksburg had no good means other than the railroad to reach their destination.[11]

The Piazza Hotel meeting led to the Vicksburg National Military Park Association, a lobbying group determined to persuade Congress to pass a law establishing a national park on the Vicksburg battlefield. In November, an executive committee of the association met to draft a bill that would establish a park at Vicksburg. The old veterans agreed that the park should not be more than 4,000 acres and should include Union and Confederate earthworks and Pemberton's and Grant's headquarters. The veterans envisioned "an ample roadway" running the length of both Union and Confederate lines.[12] Merry did not help write the bill, nor does his name appear on any of the long lists of officers in the association. He was, after all, not a Vicksburg veteran himself. But Merry went to Washington in 1895 to lobby for the bill. He said later that he journeyed to the capital with trepidation, not knowing how his idea would be received.

In 1895, Iowa had thirteen congressmen and senators in Washington. Merry had decided to focus on three with Civil War connections. Senator William Boyd Allison of the Appropriations Committee had been lieutenant colonel of volunteers, working to outfit Iowa troops for Civil War service. His rank, though, was honorary; Allison never served in the army. Iowa Congressmen David Bremner Henderson of the rules committee had lost a leg at Corinth while serving in the 12th Iowa. John Albert Tiffin Hull—Merry called him "captain" because he commanded a company in the 23rd Iowa—chaired the House Military Committee. All three ardently supported the Republican Party, meaning that they counted on Union veterans' votes. Allison had nominated Lincoln for president at the 1860 Republican convention. Merry hoped these three Iowans would be receptive to his idea for a park in Mississippi.[13]

Merry said he got the idea for a Vicksburg park from the national parks in Gettysburg, Antietam, Chickamauga, and Shiloh. Congress had authorized Chickamauga and Chattanooga in 1890; Shiloh came in 1894 and Gettysburg a year later. These parks had emerged from years of local and state authorities' preservation efforts. Pennsylvania Governor Andrew Curtin visited the Gettysburg battleground within days of the battle and set in motion plans to buy a section of the battlefield for a memorial. David McConaughy began buying parts of Culp's Hill and Little Round Top. Pennsylvania chartered the Gettysburg Battlefield Memorial Association on April 30, 1864, not a year after the battle. Northern states and veterans' groups allocated money for memorials decades before Congress created a national Gettysburg Park. The First Minnesota put up its Gettysburg monument in 1867. A monument to the Pennsylvania general John Reynolds went up in 1872, crafted by one of the best portrait sculptors of the time, John Quincy Adams Ward. Northern states made generous appropriations: New York provided $300,000 and Pennsylvania $200,000 for their Gettysburg memorials. At least until the federal government took control, northerners made the battlefield into a shrine to northern patriotism.[14]

In 1888, two Union officers riding across the Chickamauga battlefield conceived the idea of a national park that, unlike Gettysburg, would celebrate the valor of both northerners and southerners. Two years later, Congress easily passed legislation to create national parks at Chickamauga and Chattanooga. Charles H. Grosvenor of Ohio introduced the bill, and the House Committee on Military Affairs endorsed it purely as a recognition of soldierly valor. "The political questions which were involved in the contest" should not trespass on the park. Thirteen veterans of

Chickamauga and Chattanooga sat in the House; the bill passed that body in twenty-three minutes. Twelve senators had served at Chickamauga and Chattanooga. The Senate passed the bill in twenty minutes, without a dissenting vote. When President Benjamin Harrison signed the bill, it authorized a 7,600-acre park and appropriated $125,000 for its operation.[15]

Nothing in Vicksburg even remotely matched these efforts. On July 4, 1864, Union troops put up a monument on the spot where Pemberton had surrendered to Grant. Vicksburg citizens had originally intended the shaft as a commemoration of their soldiers' contribution to the Mexican War. But invading Yankees found the unfinished monument in a stonecutter's yard and appropriated it to commemorate Vicksburg's fall. For years, this recycled shaft alone commemorated the battle.[16]

Ironically, some in Congress thought approval of the earlier parks put Merry's plan at a disadvantage. Too much money had been spent on parks already, fiscal conservatives grumbled. Henderson, a native of Scotland representing Dubuque, Iowa, received Merry but then bluntly told his visitor that persuading Congress to create another military park "simply can't be done." Ten years ago, Henderson explained, Congress would have readily passed such a bill. But in 1893, a panic on Wall Street had touched off a major depression. The homeless rode the rails, farmers lost their land, and masses of desperately unemployed marched on Washington. In January 1895, the treasury reached desperate straits—Congress faced an alarming deficit. "The boys" in Congress, Henderson told Merry, had decided against spending more money on Civil War parks. "It's too late now," Henderson sadly informed him.[17]

Nonetheless, Henderson agreed to go with Merry to see Allison and Hull. Contrary to Henderson's gloomy prediction, both Allison and Hull seemed remarkably unconcerned by the depleted treasury, and both expressed enthusiasm for the project. "I think you ought to have it," Allison exclaimed. For his part, Hull enthused that "by all means a military park should be established."[18]

147

And so Vicksburg National Military Park got started—according to Merry's 1908 recollection, while reminiscing in a Vicksburg newspaper editor's office.

There are reasons to question at least the details of his narrative, particularly the claim that Henderson thought that while he would have easily passed his bill ten years earlier, no park bill could pass in 1895. Merry has Henderson making his ten-year comment at exactly the time Congress was about to pass House Bill 8096, creating Gettysburg National Military Park. The Gettysburg bill emerged from committee on December 18, 1894, and passed into law the following February.[19] It was not true that the House and Senate would not pass *any* new park bill. It may be more accurate to say that Merry came along after the Congress had already committed itself to Gettysburg.

More to the point, when Merry came calling on Henderson, the Iowa congressman still licked his wounds from his successful but bruising effort to build a national park on the Shiloh battlefield. In 1894, Henderson, a Shiloh veteran himself, had written a bill proposing a national military park on his old battleground. The bill won committee approval, but Henderson faced trouble on the House floor. The congressman wisely held off pushing the bill until after the 1894 elections. As Henderson feared, when he offered his bill on December 4, southern Democrats responded with hard, probing questions, rattling the old veteran. A Mississippi Democrat successfully amended the bill to state that "no discrimination shall be made against any State" at the park. More seriously, the House caved on southern Democrats' demands that Henderson's proposed appropriation be halved. Henderson got only $75,000. During debate, the Democrats had warned that the Shiloh bill was "an entering wedge to an immense mass of business" costing the government "thousands and hundreds of thousands of dollars." Francis M. Cockrell of Missouri, who had been a Confederate colonel at Vicksburg, commanding Missouri infantry, accused northerners of wanting a park on every battlefield. Despite this opposition, Congress passed the bill, and President Grover Cleveland signed it on December 27, 1894. The ex-Confederates had been tougher than Henderson had anticipated, and Cockrell had clearly announced his hostility to further park appropriations.[20] Those warnings still echoed in Henderson's ears when Merry came to his office, proposing that he start all over again with a new park.

While Merry's later account forgot Gettysburg, Shiloh, and Confederate Colonel and Congressman Francis Cockrell, it also failed to link Allison's more favorable response to the Iowa senator's presidential ambitions.[21] Allison was a serious presidential contender in 1895; his followers drafted campaign songs and advised him on cabinet appointments. As a candidate, Allison counted on Union veterans' support, advertising himself as a "constant and persistent" advocate for veterans even though he personally had never donned a uniform. Every Union pensioner in Iowa directly benefited from Allison's service in Congress, the senator claimed. In a campaign flier titled "Senator Allison and the Union Soldier," Allison said he supported every war measure and soldiers' pension bill since 1863.[22] Merry, representative of the Grand Army of the Republic, offered the park as one more veterans' measure.

Allison may also have felt that supporting a monument to the North's war against slavery might help his standing with African Americans. In 1895, a Republican presidential candidate could not yet afford to forget black voters. His southern supporters warned him that even though their states disfranchised black voters, those voters would still influence the delegations southern states sent to the Republican national convention. And Allison needed the support of southern states at the convention. In a pamphlet titled "What Senator Allison Has Done for the Colored Race," Allison reminded black voters that he had supported all three Civil War amendments and worked to convict Andrew Johnson at his Senate impeachment trial.[23]

Merry's railroad connections may also have increased his chances at winning a favorable response from Allison. Just as he counted on veteran voters and blacks, Allison's presidential campaign depended on railroad corporate support.[24] Allison's extensive collection of correspondence includes a letter from the president of the Burlington, Cedar Rapids, and Northern Railway writing on behalf of a bill to modify the Interstate Commerce Act. C. J. Ives's letter is no smoking gun proving bribery, but in it he refers to congressional "friends of railways" in a way that apparently included Allison. Ives seemed puzzled that some Iowa congressmen "who are largely indebted to their railway friends for the positions they hold" did not support the proposed bill. Allison's chief campaign adviser counted on railway corporations' support "to get delegates and cover expenses."[25]

Ives does not name the Iowa congressmen he thought owed their jobs to the railways, but John Albert Tiffin Hull may have been one of them. His enemies described him as "the friend of corporations, his interests having always been identified with theirs." But Hull could also have embraced Merry's proposal for reasons having nothing to do with railroad business. He was heavily committed to the myth of war. His ringing descriptions of battles in his speeches fairly reek of nostalgia for soldiering and combat. "Do you not remember," he invited one crowd of veterans, "how firing on the picket line, or by the skirmishers, told us of a battle begun?" First came irregular gunfire, he recalled, then the artillery, and finally "the full and continuous roll of musketry." "Thus the carnival of death was begun," Hull continued, remembering the "maddening intoxication of battle" when "every man's life is in the balance." In Hull's recollection, there were no phony "red badges of courage"; instead, "not a man wavers." In Hull's vivid battle descriptions, short, hard sentences march and attack like the heroic soldiers they described:

"A charging army must not stop to fire.

"The orders are promptly given and as promptly obeyed.

"Fix bayonets! Forward march! And when all are in motion out rang the shrill bugle or more cheering human voice—charge!"

Hull waxed eloquent in his description of the charge: "The grandly terrific sight of vast bodies of men in full run with bayonet and gun barrel and saber glistening in the sun with the starry banner in the front and inspiration of victory, sweeping across fields, over breastworks of the enemy, answering his guns, bayoneting and sabering his gunners . . . until the glad triumphant shout of victory told of battle won."[26]

Hull left military service shortly after the Vicksburg campaign. Confederate marksmen shot him twice as he led his company at the Big Black River, injuries that left him laid up for months. After healing, he chose to go home rather than return to the 23rd Iowa, a fact his political enemies pointed out during political campaigns. Perhaps his brief service, just thirteen months, made it easier for Hull to remember war as beautifully gallant. Hull, however, fought through the worst of the Vicksburg campaign, was shot twice, and saw many friends die in battle. He once eulogized William H. Kinsman, the colonel commanding the 23rd Iowa, as a "close and warm friend" cut down by rebel bullets, "struggling to his feet he advanced but a few steps," Hull remembered, "and again fell shot through the lungs." Hull recalled clutching his friend's hand as he died.[27] Henderson lost a leg at Shiloh and did not fight at Vicksburg; Allison never left Iowa. Alone among the three politicians, Hull was a genuine Vicksburg veteran. He enthusiastically endorsed Merry's proposal.[28]

After his success in Washington, Merry set to work cultivating his Iowa contacts on behalf of the park. His Grand Army of the Republic (GAR) comrades immediately fell into line, and GAR leaders urged the rank and file to purchase stock in the park association. Resolutions predicted that a Vicksburg park "would become a Mecca" attracting "the scarred and aging veterans, and Stalwart Sons of Veterans, the students of history of our country."[29]

One of the "Original Nine," as Merry's little group came to be called, was William T. Rigby. The other vets chose Rigby as their secretary. Newspapers sometimes called Merry the "father" of Vicksburg park, a designation he bore with some pride. But if Merry fathered the park, perhaps we should call Rigby its mother. Unlike Merry, Rigby never walked away from the project. He went to Vicksburg to birth it and then stayed to raise it. Rigby would work for decades at the park, devoting his career to building Civil War monuments. The park became his life's work.

The modern reader searches Rigby's extant correspondence for clues as to why he became so devoted to the Vicksburg battlefield. Born in Cedar County, Iowa, in 1841, he joined the 24th Iowa in 1862 as a second lieutenant. It must matter that, as a

This photograph, made around 1899, shows members of the Vicksburg National Military Park Association. William T. Rigby, appearing second from the left, made the Vicksburg National Military Park his life's work. James Grant Everest, fourth from the right, became one of the three original commissioners. He lobbied the Illinois legislature for an impressive monument. Stephen D. Lee is in the center. Old Court House Museum photograph.

young lieutenant, Rigby first experienced combat at Vicksburg. In April 1863, Rigby's regiment had piled onto transports, expecting to land at Grand Gulf. After a furious firefight between Confederate artillery and Union gunboats, the northerners backed off, leaving the Confederate gunners still active. Clearly, Grant could not land his infantry in the face of such Confederate firepower. On April 30, Rigby and his fellow infantrymen finally made their landing on Mississippi soil, going ashore at Bruinsburg. Thereafter, they marched toward Port Gibson. Rigby recounted later walking into his first battle. He and the other men unslung their knapsacks as they prepared for combat. He lamented later that he never saw his blanket again. Rigby remembered the fighting, once it started, as furious. The older soldiers told the younger men, including Rigby, that the firing was as heavy as what they had encountered at Shiloh. Like most soldiers coming under enemy fire for the first time, Rigby monitored himself, checking his own reactions. "I felt," he wrote home, "I was not at all scared but I could notice an excitement of the nerves which I allways feel on important occasions." Rigby remembered later that he willed himself not to be overwhelmed by his "excitement of the nerves." In fact, Rigby claimed that he had felt more agitated when called on to recite spelling words in front of his class as a schoolboy. Rigby said he overcame his wartime fear by forcing his mind not to dwell on the danger. "My plan all day was to think of nothing but my duties," he wrote.[30]

As the battle around Vicksburg unfolded, Rigby found that he actually enjoyed the excitement that combat offered. Chris Hedges compares the "rush of battle" to a drug, one that leaves its recovering addicts nostalgic for "war's simplicity and high," the comradeship, and contemptuous of ordinary life's routine. Hedges, a twentieth-century correspondent, not a Civil War soldier, did not fully imbibe war's narcotic effect. Civil War soldier David West gives a better sense of soldiers' high when he marveled that "when one is in the engagement he has no fear of Death before him & he can plunge his Bayonet plum through his fellow man and laff at the sight," but after the battle walking over the field "always causes my soul to shudder and my hart proves sick within me."[31]

Rigby's letters suggest that he became a bit addicted himself to the "the rush of battle." When his company guarded a hospital, assisting the wounded out of the ambulances, Rigby's reaction is interesting. "It is," he wrote grimly, "a duty I do not wish to perform again, all the worst features of the battlefield are gathered around the hospital & there is none of the excitement & action which is found on the field."[32] In another letter, Rigby lamented that his unit had missed the battle over Champion's Hill. "I can never think of that day without regret that I lost the experience which such a conflict gives & which can only be obtained in the front of the fight where the real work is done."[33]

Many northern soldiers stayed in Vicksburg after the siege, but not Rigby. No carpetbagger, he went home after the war, going to college and then becoming a farmer in Cedar County, Iowa. Though never elected to office, Rigby nonetheless had political connections. In 1879, he became a member of the Cornell (Iowa) College Board of Trustees. Five years later, the legislature named him to the Iowa State Agricultural College Board of Trustees.[34]

Becoming secretary of the park association energized Rigby. He campaigned for the park across the North, drafting resolutions for Union veterans' groups in Iowa, Illinois, Indiana, Ohio, Wisconsin, New Jersey, and Pennsylvania. The resolutions that Rigby mailed pledged the veterans to lobby their congressmen for a Vicksburg park. They further claimed that the Vicksburg siege marked a turning point in the Civil War, "an epoch in the history of our country." Rigby's resolutions sought to make the Vicksburg park into a memorial to Ulysses S. Grant, "the great commander whose genius planned the Vicksburg campaign and carried it to a successful issue." Rigby contacted Frederick Grant, asking him to approach members of Congress on behalf of the park.[35]

While Rigby worked to turn the battlefield into a monument to Grant, Confederate champions of the Lost Cause marshaled their own forces. In the 1890s, Vicksburg's Confederate veterans demanded an exclusively white southern war memorial. The United Confederate Veterans organized in 1889, and Vicksburg Confederates formed their own "camp," meeting, most often, at the Vicksburg Building Association. Like their Union counterparts, the Confederate veterans needed money to build a memorial. Unlike Rigby, they could hardly look to the Republican-dominated Congress or the cash-strapped Mississippi legislature for support. Some old soldiers complained that the legislature turned a blind eye to veterans' appeals anyway. There seemed no hope, but then, in 1895, a wealthy Confederate veteran offered $100,000 toward construction of a Confederate memorial hall or battle abbey of the South. There would be a contest among cities across the South to prove themselves worthy of the great prize. Vicksburg's old Confederates went to work, hoping to beat out less deserving rivals and bring the memorial to their town.[36]

The offer came from Charles Broadway Rouss, born Charles Baltzell Rouss. Money, not war, was the force that gave Rouss's life meaning. He quit school at age fifteen, finding his studies "tedius, tiresum, ful of anxiety, care and wear and tear."[37] Perhaps because he left school so early, Rouss became an aggressive misspeller, developing his own phonetic form of English that he used in personal letters, even ones dictated to subordinates, and in his *Monthly Auction Trade Journal*. Rouss's spelling became such a trademark that his son continued it after he took control of the *Trade Journal*. A genius at merchandising, Rouss started his first business in Winchester, Virginia, at age eighteen. He made a small fortune before the war, lost it, made another fortune after the war, lost that in the 1873 panic, and then became a millionaire in the 1890s. The owner of a vast store in New York and a chain of retail outlets across the country, he lived in a palatial mansion. He delighted in watching the street urchins claw the pavement for coins he tossed from his carriage, a habit his admiring biographer sees as a positive character trait.[38] Another friend remembered Rouss as "a great admirer of beauty" because he once saw a pretty girl and ordered his flunky to reward her with five dollars.[39]

In the Civil War, Rouss joined the 12th Virginia Cavalry. In 1896, his first biographer claimed that "he fought in all the famous battles of the Stonewall Jackson brigade."[40] Not true. He spent most of the war in Richmond, speculating in merchandise smuggled in by blockade-runners. He did not join the army until January 30, 1864. By then, Stonewall Jackson was dead, and his troops were increasingly demoralized. Rouss missed Fredricksburg and Chancellorsville; he joined in time for the Wilderness and Appomattox.[41] Rouss's old commanding officer, Thomas L. Rosser, remembered Private Rouss as "an excellent, gallant and patriotic soldier." Perhaps the general really remembered Rouss that way, but Rosser did make this observation after Rouss made his $100,000 offer to preserve the Lost Cause.[42]

After the war, Rouss pursued his dream of riches. He had invested his fortune in Confederate bonds and went to New York $11,000 in debt. Thrown in jail, he scratched his determination to achieve wealth on the wall of his cell. He pursued riches with single-minded determination, filling his *Monthly Auction Trade Journal* with military metaphors. "WE FITE," he quoted Nathan Bedford Forrest. "In the great batle of life . . . suces is with those who ar up with the lark, and while that bird is catching the erly worm, tha, too, ar redy to serv the first customer that cums along at the break of morn, as well as the last one." He saw "bisnes" as a "dedly and final grapl between KING CREDIT and its master MONEY DOWN." Rouss said no to the "periodical pay-day fiend" and always demanded "CASH BEFORE DELIVERY."[43] His philosophy apparently worked; he became a multimillionaire, the master of a retail empire.

By the summer of 1894, Rouss had begun to go blind. In August, he wrote that "my site is almost gone, and I spose in a month or so it wil hav uterly darkend."[44] Depressed, he admitted that after he passed fifty (in 1886), he found little pleasure in life.[45] Life was not worth living, he sadly told confidants.[46] Looking back over his life, Rouss thought he had thrown his time away chasing money. Now that he had attained his dream of wealth, Rouss asked, "What is the mony and gratification worth? It wil not buy me apetite if I am not hungry nor sleep if I am wakeful, nor youth in my old age."[47] Nearly blind, depressed, and bitter, Rouss made his offer of $100,000 toward construction of a Confederate battle abbey in 1894. He required that his donation be matched by contributions from ordinary southerners. Probably he thought he could achieve greater fame for himself and redeem his wasted life by involving as many people as possible. "Two things . . . go agenst me," he wrote a friend. "One is the xtreme poverty of our Confed. peple, the other is, that evry one wants it in his own state."[48]

He may well have seen his battle abbey as a way to promote nationalism more than the Lost Cause. Rouss, his biographer reports, was a "flag waving enthusiast who felt it was America's destiny to rule a vast part of the globe."[49] That view appeared in Rouss's *Monthly Auction Trade Journal*. In private, while Rouss questioned the Spanish-American War,[50] his letters suggest that he really believed in "the agresiv atitude of our cuntry." He expected America to surpass England as a superpower: "We will imitate England, we wil agrandize, acumulate, and civilize, we wil claim for our batlfield the whole face of the erth."[51]

White Vicksburgers thought they had a real chance to capture Rouss's prize for themselves. But in 1895, the cities of Richmond and Washington also competed for Rouss's money, and the veteran organizations in each thought they had the inside track. By October 1895, the *Washington Post* boasted that "if all signs do not fail . . . Washington will have what will be known as 'The Battle Abbey of the South,' adorning one of her principle thoroughfares."[52] Meanwhile, the *Richmond Times* reported that several members of the site-selection committee had indicated a preference for Richmond, with none showing any inclination for Washington or any other city.[53] When the committee met, delegations from Meridian, Mississippi; Tuscaloosa, Alabama; Anne Arundel County, Maryland; Little Rock, Arkansas; Dallas, Texas; McAllister, Indian Territory;

New Orleans, Louisiana; Pensacola, Florida; and Nashville, Tennessee, all made pitches for their cities. No one showed up to represent Vicksburg.[54] One faction of Washington veterans dreamed of a battle abbey even more grand than Rouss had originally planned. They wanted more than "a mere museum of relics, or a simple 'battle abbey,'" imagining, instead, a million-dollar enterprise with a battle abbey hall but also "a complete historical department, a department of art and sculpture, one devoted to industrial and agricultural resources," and a vast theater. This scheme came from Virginia veterans living in Washington and working within the Washington chapter of the United Confederate Veterans to sabotage Washington's chances in favor of Richmond. They hoped that by proposing such a mighty educational institution for the South, they would make it impracticable to place it in Washington, so far from most of the South.[55]

Unaware of these machinations, people in Vicksburg went to work raising money for their city. Much of this labor fell to the city's female population, as it did in other cities. Vicksburg women organized moonlight excursions for donations. The veterans called on the Mississippi legislature to fund a memorial hall in Vicksburg. They tried to flatter Rouss by calling it "Rouss Battle Abbey." According to the camp minutes for 1896, the veterans "earnestly" discussed the battle abbey. They also talked about the proposed military park, but the minutes do not describe their conversation as particularly "earnest" on that subject. The veterans decided to sponsor a series of lectures to earn money for their abbey and also help out "poor worthy comrades in distress." John Cashman's *Vicksburg Evening Post* announced that Vicksburg had history and geography on its side, "and we believe it will be the fault of our own people if the Abbey is not located here."[56] Left unstated was Vicksburg's connection to Stephen D. Lee, who would serve on the committee of generals slated to pick the winning city.[57]

In June 1896, Vicksburg's lobbying efforts reached their crescendo. Newspapers reported that "the ladies" and the veterans worked "zealously." Reports from various Mississippi politicians encouraged the Vicksburgers to believe their state legislature might contribute money to their cause.[58] But it was also in June that a *Vicksburg Evening Post* correspondent signing himself "WTW" threw cold water on the Vicksburg enthusiasts. Richmond, as the Confederate seat of government, had a strong claim on Rouss's money, WTW pointed out. South Carolina might also win the money; it had the honor of being the first state out of the Union. WTW argued that the idea of a national park at Vicksburg in no way obviated local Confederates' need for a battle abbey. The national park would commemorate both the North and the South, WTW wrote, perhaps honoring the North more than the South. The Rouss Battle Abbey would be dedicated solely to the Lost Cause.[59]

The campaign for the battle abbey may have been the only time in the history of Vicksburg Civil War commemorations when the town did not have to worry about competition from Gettysburg. No one suggested building the battle abbey on that northern site. In this fight, Vicksburgers most feared New Orleans. The *Evening Post* sounded defensive when it wrote that "the ladies of Vicksburg" had worked harder than the New Orleans women. "Taking into consideration the population of the two cities," the *Post* explained, "the ladies of Vicksburg had raised more money in proportion than the ladies of New Orleans." We have the best, most ardently patriotic women, the *Post* essentially said.[60] There were also more generalized paeans to white southern womanhood. The Vicksburg veterans insisted that when white southerners built their battle abbey, space must be reserved to celebrate the contributions of Confederate women. Southern women held the white South's "sacred trust" and "have never yet faltered or failed in the performance of any duty . . . for the Southern cause."[61]

On June 19, 1897, Vicksburg served notice on the Confederate Memorial Association that it wanted to be considered for the Rouss Battle Abbey. The Confederate Memorial Association's board of trustees did not make its decision for another year. On July 30, 1898, the board heard a petition from Vicksburg. Nashville and Richmond sent delegations to present their respective cases. Probably the board had already decided on Richmond. Before Vicksburg and Nashville even made their appeals, one trustee had already made a motion for Richmond. The minutes do not reflect a single vote for either Nashville or Vicksburg, though one delegate still held out for Washington.[62]

While Vicksburg's ex-Confederates tried and failed to win the Rouss Battle Abbey, Rigby, busy as ever, recruited Mississippi Congressman Thomas C. Catchings to fight in Washington for the national park. The available evidence suggests that Catchings was as committed to sectional but not racial reconciliation as Rigby. Catchings had joined the Confederate army at age fourteen, but his constituents called him "general" for his stint as state attorney general, not for his military rank, which fell well short of general. Though a Democrat, Catchings could count on local white Republicans to take his side when Washington Republicans contested his 1888 win over a black candidate. White Democrats expressed outrage that the Republicans had insulted the district by nominating a black candidate. In fact, veterans of the Union army living in Vicksburg told a congressional investigating committee that while they always voted with the Republicans in national elections, they sided with the Democrats locally. They just would not vote for a black candidate.[63]

In January 1896, Catchings introduced a bill for the park, requesting $75,000 to both purchase the land and administer the park. The bill envisioned a park of 1,200 acres, only a portion of the actual battlefield, a fact that surprised and disappointed some veterans. The proposal went to the House Committee on Military Affairs, where Rigby testified on its behalf. Stephen D. Lee, serving as first president of Mississippi's Agricultural and Mechanical College (now Mississippi State University), had no time to spare from lobbying the Mississippi legislature on behalf of his college to go to Washington for the park bill. After listening to

Rigby, the committee issued a brief but favorable report arguing that the Vicksburg battle should be memorialized because it won the Civil War for the North. Vicksburg was as important as Gettysburg, the committee concluded, saying, "Your committee are of the opinion that both of these places should be preserved as historic fields."[64]

While Congress considered the bill, Rigby was in Vicksburg, researching the land he wanted for the park, contacting owners ,and negotiating terms, confident that Congress actually would authorize the park. An Army Corps of Engineers officer drew up a map of the battlefield, marking property lines and Civil War fortifications.[65] Rigby organized such a massive letter-writing campaign on behalf of the park that one congressman asked him to turn it off. "I think the bill will pass," John A. T. Hull predicted before adding that he doubted that "it strengthens the situation any to pile them in."[66] Rigby's energy impressed Stephen D. Lee. "You have certainly won your spurs by your work in the interest of the Park," the old Confederate general told the younger Iowan.[67]

By spring, though, it seemed clear that Rigby's herculean efforts had run afoul of the powerful Speaker of the House. In Rigby's voluminous files, petitions directed to the Speaker began to appear. "The undersigned," one GAR post wrote on March 21, "will feel gratified if you will give such assistance as may be necessary to bring the matter before the House of Representatives."[68] Rigby's Capitol Hill informants agreed that the Speaker of the House, Republican Thomas B. Reed of Maine, alone would determine the fate of the park proposal. A majority in Congress would vote for the measure, but Reed could make sure that they never got the chance. In the 1870s and 1880s, House speakers enjoyed increasing discretion over recognizing members on the floor. One Democratic speaker had once described his right to ignore clamoring members as "absolute." In 1896, Reed was at the zenith of his powers, holding the House at his mercy with his prerogative to ignore members. He so perfectly commanded his fellow Republicans that it was said that he could force them out of their seats and return them en masse with a simple gesture up or down. A massive man physically, dressed entirely in black, Reed commanded the house with his sardonic wit, penetrating intelligence, and impatience with dilatory tactics. After once leaving an opponent momentarily speechless, Reed cut in to announce that he had "embedded that fly in the liquid amber of my remarks." When another congressman began his remarks by saying, "I was thinking," Reed interrupted to commend "the gentleman's remarkable innovation." Reed ended the Democrats' practice of silently filibustering with frequent demands for roll-call votes and then denying a quorum by not answering when their names were called. Reed simply recorded the silent members as present and proceeded with business, a procedure that outraged the Democrats. Reed favored woman suffrage, resisted imperialism, and promoted federal protection for black voters. In 1890, white southerners feared that Reed angled to be the next Republican candidate for president. That was how they explained his support for the "Force" bill, a measure to compel the South to allow black voting or face a reduction in representation. The *New Orleans Picayune* accused Reed of scheming to win black votes as a way of making himself "a man of destiny" and president.[69] The *Picayune* was right to worry. At the end of 1894, some journalists calculated that Reed's presidential ambitions posed the greatest challenge to Allison's candidacy.[70]

Rigby, the champion of the park, and Reed, master of the House, simply were not kindred spirits. They were roughly the same age: Reed born in 1839 and Rigby in 1841. But while Rigby volunteered for the army in 1862, Reed, in the words of his biographer, managed to escape the "impulse of patriotism."[71] For Rigby, his combat experience around Vicksburg may have defined his life, but Reed served in the Civil War only briefly, not joining until 1864 and then choosing the navy, not the army. Reed did not see his Civil War experience as a turning point in the same way as the veterans, especially Rigby, who pushed the hardest for the park. Instead, Reed made light of his service, telling amused listeners that he had "kept a grocery store for the government" during the war. Reed described his gunboat duty as "charming," "a delightful life," a time when he got "thirteen hundred dollars a year and one ration, and nothing to do." According to Reed the raconteur, his most terrifying Civil War moment came when he drew $5,000 from the bank and then thought he had miscounted it.[72]

Rigby was exactly the kind of promoter that Reed most distrusted. The Speaker despised "pork," federally funded projects of chiefly local benefit. Reed hardly disguised his contempt for the "promoters of public improvements." Although Rigby himself was a northerner, it probably did not help his standing with Reed that he advocated a southern project. Reed's continuing hostile attitude toward the South was no doubt a Civil War artifact, one that he would not put away in the name of reconciliation. For Reed, white southerners' continuing violence helped keep sectional anger alive in a way that it did not for Rigby. Reed's reaction to the 1898 Frazier Baker lynching offers an opportunity to see both his combative attitude toward white southern racists and his determined resistance to imperialism. White South Carolinians murdered postmaster Frazier Baker because they could not stand the idea of a black man handling their mail. Reed clipped a newspaper story about Baker's death and captioned it "Another Outrage in Cuba, Body of a Patriot Riddled with Bullets and Thrown through the Burning Rafters of his Dwelling." He handed his captioned clipping to a white South Carolina congressman who had been calling for intervention in Cuba. Reading the caption, the congressman eagerly took the bait but then read the article only to exclaim, "This isn't Cuba." "No," Reed coldly answered, snapping his trap shut. "It isn't." The unreconciled Reed distrusted the unreconstructed South and did not want to lay aside his sectionalism for military interventions. The fully reconciled Rigby had no such hesitations. He advocated a park to commemorate military valor at a time when many in Congress sought to mobilize united American militarism on behalf of imperial adventures.[73]

A lesser man would have been scared away by Reed, master of the savage invective, capable of withering sarcasm, and plainly invulnerable to the wiles of lobbyists. If Rigby hesitated for a moment, his papers fail to document the lapse. Once he had identified his target and realized the folly of frontal assault, Rigby maneuvered to make contact with the Speaker through intermediaries. This was no easy task; Reed did not exactly maintain friendships indiscriminately. Nonetheless, Rigby learned the names of Reed's cronies and persuaded one of them to push the measure. That did not work.[74] Rigby then prevailed on another Republican, Iowa Congressman Robert G. Cousins, to press Reed. Unlike most of the Iowans whom Rigby mobilized for the Mississippi park, Cousins, born in 1859, had never served in the Civil War. Apparently, he simply acted on behalf of an Iowa constituent. In any case, he struck out. When Cousins spoke for the bill, Reed responded by naming fifteen other propositions "for which he said it was claimed that there were special reasons for passing." Reed doubted the budget would allow funding for any of them. Rigby, his enthusiasm unvanquished, responded to Cousins's gloomy report by asking what more he could do. Cousins could think of nothing. Veterans' organizations and state legislatures all over the country had supported the bill: "I do not see how any greater influence could be brought to bear." Reed, Cousins concluded, would decide for himself, "looking at it from his standpoint, and there is not much use in besieging him on such matters."[75]

Reed's recalcitrance frustrated Rigby to no end but represented the views of fiscally conservative Republicans. Henry Cabot Lodge explained that purchasing Civil War battlefields cost the government enormous sums of money and then more money for their maintenance. While Lodge agreed with the argument that Grant's genius should be commemorated, he suspected that such parks really meant more for their localities than for the national government.[76] Even Stephen D. Lee found such arguments reasonable. "The trouble is the empty treasury," he wrote, "and Mr.

164

Reed has good arguments on his side." From Lee's point of view, passing a park bill under such circumstances was another lost cause. He had grudging admiration for Reed. "Mr. Reed is a man after his own mould," Lee decided, "and I don't believe any one can influence him against his decision when he has deliberately made up his mind."[77]

Despite such doubts, Rigby pressed ahead. He continued to circulate resolutions and memorials, always emphasizing the park as a monument to Grant's genius. Northern veterans found this argument positively irresistible, and so did state legislatures. In 1896, Mississippi, Iowa, New York, Massachusetts, and Rhode Island passed joint resolutions endorsing the park and calling on their congressional delegations to vote for its passage. The following year, Minnesota, Wisconsin, Michigan, Illinois, Indiana, Ohio, and Pennsylvania followed suit.[78] At the end of 1897, five members of the House Committee on Military Affairs traveled to Vicksburg to inspect the battlefield. By this time, Rigby's argument that the park would memorialize Grant had even been absorbed by ex-Confederates. Cashman's *Vicksburg Evening Post* published an article saying that "it was here at Vicksburg that General Grant's greatness dawned upon the Nation like a burst of sunshine." The arrival of the dignitaries aroused new hopes that Speaker Reed would allow a vote on the bill.[79]

Rigby and other park supporters had to wait another year before that happened. In that year, a new militarism swept the nation. Republican jingoes demanded Cuban independence from Spanish rule. Some historians have argued that calls for intervention came in an increasingly bellicose time, an era with enthusiasm for boxing and football, which grew in popularity as American men tried to prove their manliness in industrialized times.[80] Perhaps, but some in the white South resisted the martial spirit as "sentimental." The *New Orleans Picayune* denounced "sympathy wars." The Civil War had been a "sympathy war," the *Picayune* said, explaining that misplaced sympathy for slaves led to northern aggression. From this perspective, a war with Spain on behalf

165

of Cubans struggling for liberty seemed simply another "sympathy" war. The *Picayune* sarcastically calculated that freeing four million slaves cost a million white lives; since some Cubans were white and therefore worth more, according to the *Picayune*, it might be worth half a million white lives to free a million Cubans.[81] John Cashman of the *Vicksburg Evening Post* thought the war against Spain "cowardly" and scorned comparisons of McKinley to Lincoln. Lincoln, Cashman pointed out, freed the slaves without killing them, while McKinley "butchered" thousands of Filipinos in his quest to free them. The martial spirit historians have found sweeping the nation in the 1890s did not reach every corner of the South.[82]

Nor did it reach every corner of Maine. Reed opposed fighting Spain and all imperial adventures, once acidly telling a member with an interest in the marble industry that the war would "make a large profit for gravestones."[83] Reed could control the House but not the nation's appetite for war. In February, a New York newspaper published a private letter written by the Spanish minister to the United States calling McKinley weak. On February 15, the U.S.S. *Maine* exploded and sank in Havana harbor. Two months later, McKinley asked Congress for authority to intervene in Cuba. Reed seemed sadly puzzled by his nation's headlong rush to war.[84]

One year later, on February 6, 1899, as war continued in the Philippines, Reed recognized Hull, and the Vicksburg bill reached the House floor. If further evidence were needed that only Reed had stood between Rigby and his park, it was supplied by the desultory remarks made as the House hurried the bill into law. "I suppose there is going to be no opposition," a Texas Democrat wearily said before asking that the bill at least be read into the record. "I understand that is all there will be about it."[85] The Senate said little more, a Mississippi senator claiming that because every GAR encampment had endorsed it, "I presume no objection will be made to it."[86] President McKinley signed the Vicksburg park bill into law on February 21. Under the law Congress enacted, three commissioners had the job of purchasing 1,200 acres of land for the park for a total price of just $40,000. Lee, Rigby, and James Grant Everest became the first commissioners. The trio represented the three states with arguably the most at stake in Vicksburg: Rigby of Iowa, Lee of Mississippi, and Everest of Illinois. Meanwhile, in Washington, Speaker Reed resigned his seat and quit politics altogether in September 1899.[87]

Everest, like Merry, was a Union army veteran working for a railroad company. Enlisting in 1861 as a private in the 13th Illinois Infantry, Everest had worked his way up to captain and had commanded a company at Chickasaw Bayou, where he had re-coiled, like all of Sherman's soldiers, before Stephen Lee's defenses. Since the war, Everest had served as general travel passenger agent for the Chicago, Milwaukee & St. Paul Railway.[88] No mindless champion of reconciliation between Confederate and Union veterans, Everest, in 1894, as a leader in the Chicago GAR, had indignantly demanded that Confederate veterans disavow the treasonous sentiments they had championed in 1861.[89]

Just a month after the park bill became law, Lee and Rigby had set up an office in Vicksburg and had begun buying the land necessary for the park. The commissioners worked under the War Department, reporting directly to the secretary of war, Russell A. Alger, a strong supporter of the park and a Civil War veteran himself. Rigby rather than Lee did most of the work, negotiating with local landowners. This was critical to the park's success. Some owners demanded more than $100 an acre. With his small budget, if Rigby gave in to such demands, there might be no park—or so Rigby warned the recalcitrant owners. He had to persuade the landowners to sell at no more than $25 an acre, or he could not possibly buy enough land to even have a park. By April 28, Rigby, through hard bargaining, had bought enough land to guarantee that there would in fact be a park. But he did not announce this publicly, fearing the news would drive up prices for the remaining land. He preferred to insist that the park's future remained in doubt unless he could buy all the land for $40,000. He wanted the landowners to know that without a park, their rugged acreage would be worth very little.[90]

Even though the law establishing the park set out its perimeter, Rigby also worked long hours through the summer of 1899, marking off the precise boundaries on the ground. He took an engineer with him, but "as usual, the decision rested with me." To his wife, Rigby wondered if "the time will come when some one will take the burden of responsibility from me." Only death would do that.[91]

Some of the owners Rigby contacted were black. Rigby put off negotiating with them until after he had settled with most of the white owners. Rigby wanted to give the "Darkeys," as he called them, a fair price, but that would be less than what they had paid originally. "When a Darkey buys land," Rigby explained to his wife, "he has to pay a stiff price for it." Whites did not like to sell blacks land, and they did so only at premium prices. Rigby would not be paying any stiff prices, and it nagged his conscience. One black woman especially troubled Rigby. Catherine Ruffin had increased the value of her property by building an "unusually good house for a Darkey." She had been, Rigby heard, the mistress of a white man. Once he decided to get married (to a white woman, of course), he gave Ruffin a piece of land and built a thousand-dollar house on it. While talking to Ruffin in her yard, Rigby's eyes strayed to her children. He especially admired one sixteen-year-old girl, a "seductive looking creature, alert and agile as a gazelle." She had a "lithe active body that makes her agreeable to look upon," Rigby told his wife.[92]

After meeting with Ruffin, Rigby returned to his hotel hot and tired, only to find more "colored" supplicants. Mr. and Mrs. Jones owned a little house on the battlefield—all they had in the world, they told Rigby. Rigby regretted that they too would get only $25 an acre, though he vowed to try to find them some land outside the park at a price more reasonable than black people usually paid. "These are the cases in which one likes to be liberal," Rigby thought, but there was not much he could do about it other than regret that Congress had not appropriated more money.[93]

Everest stayed in Illinois, but Lee, who was in Mississippi, played no role in these negotiations either. Within a month of becoming president of the commission, his wife's health deteriorated frighteningly, leaving her in constant pain. By December, Lee decided that his wife's situation did not permit him to serve even as the formal head of the commission. He contacted the secretary of war and announced that he would be stepping aside as president of the commission in favor of Rigby. He could continue on the commission, he said, but not head it. Lee promised to one day again take charge.[94]

By establishing the commission, Congress essentially employed lobbyists to lobby itself. Within a year, the commissioners had begun working to enlarge the park's size and increase its appropriation.[95] The commission also labored to persuade northern states to pass laws establishing state commissions and appropriating money to build state monuments in the park. Rigby often drafted the legislation himself, sending the texts of laws he wanted passed to his allies in various northern states.[96] By 1901, the commission had persuaded New York, Massachusetts, and Rhode Island to create Vicksburg park commissions. With these states in the bag, the commission began appealing to the holdouts' pride. Surely New Hampshire did not want to be left behind, Rigby told his contact there.[97] Through all these negotiations, the commission touted the park as a monument to Grant's brilliance.[98]

Rigby personally traveled across the North, visiting the various legislatures, though not always successfully. In April 1901, he journeyed to Lansing, Michigan, only to find that he had arrived too late for that session of the legislature. Hurrying to Indianapolis, he again found himself too late. "The fault lies with General McGinnis and with Admiral Brown," he grumbled. His associates had not kept him informed about the legislative calendar. In truth, none of his friends took this project as seriously as he did, and none could possibly match his commitment, energy, and determination. In Madison, he found success with the Wisconsin legislature, making a connection with the former colonel of the 12th Wisconsin, one of Grant's regiments at Vicksburg.[99] Rigby did not go to Illinois, though he and the other Iowans realized that Illinois could be, and should be, the most generous state. Illinois had sent more troops to Vicksburg than any other state; that meant Vicksburg veterans formed a larger portion of the voting population in Illinois than in any other state. Illinois Republican politicians owed a lot to Vicksburg veterans, their loyal constituents. Rigby hoped for a big memorial from the Illinois legislature, and he expected Everest to deliver the victory. Everest knew the governor of Illinois and worked the legislature, lobbying for the largest Illinois monument possible. Rigby felt comfortable leaving Illinois in his hands.[100]

The commissioners lobbied Congress every year for more money and, sometimes, more land. In Washington, the commissioners had an important ally in Secretary of War Russell Alger. One historian has called Alger a "vain schmoozer,"[101] but Rigby liked him as a friend and supporter of the park. Unfortunately, the press and public pilloried Alger for his conduct of the War Department during the Spanish-American War. Within months of congressional approval of the park, McKinley forced Alger from office, a departure that shocked the commissioners,[102] but the worst was yet to come. The new secretary of war turned out to be Elihu Root. Even Root's friends described his personality as dominating, aggressive, and scornful of weaknesses, either mental or moral. A corporate lawyer, Root gave up an $80,000 salary for a salary one tenth that amount as secretary of war. He took the job out of contempt for Alger, believing the War Department to be chaotic and poorly managed, in need of stern management. No doubt Root's personality would have inclined him to vigorous remedial measures anyway, but following a slacker put an edge on his vigor that might not have been there otherwise. It would not be long before Vicksburg National Military Park felt the sting of Root's management methods and fiscal discipline.[103]

More than Root's personality drove his questioning of the Vicksburg commissioners. Some in Congress thought expenditures for parks had gotten out of hand. Between 1901 and 1904, Congress entertained thirty-four bills proposing new parks, commemorating historical events all over the nation. These bills went to the House Military Affairs Committee, chaired by Richard Wayne Parker of New Jersey. Unlike J. A. T. Hull, Parker, born in 1848, had never served in the Civil War or any war. Parker asked Root how much the existing military parks had cost. The answer, more than $2 million, unsettled the committee.[104]

With Congress breathing down his neck, Root took a much more skeptical approach than the aging Alger to Rigby's expenditures and requests for additional funds. He first sent a letter to Stephen D. Lee wanting to know just exactly what it would cost to finish the park and then maintain it once completed.[105] Rigby responded with a lengthy letter detailing ongoing negotiations for land purchases and his plans for proposed roads. Rigby pointed out that the terrain was broken and rugged. Twelve bridges would have to be built, he said, some more than 350 feet long. Roadways had to be graded. Material for surfacing the new roads would have to hauled in. Rigby wanted to restore "many miles" of Civil War earthworks and remount "a great number of guns." Rigby guessed it would cost $650,000 to finish the park.[106]

It seems reasonable to conclude that Root and Congress agreed that the Vicksburg Park had less value for the nation than other parks. In 1902, Root would report to Congress that the Vicksburg Park had cost, up to that point, $140,790, a paltry sum compared to $423,322 spent on Gettysburg. Even if Root had agreed to ask Congress for the whole proposed by Rigby, the sum would still have been far less than the amount Congress appropriated for Gettysburg.[107] Nonetheless, Root decided to cut costs in Vicksburg. To the commissioners' shock and dismay, Root insisted on a cheaper park, with fewer bridges and roads.

Unlike his predecessor, Root refused to deal directly with the commissioners, forcing them to communicate their requests through his subordinates. When Root would not accept their budget recommendations, Everest erupted in anger. Lee fumed that Root had reduced the three commissioners to "mere figureheads." Both Everest and Lee feared Root endangered the whole project. Lee predicted that the park "will be a small affair, and not what its friends hoped it to be and not what the survivors of the great armies desire." In September 1901, Lee took his frustrations to the newspapers. For his part, Rigby decided to stay "cool and philosophical." Even in the face of Root's "blow to our pride," Rigby remained determinedly optimistic. "I think that everything will, in the end, come out right and straight," he said.[108]

In 1900, Iowa legislators had considered a bill to set up a commission composed of representatives from every Iowa regiment at Vicksburg. Veterans would travel to the battleground and locate their old positions so that markers could be placed commemorating their service. This was very much a veterans' bill. Elmer J. C. Bealer spoke on behalf of the monument, describing himself as still haunted by his memories of the siege. Images of Iowa soldiers strewn over southern hills burned in his mind, Bealer said. Bealer lauded the heroism of Iowa soldiers, the first Union troops on Mississippi soil in the campaign, for such men had "nourished" the "flower of liberty" with their blood. And Bealer told legislators that the Vicksburg park would be the greatest in the world, recapturing the battle lines of both sides.[109] The *Iowa State Register* conceded that younger citizens might question the expenditure of their tax dollars on such an effort, but, the *Register* scolded, Vicksburg and Gettysburg had determined the nation's future.[110] The legislature agreed with the *Register* and approved the bill on March 29, 1900. Commissioners met at Des Moines on September 18, journeyed to the Vicksburg battlefield, and finished their report by the end of 1901.[111]

The Iowa legislature then passed a bill creating a new commission to build a monument and appropriating $150,000 for construction. John F. Merry headed this commission, which vis-

ited various monuments in Washington, Richmond, Chickamauga, and Gettysburg to get ideas. Once the commission met at
Little Round Top on the Gettysburg battlefield, its secretary taking his notes on the barrel of a cannon. In 1903, the commissioners journeyed to Vicksburg, where they enjoyed strolling about
the battlefield, picking spots to erect memorials to the various
Iowa regiments. A subcommittee selected a Boston artist's design
for the monument, but some commissioners wanted to know why
the subcommittee had settled on one artist without throwing the
selection process open to a competition. The design seemed
grandiose and failed to recognize ordinary soldiers. In any case,
the commission asked the artist to revise his plans. A year later, in
1904, Henry Hudson Kitson submitted a smaller version of the
proposed monument. The commission liked the revised design
better, calling it "more distinctly a Soldiers' Monument."[112]

In Illinois, Everest campaigned first for a state commission to
pick the most appropriate location on the battlefield for an Illinois memorial. With that accomplished, Everest moved to the
second phase. He wanted the legislature to appropriate money for
a truly grand monument. Everest followed Rigby's modus
operandi, attending GAR encampments to enlist grassroots support among the old veterans.[113] Everest made repeated trips to
Springfield, going to legislators with tediously detailed arguments
for the park. In 1901, he cautioned Rigby that Illinois did not have
as much money available as Iowa. Nor was the Republican party as
strong in Illinois as it was in Iowa. Illinois Democrats could be
counted on to oppose Civil War commemorations.[114]

Everest could only marvel at the tangled web of Illinois politics. By the end of 1901, the legislature had created a commission
to determine a site for the state's monument. But even legislative
victory did not bring an end to the political intrigue. As the
names of potential Illinois commissioners began to circulate,
Everest realized the governor planned to reward his supporters
with seats on the commission. At least one member had never
served at Vicksburg, and three members came from the same

regiment. Everest thought the commission should represent as many regiments as possible. Nonetheless, despite these shortcomings, Everest called the Illinois commissioners strong men who would effectively lobby the state for a large monument.[115]

As Everest negotiated Illinois politics, Stephen D. Lee scratched for money in the barren fields of the southern legislatures. The resistance he encountered came in a variety of forms. Some thought the money he sought for monuments would be better spent on services for living Confederate veterans.[116] In 1901, Mississippi Governor Andrew H. Longino apparently revealed his indifference to Civil War memorialization when he dismissed a United Daughters of the Confederacy petition on behalf of Jefferson Davis's birthday as "rot." Longino's "rot" remark created a minor scandal, and he quickly mouthed the proper Lost Cause platitudes, but many felt they had caught a glimpse of the governor's true feelings. He had made his statement privately to the chairman of the railroad commission, not expecting his offhand thoughts to become public.[117]

Longino's enemies charged him with disrespecting Confederate veterans, but the veterans themselves were not so sure they wanted a monument on the federal park. Five years after Longino's "rot" comment, "considerable" veteran opposition to a state battlefield memorial surfaced in Mississippi's legislature. The veterans did not want to spend state money to build a Mississippi monument in a park celebrating a Union victory. Fortunately for Rigby and the other commissioners, more legislators favored building a Mississippi memorial on park grounds, and the measure passed the legislature in February 1906.[118] The legislature appropriated $50,000. A commission chaired by Governor James K. Vardaman decided to spend $500 on twenty-six markers commemorating various Mississippi units stationed around Vicksburg. The rest of the money went to a "grand state monument" celebrating Mississippi soldiers' "heroism, prowess and fidelity to duty." Frank Triebel, working in Florence, Italy, created bronze reliefs and sculptures of Mississippi soldiers for the monument. In 1909, Mississippi dedicated its monument, though construction would not be complete for three more years.[119]

Other southern states were even less willing than Mississippi to memorialize the Civil War. Lee found the situation in Louisiana "chaotic." He went from one newspaper office to the next, trying to drum up editorial support. Lee made a passionate speech to the legislature, praising the bravery of Louisiana troops. His hard work in Louisiana seemed to pay off when the legislature finally appropriated $100,000 for a Louisiana monument on park grounds. But the Lost Cause did not have a stranglehold on the governor, and he vetoed the appropriation. In a private letter to Lee, Governor Newton C. Blanchard explained that legislators had spent beyond the state's means. Friends of the park in Louisiana scoffed at Blanchard's explanation. It is "all rot," A. L. Slack of Tallulah exclaimed. Blanchard had money for projects he favored, like new courthouses. For all his "hot air over the bare-footed [Confederate] soldiers," his veto showed where he really stood. Slack thought white southerners had generally lost interest in the Civil War. "It looks," he wrote Rigby, "as the sentiment and a love for the heroism and memories of the past are fast fading from our people."[120]

Before the Georgia legislature's appropriations committee, Lee made what he considered his best speech. As in Louisiana, though, the Georgia legislators had other priorities. "There is a flood of bills ahead of it," one Georgian explained to Lee. Georgia did not dedicate its modest Vicksburg memorial until 1962.[121] In Alabama, Lee made a speech that brought tears to the politicians' eyes. "I insist that it is Alabama's duty," he orated, "to commemorate its Confederate veterans for their heroism." No doubt many agreed, but Alabama did not dedicate its monument until forty-four years after Lee told the tearful legislators that they had a duty to the veterans.[122]

Lee came closer to success in Texas, but there too he found it necessary to overcome indifference and carelessness. Lee had trusted a legislator he knew as Captain Kyle. Kyle introduced the bill as he had promised but then neglected it, and it appeared the proposal for a Texas commission had died by September 1901. Lee enlisted Senator Thomas N. Waul to reinvigorate the park proposal in Texas. At Vicksburg, Colonel Waul had commanded a cavalry battalion. The old Confederate colonel sought out Kyle, whom he found to be a fellow veteran, aged and feeble, and seated so far from the Speaker of the Texas House of Representatives that he could not gain recognition. He also found a segment of the House strongly opposed to the measure. Finally, in October, Texas passed its bill, and the governor named three commissioners to go to Vicksburg. Despite this progress, Texas did not dedicate its monument until 1961. Lee died in Vicksburg on May 28, 1908. Of the southern states, only Virginia had dedicated a state monument at the time of Lee's death.[123] If the Lost Cause had such a stranglehold on white southern minds and if Confederate memorialization were so crucial a cog in the machinery of racial oppression, why did he die so frustrated?

Southern legislators' reluctance to appropriate money for state monuments sent the irrepressible Rigby to an alternate strategy. Rigby conceived the idea of commemorating every brigade and battery commander with a portrait monument. No other battlefield commission attempted such a comprehensive scheme. The beauty of the plan was that it required no legislative action. Rigby went to the families and friends of the commanders, soliciting contributions. To fill in when those funds did not materialize, Rigby used his park's annual appropriation to memorialize officers. Pemberton got his monument in this fashion thanks to Rigby.[124] In 1902, when the Illinois veteran Stephen Beck returned to Vicksburg, "this hauty and wicked city," he found Rigby anxious to find the exact spot where an artillery captain named Henry A. Rogers had died. Beck and Rigby hiked to the spot where Beck's regiment, the 124th Illinois, had camped. Beck recounted Rogers's death, telling Rigby how he had bled to death. Rigby took notes and then said, "Well, you take this hatchet and drop it where you may think Rogers was killed and down goes this stake." Beck dropped the hatchet and later found a granite stone monument on the spot where he placed the hatchet.[125]

Meanwhile, the northern states vigorously moved ahead. In 1900, Massachusetts sent its commission to Vicksburg, making the first appropriation for a state monument on park grounds. In 1903, its delegation made its way South to dedicate the first monument in the park, nervous and uneasy about the reception it would receive. "I expected to see scowling faces," E. T. Raymond remembered later. Instead, the aged Confederates warmly greeted the old Yankees, offering flowers and patriotic songs. Vicksburg children, Raymond happily observed, had been taught to think of themselves as Americans first and southerners second.[126] In 1904, New Hampshire became the second state to build a monument. Ohio followed a year later with smaller monuments for each of that state's thirty-nine regimental and battery units stationed at Vicksburg.[127]

Once the states decided to build a monument, they created new commissions to select a design and write the inscriptions. Some states held contests where artists offered competing designs. The War Department supervised all these deliberations, taking a detailed interest. Missouri's monument commission had wanted one of its markers to read as follows:

U.S.
MISSOURI
Marks the place where Captain
Robert Bucanan, commanding Seventh Missouri
Infantry, U.S. Volunteers, met
Major General John S. Bowen, carrying
General Pemberton's flag of truce,
on the afternoon of July 3, 1863.

The War Department rewrote this to read:

U.S.
MISSOURI

Marks the place where
General Pemberton's flag of truce was met
on the afternoon of July 3, 1863.[128]

Illinois outpaced every other state, appropriating $260,000 for its imposing monument. As the builders finished work on the awesome Illinois memorial, the *Vicksburg Evening Post* noted that ten states had taken steps to build monuments on the battleground. Pointedly, the *Post* observed that every one of the ten states was northern. And the impressive Illinois monument, modeled on Rome's Pantheon, seemed designed to show off the North's wealth. Inside its round walls, bronze tablets displayed the name of every Illinois soldier stationed around Vicksburg, some 36,000 names in all.[129]

The Illinois Monument under construction. Old Court House Museum photograph.

178

Dedicating the Illinois monument promised to be a massive celebration of North–South reconciliation, a vast outpouring of Civil War sentiment that would dwarf earlier states' festivities.[130] The great day finally came on October 26, 1906. Two thousand Illinoisans came to town. Merry had used his Illinois Central connections to arrange a special train from Illinois to Vicksburg. The train carried distinguished Illinois politicians and Illinois veterans. Two troop trains carried national guard units. Both the *Vicksburg Evening Post* and its rival, the *Vicksburg Herald*, printed special souvenir editions of their papers to celebrate the event.[131]

A huge parade of Illinois and Mississippi militia troops marched from downtown out to the park for the dedication ceremonies. Mississippi's governor spoke first. The writer William Alexander Percy once characterized James K. Vardaman as a "vain demagogue unable to think, and given to emotions he considered noble." Vardaman wore long black hair that he brushed "until it glowed," according to his biographer. He dressed in white, and his followers called him their "White Chief." The truth is, Vardaman did not try to appeal to the likes of snooty elites such as William Alexander Percy. He practiced a kind of brutal racial populism, attacking big business, child labor, and imperialism while championing a graduated income tax. In his campaign speeches, he typically won his greatest applause by railing against blacks, the inferior race. The Fifteenth Amendment, he told campaign rallies, had to be repealed. Black "fiends" lusted after white women, he shouted to his cheering crowds, and white men had to guard against that menace.[132]

Vardaman knew his speech at the Illinois dedication, with an audience full of friendly northerners, could not be quite like his campaign speeches. According to the *Vicksburg Herald*, he turned in a "remarkably eloquent effort."[133] Vardaman defended the South. In a sly allusion to New England's reputation for disloyalty in the War of 1812, often cited by southerners as evidence of their constitutional right of secession, Vardaman declared that "if

179

the South was in error, if secession was wrong, she learned the most convincing lesson from the example of Massachusetts." Vardaman continued, "One thing is certain—the men and women of the South believed that they had a constitutional right to do what they did." Vardaman sounded even more defensive when he conceded to the crowd that Mississippi had yet to build its monument. It would do so, he promised, "not as costly, or as fine as yours, but it will be as fine as the state of Mississippi can afford." He explained that the South—unlike the North—had little money for monuments because it had borne the brunt of the war's expenses. ("The war had a great price and this the South had to pay.")[134]

Famous for his demagogic appeals to Mississippi's white voters, Vardaman in Vicksburg fascinates for what he said to an audience of northerners, including Union soldiers, as well as southerners. But his speech was not the major oration of the day. That honor went to William J. Calhoun. Born and raised in the North, Calhoun tried to make sense of the Civil War, a task he found almost impossible in the racial climate of 1906. At the time of the war, Calhoun explained, his sympathies naturally went entirely with the North. But in the years after the war, he had come to appreciate the southern point of view better, he told his audience. White southerners and northerners belonged to the same "great racial movement" through history. Calhoun made the white race seem a force of nature, comparable to volcanic eruptions or the tides. "The Anglo-Saxon has ever been a migratory, adventurous spirit," he said. Why would people of a common racial heritage fight each other? Part of the answer, according to Calhoun, lay in the fact that the South and the North each sincerely believed in the rightness of their cause. Patriotism stirred the hearts of southerners and northerners alike. But Calhoun's speech also explored the "attractive force in war." "Why," he asked, "does the beat of the drum and the call of the bugle quicken the blood and thrill the hearts of men?" Perhaps, he suggested, "the spirit of the savage, of the barbarian, still lurk[s] in the human heart." In 1906,

Calhoun continued, the country might have to call on that savage spirit again. The nation faced enemies that required unity. The North and South must combine against the red flag of anarchy, he said. Where the light of intelligence is dim, he warned, where the love of country is weak, the seed of socialism would take root.[135]

Katie Cashman Conway of the *Vicksburg Evening Post* celebrated the Illinois dedication by assembling a collection of white female siege narratives. Jane Bitterman's story excused Confederate men for failing to protect her, but she reminded her readers that she really did not approve of the surrender. She remembered July 4, 1863, as a day of deep regret and throbbing heartache, crushing all hope. Another woman remembered traveling without a male escort, fearing both the slaves and the Yankees. The wife

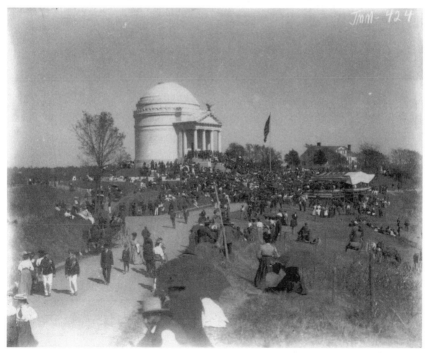

Dedication ceremonies at the Illinois Monument. Old Court House Museum photograph.

181

of the *Post*'s founder and editor (and the mother of Katie Conway) argued that with emancipation blacks became lazy, aggressive, and insolent.[136]

And then it was over. The visitors left town, and locals returned
to their routines. Vicksburgers thought that their town seemed
dead after the Illinoisans left. The quiet, though, was just a respite.
Just a month later, Iowa sent its veterans and dignitaries to dedicate
its not-yet-completed memorial. Merry did not want to wait until
construction had actually finished, he said, because every day more
veterans died. Delay would simply shrink the number of people to
be commemorated.[137] Once again, trains delivered vast crowds.
Unlike Illinois, Iowa sent no troops, and the parade to the park had
a more pacific flavor than had been the case the month before.
Vicksburg put on an elegant reception where delighted Iowans discovered the punch had been spiked with alcohol.[138]

Then came the speeches with their celebrations of racial
unity. Like the Illinois governor, Governor Albert B. Cummins of
Iowa praised the South for the sincerity of its secession. Cummins reassured his audience that Civil War soldiers fought not
over "the status of the negro" but rather to make the union permanent. Perhaps encouraged by what he had heard at the Illinois
ceremonies and by Cummins's speech, Vardaman made a more
openly racist appeal than he had the month before. How could
white northerners and southerners fight each other, he asked, repeating Calhoun's theme. How could men "of the same flesh"
snarl and quarrel "like wild beasts or dyspeptic children?" Vardaman solved the puzzle by speculating that "it must have been
because the North and South did not know each other."[139]

White Vicksburgers took comfort from the presence of General James B. Weaver in the Iowa delegation. Weaver had commanded the 2nd Iowa during the Civil War. Thereafter, he had
run twice for the presidency, as a Greenbacker in 1880 and as a
Populist in 1892. Weaver, the *Vicksburg Evening Post* explained,
believed that all men were created equal but that the government
was intended for white men only.[140] When Iowa dedicated its

182

monument at Shiloh, Weaver urged that "the whole negro race in this country . . . set their faces toward Africa and a Black Republic." Northerners increasingly found blacks "distasteful," Weaver reported, so diffusing blacks through the North offered no solution. Keeping them in the South was no answer either. Soon there would be too many blacks for the South, Weaver warned. Weaver thought Africa offered a solution. "These people were brought here in chains in the dismal holds of slave ships," Weaver concluded. "Let them return as freemen in our modern ocean steamers."[141]

Although Weaver's presence and the promise of his racism tantalized the Vicksburg press, the great Greenbacker and Populist did not speak at the Iowa dedication in Vicksburg. The principal orator was Colonel Charles A. Clark, a Maine winner of the Congressional Medal of Honor who settled in Iowa after the war. Iowa veterans elected him GAR department commander shortly before the dedication ceremonies.[142] Like Calhoun and like his governor, Clark deprecated the role of slavery in the Civil War. "This war," he said flatly, "was for the Union," and genuine but rival patriotisms animated both sides. Clark, hero of Fredericksburg and Rappahannock, went to great lengths to explain away emancipation. Clark quoted Lincoln as saying he wanted to save the Union regardless of whether doing so saved slavery. The destruction of slavery helped save the union, serving the higher purpose. Clark did not want his audience to think that he blamed the South for slavery; it was a national crime, he assured his listeners, its existence as chargeable to the North as the South since the North profited from it.

The Constitution, Clark continued, had been distrusted by the North and the South, its ratification hotly contested. Some of the northern states were the last to ratify. Resistance to the Constitution's creation of a powerful national government made civil war inevitable, Clark said. "The hand of God" guided the nation into war at just the right time: "Delay would have made the peril to the Union more deadly, and the result more doubtful." Modern arms and artillery would have given southern defenders an advantage the North might not have overcome. Given his view that God timed the war so the North could win, it is no wonder that Clark viewed fighting for the Union as almost a holy crusade. "Destruction of the Union would have been the greatest crime of the ages," he said.[143]

The speakers at Vicksburg's various monument dedications articulated what became orthodox Civil War cant in some quarters, though certainly not everywhere. According to this enduring view, only the gullible thought that the North fought for racial egalitarianism. "The myth," writer Edmund Wilson said in 1962, that the North fought "to free the slaves is everywhere except in the South firmly fixed in the American popular mind." Wilson took the South's side. In his 1962 book, Wilson could still say that, in reality, the Civil War simply pitted "two contending power units" against each other. The North and the South were no better than any two European countries. Slavery had little to do with the North's war against the South, Wilson insisted; it simply supplied "the militant Union North with the rabble-rousing moral issue which is necessary in every modern war to make the conflict appear a melodrama." Moreover, secession was not so wicked, Wilson wrote. New England itself had debated seceding. Wilson's words repeated exactly sentiments found in southerners' speeches delivered in Vicksburg almost sixty years before.[144]

When cheering faded and the Iowans returned home, Rigby remained behind. He knew there was much work to be done, more monuments to be dedicated, and many more states to be heard from. Yet he could take satisfaction that with the Illinois and Iowa monuments in place, the park was fully established, ready to be used by the nation as a patriotic resource.

Notes

1. Roy P. Basler, ed., *Walt Whitman's Memoranda during the War [&] Death of Abraham Lincoln* (Bloomington: Indiana University Press, 1962), 5.

2. *Vicksburg Commercial Herald,* June 11, 1887.

3. *Vicksburg Commercial Herald,* June 11, 12, 1887; *Vicksburg Evening Post,* June 13, 1887.

4. *Vicksburg Commercial Herald,* June 11, 12, 1887; *Vicksburg Evening Post,* June 13, 1887.

5. *Vicksburg Commercial Herald,* June 11, 12, 1887.

6. *Vicksburg Evening Post,* November 30, 1908.

7. *Vicksburg Evening Post,* June 8, 1908.

8. Vicksburg National Military Park Association minutes, October 22, 23, 1895, box 10, Memorial, Monument and Exposition Commissions, RG 12, Mississippi Department of Archives and History, Jackson (hereinafter cited as Association Papers); *Vicksburg Evening Post,* November 30, 1908; November 10, 1906.

9. Chris Hedges, *War Is a Force That Gives Us Meaning* (New York: Public Affairs, 2002), 3.

10. Jacob A. Swisher, comp., *The Iowa Department of the Grand Army of the Republic* (Iowa City: State Historical Society of Iowa, 1936), 135.

11. Ernest A. Sherman, *Dedicating in Dixie* (Cedar Rapids, Iowa: Record Printing Company, 1907), 14–15; Swisher, *The Iowa Department of the Grand Army of the Republic,* 135; *Vicksburg Evening Post,* November 30, 1908; *New Orleans States,* April 5, 1911, quoted in *Vicksburg Evening Post,* April 6, 1911.

12. Vicksburg National Military Park Association minutes, November 22, 1895, Association Papers. President George W. Bush signed a bill adding Pemberton's headquarters (1018 Crawford Street) to the park in October 2002. *Vicksburg Post,* October 13, 2002.

13. *Vicksburg Evening Post,* November 30, 1908; *Biographical Directory of the American Congress, 1774–1961* (Washington, D.C.: U.S. Government Printing Office, 1961).

14. This story has been told many times. It seems a particular favorite of dissertation writers. Perhaps the most detailed version appears in Amy J. Kinsel, "'From These Honored Dead': Gettysburg in American Culture, 1863–1938" (Ph.D. diss., Cornell University, 1992), 90–306. See also Michael Wilson Panhorst, "Lest We Forget: Monuments and Memorial Sculpture in National Military Parks on Civil War Battlefields, 1861–1917" (Ph.D. diss., University of Delaware, 1988), 8–14; Mary Munsell Abroe, "'All the Profound Scenes': Federal Preservation

of Civil War Battlefields, 1861–1990," 2 vols. (Ph.D. diss., Loyola University [Chicago], 1996), 66–81; Benjamin Yarber Dixon, "Gettysburg, a Living Battlefield" (Ph.D. diss., University of Oklahoma, 2000), 47–52, 72; Ronald F. Lee, *The Origin and Evolution of the National Military Park Idea* (Washington, D.C.: National Park Service, 1973); Carol Reardon, *Pickett's Charge: In History and Memory* (Chapel Hill: University of North Carolina Press, 1997), 177–78.

15. Abroe, "'All the Profound Scenes,'" 178–91; Panhorst, "Lest We Forget," 26–27.

16. Panhorst, "Lest We Forget," 15–16, 43, 157.

17. *Vicksburg Evening Post*, November 30, 1908; Samuel W. McCall, *Thomas B. Reed* (Boston: Houghton Mifflin, 1914), 214; Allen Weinstein, *Prelude to Populism: Origins of the Silver Issue* (New Haven, Conn.: Yale University Press, 1970); Gretchen Ritter, *Goldbugs and Greenbacks: The Antimonopoly Tradition and the Politics of Finance in America, 1865–1896* (Cambridge, U.K.: Cambridge University Press, 1997), 152–207.

18. *Vicksburg Evening Post*, November 30, 1908.

19. *Congressional Record*, 53d Cong., 3rd sess., vol. 27, 105, 402, 1607, 1715.

20. Timothy Brian Smith, "Shiloh National Military Park: An Administrative History, 1862–1933" (Ph.D. diss., Mississippi State University, 2001), 41–78.

21. J. F. Merry to Allison, November 25, 1895, box 299, William Boyd Allison Papers, State Historical Society of Iowa, Des Moines.

22. "Senator Allison and the Union Soldier," John Alfred Tiffin Hull Papers, State Historical Society of Iowa, Des Moines.

23. G. M. Humphreys to Allison, December 18, 1895, box 298, Allison Papers; "What Senator Allison Has Done for the Colored Race," Hull Papers.

24. James S. Clarkson to Allison, December 23, 1895, box 296, Allison Papers; James S. Clarkson to Allison, December 14, 1895, box 296, Allison Papers.

25. C. J. Ives to Allison, January 7, 1894, box 294; James S. Clarkson to Allison, December 14, 1895, box 296; and James S. Clarkson to Allison, December 23, 1895, Allison Papers.

26. Undated speech, folder 8, box 2, file 2, part 4, Hull Papers.

27. Undated speech, folder 7, file 2, part 4, Hull Papers.

28. Unidentified clipping, number 119, folder 5, box 9, file 9, Hull Papers.

29. Headquarters, Department of Iowa, Grand Army of the Republic, circular number 2, January 11, 1896, folder 158, box 7, administrative series, Vicksburg National Military Park Archives.

30. Rigby to brother, May 4, 1863, Papers of William Titus Rigby, Special Collections Department, University of Iowa Libraries, Iowa City.

31. Hedges, *War Is a Force That Gives Us Meaning*, 163, 3, 5, 7; David West to father, June 9, 1863, folder 20, box 4, Civil War Papers, State Historical Society of Iowa, Des Moines.

32. Rigby to brother, May 15, 18, 1863, Rigby Papers.

33. Rigby to brother, June 12, 1863, Rigby Papers.

34. Biographical sketch of Captain W. T. Rigby, n.d., Vicksburg National Military Park Association Papers, folder 26, box 10, RG 12, Mississippi Department of Archives and History, Jackson.

35. "Resolutions," n.d., Rigby Papers; Frederick Grant to Rigby, January 17, 1896, Rigby Papers.

36. Minutes, October 11, 1895; February 14, 1896; and March 12, 1896, UCV Camp No. 32, Vicksburg, Old Court House Museum, Vicksburg, Mississippi.

37. Rouss to Frederick William Holliday, May 16, 1894, Frederick William Holliday Family Collection, Perkins Library, Duke University, Durham, North Carolina.

38. Larry A. Mullin, *The Napoleon of Gotham: A Study of the Life of Charles Broadway Rouss* (Winchester, Va.: privately printed, 1974), 11–50.

39. *Winchester Evening Star*, March 10, 1902.

40. A. V. McCracken, *The Life of Charles Broadway Rouss* (n.p. [1896]), 5.

41. Dennis E. Frye, *12th Virginia Cavalry* (Lynchburg, Va.: H. E. Howard, 1988), 63–73, 83, 164.

42. Rosser to James T. Gray, December 21, 1895, box 3, Grand Camp Confederate Veterans, Department of Virginia, R. E. Lee Camp No. 1, records, Virginia Historical Society, Richmond.

43. *Monthly Auction Trade Journal*, November 1899.

44. Rouss to Holmes Conrad, August 3, 1894, Charles Broadway Rouss collection, Stewart Bell, Jr., Archives Room, Handley Regional Library, Winchester, Virginia.

45. Rouss to H. C. Baker, May 19, 1896, Rouss Collection.

46. Rouss to Holliday, January 8, 1894, Holliday Collection.

47. Rouss to Holliday, May 11, 1897, Holliday Collection.

48. Rouss to Holliday, December 24, 1894, Holliday Collection.

49. Mullin, *The Napoleon of Gotham*, 50–52.

50. Rouss to Holliday, May 16, 1898, Holliday Collection.

51. Rouss to Holliday, May 16, 1898, Holliday Collection.

52. *Washington Post*, October 14, 1895.

53. *Richmond Times*, October 22, 1895.

54. *New Orleans States*, November 3, 1895.

55. Samuel E. Lewis, October 19, 1895, and Samuel E. Lewis to A. G. Dickinson, December 6, 1895, box 4, Samuel Edwin Lewis Collection, Virginia Historical Society, Richmond; *Washington Star*, July 4, 1895.

56. *Vicksburg Evening Post*, May 26, 1896.

57. Mullin, *The Napoleon of Gotham*, 52.

58. *Vicksburg Evening Post*, June 8, 1896.

59. *Vicksburg Evening Post*, June 9, 1896.

60. *Vicksburg Evening Post*, June 11, 1896.

61. *Vicksburg Evening Post*, June 15, 1896.

62. Minutes, June 19, 1897; and July 20, 1898, Confederate Memorial Association Papers.

63. *Vicksburg Commercial Herald*, August 28, 1884; *Vicksburg Evening Post*, November 1, 1888; April 9, 1889.

64. W. D. Hoard to Rigby, January 21, 1896, Rigby Papers; J. H. Willard to Thomas C. Catchings, January 17, 1896, Rigby Papers; Lee to Rigby, January 29, 1896, Rigby Papers; "National Military Park, Vicksburg, Report," Committee on Military Affairs, February 1, 1896, 54th Cong., 1st sess., report no. 216.

65. Willard to Rigby, January 18, 1896, Rigby Papers.

66. Hull to Rigby, February 18, 1896, Rigby Papers.

67. Lee to Rigby, February 19, 1896, Rigby Papers.

68. Headquarters Department of Maryland, Grand Army of the Republic, to Thomas B. Reed, March 21, 1896, box 2, Rigby Papers.

69. Samuel W. McCall, *Thomas B. Reed* (Boston: Houghton Mifflin, 1914), 100, 102, 197–98, 233; Barbara W. Tuchman, "Czar of the House," *American Heritage* 14 (December 1962): 33–35, 92–102; Richard G. For-

gette, "Reed's Rules and the Partisan Theory of Legislative Organization," *Polity* 29 (spring 1997): 375–96; Randall Strahan, "Thomas Brackett Reed and the Rise of Party Government," in Roger H. Davidson, Susan Webb Hammond, and Raymond W. Smock, eds., *Masters of the House: Congressional Leadership over Two Centuries* (Boulder, Colo.: Westview Press, 1998), 34–59; *New Orleans Picayune*, quoted in *Vicksburg Evening Post*, June 7, 1890.

70. *Philadelphia Record*, November 30, 1894.

71. William A. Robinson, *Thomas B. Reed: Parliamentarian* (New York: Dodd, Mead and Company, 1930), 17–19.

72. McCall, *Thomas B. Reed*, 31–32.

73. Robinson, *Thomas B. Reed*, 39, 152–59.

74. William H. Hodgkins to Rigby, April 16, 1896, Rigby Papers. For Reed's friends, see Robinson, *Thomas B. Reed*, 105, 371.

75. Cousins to Rigby, May 8, 1896, Rigby Papers.

76. Lodge to William H. Hodgkins, February 4, 1897, Rigby Papers.

77. Lee to Rigby, February 11, 1897, Rigby Papers.

78. N. W. Hubbard, Jr., to Rigby, December 23, 1937, Rigby Papers; Report of Secretary Rigby, December 7, 1899, in *Vicksburg Evening Post*, December 7, 1899.

79. *Vicksburg Evening Post*, December 20, 27, 28, 29, 1897.

80. Jackson Lears, *No Place of Grace: Antimodernism and the Transformation of American Culture, 1880–1920* (New York: Pantheon, 1981), 98–139; David Healy, *U.S. Expansionism: The Imperialist Urge in the 1890s* (Madison: University of Wisconsin Press, 1970), 99–158.

81. *New Orleans Picayune*, reprinted in *Vicksburg Evening Post*, May 5, 1898.

82. *Vicksburg Evening Post*, February 23, 1899; Ivan Musicant, *Empire by Default: The Spanish-American War and the Dawn of the American Century* (New York: Henry Holt, 1998), 3–124.

83. Musicant, *Empire by Default*, 166; McCall, *Thomas B. Reed*, 233.

84. *Vicksburg Evening Post*, February 7, 1899; "Report of Secretary Rigby," December 7, 1899, in *Vicksburg Evening Post*, December 7, 1899; John Offner, *An Unwanted War: The Diplomacy of the United States and Spain over Cuba, 1895–1898* (Chapel Hill: University of North Carolina Press, 1992); David F. Trask, *The War with Spain in 1898* (New York: Macmillan, 1981); Lewis L. Gould, *The Spanish-American War and*

President McKinley (Lawrence: University Press of Kansas, 1982); Musicant, *Empire by Default*, 78–124.

85. U.S. House of Representatives, February 6, 1899, *Congressional Record*, 55th Cong., 3rd sess., vol. 32, 1518.

86. U.S. Senate, February 10, 1899, *Congressional Record*, 55th Cong., 3rd sess., vol. 32, 1678.

87. *Biographical Directory of the American Congress, 1774–1961*, 1506.

88. *Vicksburg Evening Post*, March 15, 1899; October 18, 1917.

89. Everest to Commander of the Lee Camp, Confederate Veterans, Richmond, June 14, 1894; and Everest to George L. Christian et al., September 25, 1894, box 2, R. E. Lee Camp No. 1, Richmond, Grand Camp, Confederate Veterans, Department of Virginia, Virginia Historical Society, Richmond.

90. Rigby to Mrs. Rigby, April 28, 1899, Rigby Papers.

91. Rigby to Mrs. Rigby, box 3, Rigby Papers.

92. Rigby to Mrs. Rigby, June 10, 1899, box 3, Rigby Papers.

93. Rigby to Mrs. Rigby, June 10, 1899, box 3, Rigby Papers.

94. Lee to Rigby, March 26, 1900, box 1, letters received, Resident Commissioner and Commission Chairman, VNPA records; Lee to Secretary of War, December 21, 1899 letterbook volume 1, VNMP records.

95. Rigby to Elihu Root, March 8, 1900, letterbook volume 1; and Rigby to Lee, May 10, 1900, letterbook volume 2, Commission Records of Letters Sent by the Chairman, Vicksburg National Military Park, RG 79, National Archives, East Point, Georgia.

96. Rigby to Senator Francis M. Cockrell, December 15, 1900, letterbook volume 3; and Rigby to Governor W. D. Hoard, December 17, 1900, Commission Records of Letters Sent by the Chairman, Vicksburg National Military Park, RG 79, National Archives, East Point, Georgia.

97. Rigby to Colonel Lewis W. Aldrich, January 4, 1901, letterbook volume 3, Commission Records of Letters Sent by the Chairman, Vicksburg National Military Park, RG 79, National Archives, East Point, Georgia.

98. Rigby to Kountz, January 19, 1901, letterbook volume 3, Commission Records of Letters Sent by the Chairman, Vicksburg National Military Park, RG 79, National Archives, East Point, Georgia.

99. Rigby to Brother John, April 5, 1901, letterbook volume 4; and Rigby to Lee, April 5, 1901, letterbook volume 4, Commission Records of Letters Sent by the Chairman, Vicksburg National Military Park, RG 79, National Archives, East Point, Georgia.

100. Rigby to Everett, May 3, 1901, letterbook volume 4, Commission Records of Letters Sent by the Chairman, Vicksburg National Military Park, RG 79, National Archives, East Point, Georgia.

101. Musicant, *Empire by Default*, 98.

102. Edward Ranson, "The Investigation of the War Department, 1898–1899," *Historian* 34 (1971): 78–99; Everest to Lee, July 23, 1899, box 1, letters received, VNMP records. In his memoir of the Spanish-American War, Alger blamed Congress for leaving the country unprepared for war. Russell A. Alger, *The Spanish-American War* (1901; repr., Freeport, N.Y.: Books for Libraries, 1971), 455.

103. *Memphis Commercial Appeal*, October 27, 1901; Healy, *U.S. Expansionism*, 144–58.

104. Ronald F. Lee, *The Origin and Evolution of the National Military Park Idea* (Washington, D.C.: National Park Service, 1973).

105. Root to Lee, December 27, 1900, box 74, Records of the War Department Relating to National Parks, Records of the National Park Service, RG 79, National Archives, College Park, Maryland.

106. Rigby to Root, January 3, 1901, box 74, Records of the War Department Relating to National Parks, Records of the National Park Service, RG 79, National Archives, College Park, Maryland.

107. Lee, *The Origin and Evolution of the National Military Park Idea*.

108. Lee to Rigby, July 29, 1901; and Lee to Rigby, October 31, 1901, box 3, Rigby Papers; Rigby to Lee, June 24, 1901, letterbook volume 4; and Rigby to Lee June 21, 1901, letterbook volume 4, VNMP Records; *Vicksburg Evening Post*, September 23, 1901.

109. *Vicksburg Evening Post*, May 22, 1908.

110. *Iowa State Register*, February 11, 1900, quoted in *Vicksburg Evening Post*, February 15, 1900.

111. *Vicksburg Evening Post*, November 14, 1906.

112. Proceedings of the Vicksburg Monument Commission, State Historical Society of Iowa, Des Moines; *Vicksburg Evening Post*, November 14, 1906.

113. Everest to Rigby, May 5, 1900; and Everest to Rigby, November 16, 1900, box 1, letters received, VNMP records.

114. Everest to Rigby, March 5, 1901, box 1, letters received, VNMP records.

115. Everest to Rigby, December 5, 1901, box 1, letters received, VNMP records.

116. *Vicksburg Evening Post*, February 28, 1907.

117. *Vicksburg Evening Post*, April 18, 19, 23, 24, 1901.

118. *Vicksburg Evening Post*, January 17, 20, 23, February 1, 21, 1906.

119. John G. Cashman to Harrison Granite Co., New York, November 19, 1906; and Frank E. Triebel to John G. Cashman, September 7, 1911, John G. Cashman Papers, Old Court House Museum, Vicksburg, Mississippi; *Vicksburg Evening Post*, November 12, 1909; and March 15, 1912; *Vicksburg Post*, November 7, 1996.

120. Lee to Rigby, June 30, 1906; Lee to Rigby, July 4, 1906; Lee to Rigby, July 5, 1906; A. L. Slack to Rigby, July 13, 1906; and Slack to Rigby, June 27, 1906, box 9, VNMP Records; *Vicksburg Evening Post*, May 16, 1901.

121. Lee to Rigby, July 5, 1906; F. M. Longley to Lee, July 26, 1906; and Longley to Lee, August 1, 1906, box 9, VNMP Records.

122. *Vicksburg Evening Post*, July 20, 1907.

123. T. N. Waul to Lee, September 9, 1901; and Lee to Rigby, October 8, 1901, box 1, letters received, VNMP records; *Vicksburg Evening Post*, May 28, 1908.

124. Panhorst, "Lest We Forget," 36, 60–61, 128–29. Panhorst, an art historian, grades these portrait sculptures poorly: "Few of these portraits are great works of art" (see 129).

125. S. C. Beck, *A True Sketch of His Army Life* (n.p., 1914), 44–45.

126. *Vicksburg Evening Post*, June 9, 1906.

127. *Vicksburg Evening Post*, December 19, 1905; *Vicksburg Herald*, October 27, 1906.

128. Minutes of the Missouri-Vicksburg Military Park Commission, Missouri Historical Society, St. Louis.

129. *Vicksburg Evening Post*, December 19, 1905.

130. *Vicksburg Evening Post*, June 15, 1904.

131. *Vicksburg Evening Post*, October 26, 1906; *Vicksburg Herald*, October 27, 1906.

132. William F. Holmes, *The White Chief: James Kimble Vardaman* (Baton Rouge: Louisiana State University Press, 1970), vii–xii, 36–42.

133. *Vicksburg Herald*, October 27, 1906.

134. *Vicksburg Herald*, October 27, 1906.

135. *Vicksburg Evening Post*, October 26, 1906.

136. *Vicksburg Evening Post*, October 26, 1906.

137. Iowa finally finished construction in 1912, dedicating the completed monument in a modest ceremony. *Vicksburg Evening Post*, April 2, 1912.

138. Sherman, *Dedicating in Dixie*, 5–36; *Vicksburg Herald*, November 16, 1806.

139. *Vicksburg Herald*, November 16, 1906.

140. *Vicksburg Evening Post*, November 14, 1906.

141. *Vicksburg Evening Post*, November 23, 1906.

142. Swisher, *The Iowa Department of the Grand Army of the Republic*, 117; *Vicksburg Herald*, November 16, 1906.

143. *Vicksburg Herald*, November 16, 1906.

144. Edmund Wilson, *Patriotic Gore: Studies in the Literature of the American Civil War* (New York: Oxford University Press, 1962), xv–xvi.

The Great Reunion

ICKSBURG National Military Park flourished before World War I. In 1917, as American soldiers prepared for European trench warfare, 10,000 Civil War veterans gathered to hear speeches about American unity and German cruelty. The reunion offered a fresh opportunity for racial reconciliation. In Pennsylvania, whites could almost ensure an all-white Civil War celebration at Gettysburg. This would not be possible in Mississippi. And white Mississippi's power structure would not control the reunion. Mississippi's leading racist very nearly boycotted the event. The national government paid for the gathering, and a Chicago Civil War veteran, a former officer in a black regiment, organized the affair.

The national authority, though, did not finance the Vicksburg reunion to heal racial wounds. Organizers claimed the money well spent because it helped prepare the country for war with Germany. In a place filled with graves of the Civil Ear dead, the park's greatest reunion became a giant pep rally for World War I.

The Vicksburg battleground saw many reunions of Civil War soldiers. The biggest and most important of these efforts before 1917 came in 1890, when Vicksburg hosted a great Blue–Gray reunion with fireworks, parades, barbecues, and a balloon ascension.[1] The 1890 reunion, like the

194

one in 1917, was rigidly segregated. It seems telling that Civil War veterans, especially the Union soldiers who liberated slaves, would segregate themselves after the war. But the 1890 reunion came in the age of Jim Crow.[2]

The Grand Army of the Republic had two Vicksburg posts, one black and one white, and black veterans played a prominent role in the 1890 reunion, parading through town, 400 strong. One white newspaper noted that many wore straw hats and badges, and some still retained and wore pieces of their old blue uniforms.[3] Ex-Confederates recognized the importance of claiming black participation in their war effort too. So they put their black veterans on display as well, evidence, they thought, of truly faithful colored people. The *Vicksburg Evening Post* reported that Henry Wyatt, colored, had served the 21st Mississippi all through the war, standing alongside his young master. Actually, Wyatt had "stood alongside" as his master's servant, not as an independent soldier. Ignoring that, the newspaper went on to say that when Wyatt's master died, the slave tried to rescue the body "in the face of galling fire." White southerners made the most of Wyatt, evidence of heroic black subservience. What they did not do, though, was ignore the black veterans.[4]

Three years after the great 1890 reunion, Vicksburgers dedicated their city's Confederate monument in the city cemetery. The dedication took place on Confederate Memorial Day, celebrated in Mississippi on April 26. That day, schools closed and businesses shut their doors early. According to the *Vicksburg Evening Post*, the largest crowd assembled in Vicksburg since the Civil War gathered at the new monument. Confederate veterans had places of honor at the monument's base. Young ladies representing each seceded state attended, as did state militia troops. The major address came from Stephen D. Lee. The *Post*'s account of his speech makes it sound like a lawyer's brief—"a succinct and intensely interesting account"—on behalf of Confederate valor. He began his argument by praising Grant as a "bold and skillful" general who admired Confederate soldiers' courage. Representing Grant as "skillful" followed Rigby's strategy for promoting the park but also represented a critical step in making his case for Confederate bravery. Southern men must have been poor soldiers indeed if they surrendered to a mediocre foe; better to be defeated by a general "bold and skillful." After building up Grant, Lee then delivered "facts and figures as to the great discrepancy in numbers and resources between the armies of the North and South." When he finished, according to the *Post*, his listeners came away more convinced than ever that Confederate soldiers fought bravely. With that fact established, "sweet little flower girls" then decorated the Confederate graves with flowers.[5]

For decades after the 1893 Memorial Day exercises, Vicksburg whites memorialized the Confederate fallen on Memorial Day. They gathered at the Louisiana Monument in downtown Vicksburg and then marched in a giant procession to the Confederate Memorial in the city cemetery.[6] The Ladies Confederate Cemetery Association always organized the festivities in cooperation with the Vicksburg camp of the United Confederate Veterans. Speakers delivered patriotic orations every year. In 1898, a minor scandal erupted when the speaker, Doctor S. D. Robbins, gave a speech criticizing Jefferson Davis for foolishly trusting the Constitution to protect southerners when they seceded. "Though not a lawyer himself, Mr. Davis had even more than a lawyer's respect for the inviolability of the law," according to Robbins. Davis never imagined that Lincoln would lawlessly act to put down the Confederacy. Davis's "fatal reliance upon the protecting power of the Federal Constitution felt by Mr. Davis himself was the cause of our defeat." Southern white men stood ready to step forward and defend their section, but Davis failed to take seriously the Yankee threat and make proper military preparations.[7]

This was precisely the sort of thing the United Confederate Veterans sought to stamp out entirely. That organization routinely monitored history books for any criticism of Jefferson Davis or the Confederate government. Outraged by the Robbins speech, the Vicksburg camp of the United Confederate Veterans censured not only Robbins but also the *Vicksburg Evening Post* for daring to print his text. The *Post* responded by pointing out that Robbins himself had been a Confederate soldier and had delivered an "excellent and instructive" speech "respectful in temper and tone." The *Post* then went further and advanced its own subtle criticism of the Old South and the Confederacy. "Preceding the war, and in the early days of the war, there was not freedom of discussion in the South," the *Post* charged. With those days happily in the past, though, there should be full liberty, the *Post* opined. "Let the truth be told, though the Heavens fall," the *Post*'s editor, ex-Confederate John G. Cashman, concluded.[8]

In 1913, on the fiftieth anniversary of the Civil War battles in both Gettysburg and Vicksburg, 50,000 veterans gathered in Pennsylvania. David Blight has astutely written that "this reunion was about forging unifying myths and making remembering safe." Organizers did not allow black veterans to participate. Blight reminds us that the Gettysburg reunion embodied Civil War nostalgia, a lost age of heroism, and civic reconciliation. These values overwhelmed the Civil War's emancipationist vision. According to Blight, this happened without the participants even realizing it. Woodrow Wilson spoke at the Gettysburg reunion, probably without even thinking about how blacks might have remembered the Civil War.[9]

On a more conscious level, the Gettysburg reunion invoked a lost heroic age in service of national patriotism. In

1913, Franz Ferdinand lived unassassinated. State governments, as well as Congress, wanted to remind foreigners
like Franz Ferdinand of the strength of American patriotism and valor, and they invested significant sums in the reunion. The states had appropriated nearly $2 million for
the Gettysburg extravaganza, and Congress kicked in another $450,000.[10] Reunion proponents proclaimed the
money well spent, not just as a gesture toward old veterans
but also as an investment in America's future as an international power. Gettysburg reunionists argued that its success
advertised to the world American unity, vigor, and "strength
to carry out the nation's policies."[11] Unity made America
stronger on the global stage.

The success and enormous publicity surrounding the
Gettysburg celebration inspired Vicksburg veterans to
push for their own reunion. No one seems to have seriously
considered carrying out such a project with private funds.
No Charles Broadway Rouss stepped forward. Congress
had to foot the bill, as it had in Gettysburg, or there would
be no reunion. Veterans—and everyone else—saw lobbying
Congress for reunion money much as they saw asking for
pensions or government hospitals. A state-sponsored reunion was a benefit, an entitlement for those who served.
The National Association of Vicksburg Veterans became
the lobbying agent for a Vicksburg reunion, arguing that
Gettysburg, while drawing tens of thousands, had left out
many Civil War veterans. The Vicksburg veterans pointed
out that the Gettysburg reunion had been "distinctly an Atlantic coast affair."[12]

The push for a Vicksburg reunion came more from the
North than the South. The leading proponent of a Vicksburg reunion was Frederick A. Roziene of Chicago, president of the National Association of Vicksburg Veterans.
The 1913 Gettysburg extravaganza inspired Roziene, just as
the Gettysburg Park had prompted Merry to push for a

Vicksburg park eighteen years before. Roziene, also like Merry and Rigby, tried to create a groundswell by sending letters to veterans he hoped would support such a gathering.[13] He included John A. Webb, John G. Cashman, and Louis Guion of Mississippi on his executive committee, but the bulk of the leadership, like Roziene himself, came from Chicago.

Born in Sweden (in 1835), Roziene had volunteered for the 72nd Illinois, known as the Chicago Board of Trade regiment since the board financed its organization. As a sergeant in the 72nd, Roziene fought at Vicksburg, participating in the failed attacks of May 19 and 22. In 1864, Roziene joined the 49th U.S. Colored Infantry as a lieutenant. Thereafter, Roziene's life had not gone well. After the war, Roziene suffered a series of "humiliating" business reverses. He told pension authorities in 1900 that he had earned no income for a decade. Roziene believed the war had ruined his health, leaving him a permanent invalid. He suffered from malaria, chronic diarrhea, "nervous debility," "affection of heart," and the loss of nearly all his teeth. Roziene claimed to have "an exclusive temperament" that made it difficult for him to admit his economic and physical reversals in public, but in 1900 he nonetheless begged the Pension Bureau for more money, asking his senator to intervene on his behalf. His application for a pension painted such a grim picture that it raises questions of whether he used the nation's Civil War memory to find meaning for an unhappy life.[14] Roziene began working for a reunion at age seventy-eight, forming his National Association of Vicksburg Veterans solely to make his vision a reality. Roziene vowed to make a reunion happen on the Vicksburg battleground or picnic on it alone with his daughter. In 1914, his chances for having more company than just his daughter looked pretty good.[15]

In 1914 and 1915, Congress considered Roziene and the other veterans' request for federal support for a reunion, or "Peace Jubilee," as Roziene called it, following the Gettysburg example. Since they had missed the anniversary of the battle in Vicksburg, they based their request on commemorating the centennial of the end of the War of 1812 and the semicentennial of the end of the Civil War.[16] Roziene enlisted the help of Mississippi Senator John Sharp Williams in his reunion crusade. Williams eagerly joined the effort, writing numerous letters and buttonholing his fellow senators for a Vicksburg reunion appropriation. Mississippi's other senator, James K. Vardaman, did little to advance the Peace Jubilee. As governor, Vardaman had attended one monument dedication after another at Vicksburg, welcoming visiting northerners. The reunion Roziene and Williams wanted promised to be similar to the monument dedications, with the same sort of patriotic speeches, bands, and parades. Vardaman, nonetheless, had considerably less interest in the reunion.[17]

Vardaman's distaste can be traced to his recognition that the celebration of the Civil War had more obviously become part of an effort to move the American military toward preparedness for war. By June 28, 1914, when a Bosnian Serb assassinated Franz Ferdinand at Sarajevo, Vardaman had come to blame war on greedy bankers and munitions manufacturers. Vardaman's skepticism about European war did not diminish when European states reacted to Ferdinand's death by declaring war on one another. When England announced its war against Germany on August 4, most Mississippians sympathized with their English cousins. Pancho Villa's raid on Columbus, New Mexico, further refreshed the fervor of Mississippians for military preparedness. American blood had been spilled on American soil. Mississippi mobilized its militia, and patriots across the state cheered. Some opponents of Wilson's program switched sides and patriotically joined their president, but not Vardaman, especially when the British began blockading cotton sales to Europe.[18]

John Sharp Williams also recognized the connection between the reunion and promoting the war effort. Williams's extant correspondence suggests that he understood Mississippi's reluctance to help pay for a reunion as the chief problem to be overcome. Pennsylvania's legislature had generously appropriated money for the veterans coming to Gettysburg. It embarrassed Williams that the Mississippi legislature refused to do likewise. Roziene, fearing Mississippi miserliness would sink his pet project, took the position that Mississippi should not feel obligated to spend money on a reunion since it would take place on federal property. Williams nonetheless remained uneasy and contacted members of the state legislature, pleading with them not to "put Mississippi and yourselves and me in the attitude of inviting people to the state . . . and yet make no appropriation for their entertainment." That would be, Williams argued, like inviting a guest to your home and then making them pay for their own food.[19]

Plans for Blue–Gray reunions always ran the risk of foundering on objections from the veterans themselves. Either side could sabotage reunion plans at will simply by bringing up issues that still festered from the 1860s. The United Confederate Veterans, rather than merely endorsing the idea of a reunion, announced they would meet with northern soldiers, but only if the northerners conceded that Jefferson Davis had been as patriotic as Abraham Lincoln. Union veterans rejected that condition: they would not allow Davis to be honored equally with Lincoln. As they pointed out, no such conditions had been put on the Gettysburg reunion. In the end, the need for military preparedness overwhelmed such quarrels.[20]

Mississippi's reluctance to pay a share of the reunion costs continued to bedevil organizers. In 1915, a northern congressman embarrassed Mississippi proponents of the jubilee in just the way John Sharp Williams had feared. Massachusetts Congressman Frederick H. Gillett asked one Mississippian if his state had appropriated anything, even a penny. It had not, and, in fact, the Mississippi legislature had defeated a proposal to do so because some former Confederates objected to a reunion. In 1915, Congress reacted by refusing to fund the reunion. "Dirty shame!!" a Union veteran wrote Rigby. Roziene kept his promise and picnicked on the battleground alone with his daughter.[21] Rigby blamed the setback on the "carnage raging in Europe." The nation, he thought, was distracted by World War I.[22]

Rigby miscalculated. Ultimately, the war would justify the reunion. The setback in 1915 hardly dampened the spirits of Roziene and his fellow reunion enthusiasts. In 1916, the veterans began their fight for a congressional appropriation anew. As they did so, the nation rearmed, expanding its army and navy for a possible entry into the European war. In June, Congress passed the Army Reorganization Act, doubling the size of the army. In addition, Congress appropriated more money for the navy. Also in June, Congress finally allocated $150,000 for the Vicksburg reunion.[23]

Vicksburgers associated the reunion with preparation for war. For months, citizens read in their papers stories and illustrations of German submariners murdering innocent white women, implicitly using the same argument to justify war against Germany as they traditionally used to excuse lynching. German savages endangered white women, the newspapers charged, just like black rapists. In January 1917, Germany announced unrestricted submarine warfare, a move that alarmed the Mississippi press.[24] Congress declared war the following April and passed a selective service act a month later. On June 5, the Vicksburg newspapers carried wire service stories reporting that "the manhood of the

nation offered itself before the altar of democracy today."
Nearly ten million men turned out to give their service to
the flag on that one day. The *Vicksburg Evening Post* ran a
drawing of Uncle Sam beckoning young men to serve. Flags
decorated the paper's front page.[25]

In Vicksburg, the young men hurried to serve in part
because the newspapers reported German barbarities.
Documents taken from German prisoners, the *Vicksburg
Evening Post* said, proved that the Kaiser gave out two million iron crosses not just for bravery but for "exceptional
ability in looting and destroying French villages and farm
houses."[26] Later the *Post* charged the Germans with racial
prejudice. Germans promoted "fantastic theories of racial
development." "The myth of Anglo-Saxon racial solidarity," the *Post* concluded, "was also 'made in Germany' and
the word itself was minted there. Historically it has no justification."[27]

Such charges of German savagery and racial prejudice, a
regular feature of American newspapers in the North and
the South, ran up against the problem of America's own
cruelties and intolerance. Woodrow Wilson asked American citizens to call off their lynching on behalf of the war
effort. "We are at this very moment fighting lawless pas-
sion," he proclaimed. Germany has made its armies into
lynch mobs. American "lynchers," he added, "emulate her
disgraceful example." American mobs help the German
propaganda effort. Wilson "earnestly and solemnly"
begged Americans, "the men and women of every community in the United States," to call off their mobs. Wilson
put his plea in patriotic terms, reminding citizens that they
had responded to his call to arms, and now, he said, they
again answer their president's summons. Yet at the same
time he implored Americans to keep the law inviolate, the
Wilson administration encouraged vigilantism against German sympathizers and slackers.[28]

Wilson's plea carried weight because it came in wartime but also because Wilson himself came from the South. More often, white southerners charged that white northerners brought up lynching only when they wanted to continue Civil War sectional hostilities. Talk against lynching, white southerners insisted, flowed from regional jealousies. Once World War I had ended, southern congressmen could more easily claim that their northern colleagues violated the spirit of reunion fostered by southern and northern Civil War veterans when they proposed federal laws against lynching. Edward C. Little of Kansas reminded the House that he had personally worked for sectional reunion. "We were not," he expostulated, "fighting for any reserve power to lynch people."[29]

"The reserve power to lynch people" did lie at the core of how some viewed the Civil War and its effects. Slavery had placed its black victims in a nearly lawless state: owners of slaves "disciplined" their property outside the law. The Union army came South to end what it called the anarchy of secession and also to place labor relations within a lawful framework.[30] White southerners resisted this and in the twentieth century still kept blacks in something approximating a semilawless state. Mississippi writer David Cohn explained that "unwritable codes" governed race relations in the delta. "Good" Negroes did not go to prison "merely to satisfy the unimaginative law." Historian Neil McMillen has written that whites selectively enforced their laws, applying some only to whites, others to blacks. One contemporary observer insisted that his town had little crime, though, of course, "Negroes knife each other occasionally, but there is little *real* crime. I mean Negroes against whites or whites against each other."[31]

In Vicksburg, white and black citizens were locked in a contest over law; whites had it, blacks wanted it. In 1894, thirty black citizens petitioned against a prejudiced white justice of the peace. "We believe that the law ought to be upheld," these citizens said, "that crime ought to be punished, no matter by whom committed." The justice of the peace had been ruthless toward blacks charged with misdemeanors and had actually killed at least one black person. This was "a wanton and reckless" act, "without justification in law or morals." The blacks appealed to law-abiding whites, seeking to forge a common bond under law across racial lines.[32]

The leading black Vicksburger fighting for civil rights was W. E. Mollison. Born in Issaquena County, educated at Fisk University, and admitted to the bar in 1881, Mollison had moved to Vicksburg a decade later. Mollison began pressing Warren County officials to admit blacks as jurors, basing his arguments on the U.S. Constitution's Fourteenth Amendment. For whites, this probed a raw nerve, raising questions about how much power the North's Civil War victory had given the national government over states' crime-fighting procedures. In 1880, the U.S. Supreme Court first ruled that states could not discriminate against blacks when choosing jurors. Even when state laws did not exclude blacks, if sheriffs discriminated in jury selection, that violated the Fourteenth Amendment. But then, also in 1880, the Court decided that the mere absence of black jurors, no matter how total and complete, did not automatically prove discrimination. States learned they could maintain all-white juries as they did not do so by law and as long as state officers did not testify that they discriminated.[33]

It was not Mollison's style to agitate. He publicly insisted that in Vicksburg "there is a good feeling between the two races." He continued, "There is no maudlin sentimentality between them, but each respects all that is best in the other." Mollison counted the triumphs he won by working within the system. And few southern black men could match Mollison for personal successes. He had been appointed superintendent of public education in Issaquena County by a

Democratic board of education over a white Democratic rival. Issaquena voters elected him clerk of circuit and chancery courts twice. A Democratic judge had appointed him district attorney pro tem. A Democratic president named him a census supervisor. He had represented Mississippi at the 1892 national Republican convention.[34]

In 1904, when Mollison pleaded with the board of supervisors to admit blacks onto juries, a white observer in neighboring Hinds County expressed surprise that the supervisors promised to "take the matter under advisement." Hinds County would never take any such petition "under advisement," this observer sternly observed.[35] A year later, when an all-white grand jury indicted Joe Hill for murder, Mollison intervened on the black defendant's behalf. For help, Mollison turned to the two most combative lawyers in town, both white men.

Harry Coleman was the son of James T. Coleman, an antebellum filibusterer and Confederate officer. Like truculent defense lawyers everywhere, Coleman sometimes quarreled with Vicksburg's police chief and city judge.[36] But it was Coleman's partner and cousin who would dominate the Hill defense team, T. Dabney Marshall. Marshall had an even stronger reputation for his fiery clashes with Vicksburg police, angry exchanges with judges, and incessant demands that prisoners' constitutional rights be protected. Marshall once charged a Vicksburg police officer with assault and battery when that officer handcuffed his black client.[37]

Dabney Marshall's road to advocacy for black rights followed a convoluted path. At the age of twenty-nine, Marshall already seemed headed for great things. A Vicksburg newspaper reported that he served as "a prominent counsel in nearly all the most noted criminal cases in this county" and "almost uniformly" won. Another newspaper called him "one of our brilliant young men of the state."[38] He spoke French, raised flowers, read omnivorously, and remembered what he read. When he died in 1928, the local newspaper recorded that he "was modest in demeanor and looked on life in a broad, sympathetic and tolerant manner." He had a reputation for unusual fairness. Voters placed him in the state legislature. In 1895, he became a candidate for the state senate.[39]

The Civil War shaped Marshall's thinking. When he spoke at Vicksburg's Fourth of July celebrations, Marshall reasoned that both the North and the South had fought for freedom. Northerners should be forgiven for fighting the South, Marshall told his audience, for they honestly believed that liberty could not survive outside the Union. But even Marshall could not believe the North fought against slavery, or, at least, he would not say so before a Vicksburg Fourth of July audience. In his vision, northerners "shouldered their guns and marched as to holy war" because they thought the southern states, separated from the Union, would fall prey to European despots. Northern soldiers did the South a favor by going to war against it, or so said Marshall.[40]

In his poetry, Marshall went even further to honor fallen northern soldiers. Sixteen thousand federal soldiers reside in Vicksburg's national cemetery, Marshall wrote, most reposing under marble markers that bear no name. "No post singles out their individual deeds of valor to shut them up in the Helicanian honey of immortal verse." Marshall imagined that they went to war seeking "the hope of posterity on the altar of their country . . . and yet they sleep unknown."

> They died they thought for man!
> And yet did their dying staunch one tear.
> Is it not the same old world of woe and want?
> Does not humanity still stagger through sorrow
> On from darkness into dark again?[41]

Marshall came from a family of lawyers, but that did not guarantee fealty to constitutionalism. He could still have drawn the same lesson from the war as S. D. Robbins and concluded that Jefferson Davis's great mistake had been to trust the Constitution. A hint that Marshall did not naturally go that way appeared in the lawyer's early sympathies for prohibition. This must document Marshall's faith that the Constitution really could eradicate alcohol consumption, an impressive confidence in the power of law.[42]

On August 9, 1895, Marshall and his cousins, R. C. Fox and Harry H. Coleman, assassinated Rufus Tilford Dinkins in a railway station.[43] The murder was sensational news. The press reported that Marshall and his cousins acted because Dinkins had been spreading foul stories about the young lawyer. The newspapers could never quite bring themselves to reveal just what awful thing Dinkins had said. The *Jackson Clarion-Ledger* called the rumor "sensational" and said it would, if true, doubtless force Marshall to give up his campaign for the state senate. Other newspapers eventually characterized the story Dinkins spread as "reports of degeneracy," "a foul charge," "a bestial act," or "bestial conduct."[44]

Newspapers described Dinkins, known as "Tip," as having a "splendid physique" combined with an "indomitable will" and "reckless courage." Unlike Marshall, Dinkins had been married twice and had two children.[45] Though Marshall had appeared in the press regularly before the shooting, journalists never described his physical appearance, instead praising his erudition, his talent as an author and poet, and his skill at winning over juries.[46] Now, though, reporters revealed that Marshall weighed less than ninety pounds and was extremely nearsighted. "He is very fragile, and has been called 'The Little Shrimp.'"[47]

The Little Shrimp had big friends and powerful connections. Anselm J. McLaurin, widely regarded as Mississippi's

best lawyer and recently nominated by the Democrats to
be the next governor, stepped forward to defend Marshall.
Congressman Catchings volunteered to serve as cocounsel.
These smart and powerful lawyers wasted no time in
putting out their client's side of the story. Marshall had
spent one night in a hotel room with Dinkins, they admitted, but not several as had been reported. Dinkins and
Marshall had used the same basin, comb, and brush and
had breakfasted together.[48]

The murder trial proved anticlimactic, to say the least.
As Marshall assembled his dream team of lawyers, newspaper readers across Mississippi eagerly anticipated a dramatic courtroom showdown, one that pitted the state's best
legal talent against witnesses who saw the shooting take
place. They surely hoped the newspapers would finally report just exactly what Dinkins had actually said about Marshall that caused all the trouble. But then, Marshall and his
fellows startled the state by pleading guilty and receiving
life sentences. Marshall's high-powered counsel had negotiated a plea bargain: Marshall, Coleman, and Fox would go
to prison for life rather than face the death penalty.[49]

That did not end the story. Almost immediately, a fresh
round of rumors swept through Mississippi. As the winner
of the Democratic primary, McLaurin was certain to be
governor in just a few months since the Republicans had no
chance in November. When Marshall and his cohorts plead
guilty, they knew their own lawyer would soon have the
power to pardon them. And so the gossips predicted that
McLaurin would pardon the trio as soon as he became governor. McLaurin answered with a statement indicating that
he would do no such thing. (Actually, he did pardon Fox
and Coleman.)[50]

An even darker explanation for the guilty pleas circulated
as well. According to this theory, Marshall had avoided a
trial to keep the details of Dinkins's allegation off the public

record. His lawyers issued a statement indicating that such evidence would have been irrelevant at trial and, therefore, that Marshall had no reason to fear a trial on that account.[51] Marshall himself wrote a letter from his cell insisting that, despite his guilty plea, he really was not guilty of murder. He had shot Dinkins, of course, but he denied the "false charge of plot and plan." He had not gone to Dinkins intending to shoot the man and had thus been guilty only of manslaughter and not murder.[52]

Marshall lied. A month after his letter denying malice appeared, the press gained access to a private letter he had written his father before the killing. In this private letter, Marshall said of Dinkins, "I learn he comes from a fighting stock which is naturally expert in firearms, I cannot tell what the result will be, in case he should refuse to do me the justice I demand." Marshall pleaded with his father to understand: "All my life [I] have been an unswerving supporter of the law, the thought of now being forced to break it perhaps, and stain my hands with human blood, is unspeakable and dreadful, even though I take the life of a slanderer who deserves no mercy."[53]

In his letter to his father, Marshall swore on his honor that "I am not guilty of the infamous charge against me."[54] Honor, of course, had everything to do with it. In his letter to the newspapers, Marshall had complained about the "public opinion which bade me kill."[55] The South's antebellum honor culture had little use for a man unwilling to fend off challenges to his reputation. A rumor had circulated disparaging Marshall's manliness in the most serious way possible. What Dinkins had said, what the newspapers did not dare print, was that Marshall had made a sexual overture to Dinkins. In 1895 in Mississippi, Marshall could not allow the man spreading such a story to live if that man would not retract what he had said. Though untrained in firearms and nearly blind, Marshall and his

210

cousins had stalked Dinkins, challenged him, and then shot him.

In 1901, McLaurin's successor as governor pardoned Marshall, and he left prison after serving six years. A fall left him even more physically infirm and weaker than when he went into prison.[56] For a moment, it appeared that Marshall's powerful connections would allow him to resume his political career. The Warren County Election Commission put his name on the ballot for state legislature.[57] But that decision did not stand. Instead, Marshall retreated from political life and, with his cousin Coleman, became the most aggressive defense attorney in town, especially on behalf of black people. Marshall sent letters to the *Vicksburg Evening Post* charging that the police mistreated black citizens. And the *Post* printed his letters. True, Marshall had been convicted of murder himself, but he came from a good family, had talent, and had killed to defend his honor. Besides, the *Post* had a rambunctious streak itself. Marshall filed a lawsuit on behalf of a black man named Julius Monroe, allegedly mistreated while imprisoned on the county farm. When police arrested Monroe shortly before his suit was set for trial, Marshall intervened, charging that the police intended to spirit Monroe away so the suit could not proceed. He filed assault and battery charges against three police officers for handcuffing Monroe.[58] In other cases, Marshall insisted that prisoners had a right to counsel, that police could not force confessions with "a sweating process," and that police officers could not kick black prisoners as they marched them to jail. The *Post* published all these challenges to Vicksburg's racial system.[59]

When the Hill case went on trial, Dabney Marshall planned to put Vicksburg's jury selection process under a microscope. He called county officers into court to examine just how they picked jurors. He needed to prove a state action, that Mississippi had all-white juries because officials wanted it that way and actively pursued a racist policy. Mollison himself testified to his efforts on behalf of black jurors. Marshall called the sheriff to the stand. J. L. Hyland tried to avoid Marshall's questions, insisting that he had never instructed his deputies not to select black jurors. "Have you ever summoned a negro since you have been sheriff on any jury up here?" Marshall demanded. "No, sir," the sheriff confessed. Under the Supreme Court's rule, that was not enough to prove discrimination. The Court had ruled that no matter how obviously and totally white the juries were, that fact by itself proved nothing. Hyland's admission accomplished nothing for Marshall.

Marshall then called the circuit clerk and established that some blacks were registered to vote and, having never been convicted of any crimes that would disqualify them from jury service, could serve. T. C. Childs next took the stand. He was the deputy who had actually selected the grand jury. The Little Shrimp bore in on the deputy sheriff. "Now be fair with us," Marshall demanded. "Don't you know that you would not summon a negro on the jury if you could get out of it just because he was a negro?" The deputy answered, "O, I don't know, I have not hatred toward the negro; I rather like them." That did not satisfy Marshall: "Do you like them as jurors?" The deputy admitted that he had never seen any as jurors. Marshall asked again if Childs excluded blacks simply because of race. "I have never given it a thought." Marshall pounced: "You never even think about it?" "Never do," came the answer. Marshall had him on the record: "The policy is so settled in this court to summon white men solely you don't even think about summoning a negro?" The answer: "Settled with me; I never give it a thought."[60] And with that, the state officer picking the jurors admitted that the policy of picking only white jurors was "settled with me."

In their brief, the two white lawyers, perhaps at Mollison's urging, argued that if Mississippi judges did not follow the Fourteenth Amendment and allow black jurors, they were no better than lawless savages, "standing on the banks of the congo."[61] The state responded that Hill's lawyers had filed their motion after Hill had been arraigned and plead not guilty. By entering the plea, Hill had accepted the all-white grand jury as legitimate. His jury discrimination complaint came too late to be accepted, they argued.[62]

Perhaps because they did not want to appear as savages "standing on the banks of the congo," the Mississippi Supreme Court justices accepted Marshall and Coleman's argument—partially. They yielded grudgingly, grumbling that "we are bound" by the U.S. Supreme Court. No ringing endorsement of the Fourteenth Amendment's equal protection clause appeared anywhere in the opinion. The court nonetheless reversed Joe Hill's conviction on the grounds that he had not been allowed legal counsel when arraigned and had therefore not knowingly given up his constitutional rights by making a plea.[63]

For a time, Warren County admitted blacks into its jury pool, an action that outraged the white jurors so much that they "came near going on strike." Newspaper accounts record that in one case "for some minutes there was a strenuous protest and various threats by different jurymen." How the judge handled this is not entirely clear from the newspaper report, but "the white jurymen were placated and consented to serving and allowing the Negro to remain." Mollison must have celebrated. However, Marshall, Coleman, and Mollison's victory proved short-lived. Supervisors placed a few blacks on juries for a time, and the local bar "tacitly agreed to object to Negroes, as far as practicable." In 1907, the Mississippi Supreme Court put an end to the whole charade when it denied "the mistaken impression, which seems to have become prevalent," that blacks had to be admitted to juries. Juries can be all white, the justices explained; there just cannot be discrimination. This decision, consistent with the U.S. Supreme Court's rulings, defeated Mollison's effort to integrate juries. The case likely taught or reminded sheriffs and their deputies all across Mississippi that, in the unlikely event another lawyer like Dabney Marshall came along, they should never admit discrimination when testifying in court.[64]

The squabble over the juries paled in comparison to whites' continued use of mob law to humiliate blacks. Every extralegal hanging of a black person accused of some crime signaled white determination to keep blacks in a slavelike state outside the law. World War I challenged this. J. William Harris has convincingly argued that World War I represented a "methodological moment" where the color line became a bit confused in Vicksburg. Harris finds that World War I challenged whites' imagined boundary between the races. In 1918, Vicksburgers tarred and feathered Dave Cook, a white man, and hung a sign around his neck that read "I am disloyal to the United States Government." Then the mob took the sign off Cook and put it around a black man's neck, also tarred and feathered. Dr. John Miller had supposedly made disloyal statements, saying his race got only half its rights. This earned him a "white man's punishment," something not possible outside of world war context, Harris believes. Harris finds that local Vicksburg elites denounced World War I–era mob violence out of fear that a wider, civilized world might condemn Mississippi and Vicksburg.[65]

In fact, one member of Vicksburg's "elite," the editor of the *Vicksburg Evening Post*, had consistently denounced lynching and mob law long before World War I. The newspaper record suggests that Vicksburg and surrounding Warren County had a high lynching rate. In 1885, the *New*

Orleans Picayune reported that neighbors in the Red Bone community had gone after Daniel Carnahan after he allegedly raped a woman. The *Picayune's* story is based on gossip ("my informant states that he has reason to believe") and cannot actually confirm that the mob caught Carnahan. The Vicksburg papers did not carry the story.[66] In 1888, the *Picayune* again reported gossip, this time that someone named Marley had been killed for murder.[67] Nor can Henry Gentry's death be confirmed in 1891. Charged with killing another black man, he may have been mobbed by African Americans.[68] A year later, the *Picayune* claimed that Warren County blacks hanged an unknown African American for violating a black woman.[69] Jesse Mims perished in 1894, beaten to death by a county convict camp guard. The guard forced other convicts to hold Mims. It could be said, then, that a "mob" killed Mims.[70] In 1900, another rumor asserted that blacks had lynched Gloster Barnes near Eagle Lake.[71]

Some newspaper reports contradicted themselves. In 1903, newspapers said that a mob hanged Ben Bryant and William Morris for murder, dropping their bodies off a bridge. Subsequently, news surfaced that Morris had escaped, but a later article claimed that he had died after all.[72] In 1907, the *Vicksburg American* said that Sam Washington was "probably" hanging from a bridge in Warren County or Claiborne County. Then a justice of the peace told newspapers that no such hanging had occurred. Later, the *American* reported that the sheriff could not find Washington and that he had probably been "spirited away."[73]

Accounts of mob law actually in the city of Vicksburg, in sight of newspaper reporters, can be read with greater confidence. A mob did hang Frederick Villarosa from a tree on Grove Street for the attempted rape of a child in 1886.[74] Two years later, a mob hanged an accused burglar, James Harris, from a tree on the east side of the courthouse.[75] A year after that, a mob hanged suspected rapist Wesley Thomas from a railway trestle.[76] A mob hanged Cato Garret from a bridge in 1903, and Ed Johnson died on East Clay Street in 1915.[77]

Though President Wilson called for an end to such behavior, some felt that world war required vigilantism. The Vicksburg newspapers said in banner headlines that "Hun Sympathizers" fought Ohio vigilantes,[78] Illinois lynchers hanged a "disloyalist,"[79] and a Louisiana mob tarred a rich planter for refusing to buy Liberty Bonds.[80] Such sensational news stories probably encouraged Vicksburg's lingering mob spirit. The Vicksburg vigilantes that tarred and feathered Cook and Miller called themselves the "Flying Squadron." In addition to Cook and Miller, the Flying Squadron hoped to tar and feather a black druggist and an attorney but could not find them. The vigilantes also tarred two African American women for not working. "The country was at war," one vigilante told a journalist, "and it wasn't any time for anybody to be loafing."[81]

The *Vicksburg Evening Post*, from its founding in 1883, unflinchingly denounced lynchings and reports of lynchings not only in and around Vicksburg but across Mississippi and the South as well. This contradicts what most historians believe about white southern newspapers. The most distinguished historian of Mississippi race relations writes that lynching "had little articulate opposition."[82] One scholar has doubted reports of the *Post*'s opposition to lynch law, saying such a claim had to be based on "fragmentary" evidence. All historical evidence is fragmentary, of course, but the *Post* has been microfilmed back to its founding in 1883. Under editor John G. Cashman, the *Post* energetically, invariably, and without exception opposed mob law and lynching. Cashman denounced governors who would not stand up to mobs and praised those whom he thought did.[83]

It was against this history that white Mississippians charged Germans with barbarity and racial prejudice. The Civil War and Reconstruction had made the federal government a player in the fight for racial justice, but only a little and only at the outermost margins. World War I, though, strengthened voices calling for a stronger national government. These demands reached Vicksburg. Patriotic Vicksburgers heard the call and could not resist, but whites remained determined to keep the national government out of their racial affairs.

On June 5, 1917, 2,506 Warren County men registered for war service. The county had a population of just over 30,000, with 9,000 males older than the age of twenty-one. Blacks made up a heavy majority of Warren County's pool of potential recruits. The county's 60 percent black population stepped forward to serve with enthusiasm.[84] Even though whites tried to soft-pedal black enlistment, more blacks than whites registered on that day in June. Some aged black men, in fact, tried to lie about their ages so that they could go to war.[85] Whites joked about the elderly black men, obviously too old but eager to serve anyway. In fact, though, whites did not think the idea of black soldiers funny at all. They had traditionally feared and despised armed black men. In 1898, when word had circulated that the War Department might organize a black regiment for service in Cuba, a spokesman for Vicksburg's black community offered to command the proposed regiment personally. Colored citizens, P. C. Hall said, wanted to demonstrate their "intelligence, patriotism, loyalty, and worth" through military service. Some whites assumed black southerners, once in Cuba, would join the enemy army, "composed of negroes and mixed breeds."[86]

In 1906, the *Vicksburg Herald* called "negro regiments" a "thorn in the side of the national military system.[87] Whites accused the 25th Infantry of shooting up the town of

Brownsville, Texas. Vicksburg whites took satisfaction when President Theodore Roosevelt dismissed every soldier in the unit, though they thought it "inexcusable" that black soldiers had ever been stationed in a southern town in the first place. When Ohio Senator Joseph B. Foraker, a Republican and Union army Civil War veteran, tried to defend the cashiered soldiers, the *Vicksburg Herald* did not disguise its contempt. Stories of misconduct by black Union troops still circulated in Vicksburg forty years after Reconstruction's supposed close in 1877. For white southerners, Brownsville had provided fresh evidence, if any were needed, that blacks should not be soldiers. The problem was that a uniform and a gun freed the slave class from the "subordination of race inferiority."[88]

As white Vicksburgers talked over the "problem" of enlisting black men as soldiers, plans went ahead for the reunion. In 1917, the War Department dispatched Colonel Willard D. Newbill and 1,250 soldiers of the 155th Infantry to organize facilities for the great reunion. Newbill, a Spanish-American War veteran who had commanded troops in the Philippines, told people in Vicksburg that he really itched for combat in France. Construction of a tent city began in August in a long, wooded valley running south from the Alabama and Vicksburg Railway to Union Avenue. This area, just east of the Railroad Redoubt, had seen fierce fighting during the siege. Newbill directed construction of a new road that ran the length of the valley. In addition, Newbill built roads and paths named for prominent Confederate and Union generals from the siege. Newbill also built a water system. The city of Vicksburg lent necessary pipe as well as fire hydrants and fire hose.[89]

At the Gettysburg reunion, the army had fed the veterans from many small kitchens, each accommodating 500 men. Working with a fraction of the budget available at Gettysburg, Newbill did not have enough cooks for that.

So he set up two large messes and fed the veterans in shifts. In Chicago, Newbill rented 375,000 square feet of canvas and acquired an additional 30,000 square feet in Kansas City. Using black labor, Newbill constructed tents of enormous proportions—one tent alone accommodated 1,300 men. Newbill told reporters that the big tent had been used by Billy Sunday and Teddy Roosevelt. "I am under the impression that it is the biggest piece of canvas in the United States," Newbill said. Newbill also acquired sixty-five Packard trucks to transport the veterans from their trains and around camp.[90]

The first veteran arrived October 6, ten days early. Freeland Romans of the 72nd Illinois seemed the embodiment of the war spirit America needed to fight the Kaiser. He told journalists, "I am early, I know, but I couldn't wait any longer." As journalists scribbled in their notepads, Romans reminisced about his Civil War duty, standing guard around Vicksburg's courthouse. Romans's enthusiasm for his time in Vicksburg echoed Rigby's letters describing his own war service. While Romans reported no happy memories of combat, he did see his military service as the defining moment in his life. "The three months I spent in Vicksburg after its fall are among the happiest days of my life," he cheerily informed reporters.[91]

When Newbill put up a twenty-four-by-twelve-foot American flag in his tent city, he no doubt thought that he championed American values—law and order, as well as vigilance. Newbill had been born in Virginia, and the Vicksburgers happily claimed him as a southern gentleman. In fact, his report suggests a military professional determined not to leave black Vicksburgers out of the celebration. Newbill never lost his focus: his job was to help unify Americans to win the war. He explained to reporters that "the reunion will build up sentiment and that is what we need in wartime."[92]

There is some evidence to support Newbill's assertion that his reunion did the job intended. Ten thousand veterans came.[93] Newspaper coverage promoted patriotism by describing the reunionists' jolly fraternization. One reporter quoted an aging Civil War veteran as saying, "If they would turn this company against the Germans we would make a showing, my boy. We fought once and could do it again." The reporter assured his readers that such sentiments could be heard on all sides. The *Vicksburg Evening Post* ran a front-page picture of doughboys marching off to war saluted by two grizzled old Civil War veterans, one in gray and one in a Union uniform. The next day, the paper carried a drawing on its front page of Civil War veterans proudly marching under an American flag, with a photograph of charging doughboys in the background. "Here and 'Over There,'" the caption read.[94]

Nonetheless, tensions erupted between the former antagonists. One old Union veteran refused to ride in one of the army trucks provided. "That wagon is full of Johnny Rebs. They might throw me out. I'm all alone." Told that a taxi would cost him a quarter, the old soldier snapped, "I don't care if it costs $500. I won't trust myself with those Johnny Rebs." At night the *Post* said that the veterans formed groups "and re-fought the war." The paper continued, saying that "the louder the band played, the higher their voices were raised in singing the praises of their favorite commander."[95]

In such gatherings, the veterans expected music, and Vicksburg did not disappoint. Newbill constructed an amphitheater, complete with a bandstand. One historian, writing about Natchez, quoted a white southerner as remembering that "one thing that we never sang was the 'Battle Hymn of the Republic.' That was a northern song."[96] Many observers noticed that after September 11, 2001, American radio stations played "America" but not the national anthem.

Vicksburg newspapers used memories of Civil War valor to promote support for American soldiers fighting in World War I at the 1917 reunion. University of Southern Mississippi.

No doubt some future historian will decipher the meaning of that choice. In 1917, black veterans, gathered at Bethel AME Church, heard "America" and the "Star Spangled Banner" performed. Then they sang "The Battle Hymn of the Republic." Newbill had encouraged the black veterans to come and participate. Because of that, the *Vicksburg Herald* commented, "He will go away . . . carrying with him the esteem and gratitude of all of Vicksburg's citizens—white and black alike."[97] At Newbill's white camp, "The Star Spangled Banner" was ubiquitous, sometimes played by the 155th Infantry band and sometimes sung by the veterans. When a black band played "Dixie," the Confederate veterans danced in the aisles. According to one newspaper account, "Even the colored waiters cake-walked." The band

221

The U.S. Army built a tent city to house Union and Confederate veterans attending the great 1917 reunion on the Vicksburg battleground. Old Court House Museum photograph.

then played "Yankee Doodle," and the Union veterans cheered.[98] Newbill and Roziene sought to use music to stress national unity in the midst of war.

Orators delivered ringing patriotic addresses. Bishop Gunn, from Natchez, said that the Civil War had produced "a united country, an indivisible, imperishable, intangible Union." The whole unified nation, Gunn claimed, had rallied around a southern president and wanted him to remain "until the world gets a taste of a real American victory, followed by a real American peace, not a pax Germanica, nor Galica, but a pax Americana."[99] The governor of Minnesota told his audience that the whole united country fought against "military tyranny and Prussian autocracy."[100] Iowa Governor W. L. Harding delivered a patriotic oratory that surpassed those of all other speakers. After praising the

222

At the 1917 reunion, the U.S. Army set up two large messes and fed the veterans in shifts. Old Court House Museum photograph.

South and North for reconciling, Harding blasted the Germans for their atrocities. Harding described a day when the allies would sit around a table and readjust the world. "And Uncle Sam will be at the head of the table. On each side of him will be two men, one wearing the Blue, the other the Gray. And behind him will be a young man in Khaki." In the meantime, Harding continued, "The sons of Confederate soldiers and the sons of Union soldiers will continue their march to Berlin."[101]

The Vicksburg reunion's tight connections to the American war effort left Mississippi Senator James K. Vardaman, the "White Chief," in a bit of a quandary. He had long celebrated the Confederacy as an articulation of states' rights and a ratification of his own racism. He enjoyed northerners'

At the 1917 reunion, the Illinois Central Railroad set up an information station. Eva W. Davis is in the picture (the second woman from the left in the back). Old Court House Museum photograph.

racial concessions and had used monument dedications as an opportunity to memorialize white solidarity across regional lines, but the war in Europe was another matter altogether. Vardaman had not denounced the Germans for sinking the *Lusitania* but had protested British restrictions on cotton sales to Europe. Vardaman feared "rampant war spirit in America," and he knew full well that the reunion had become part of that spirit. He had denounced "preparedness" as a menace to the republic, threatening military despotism. Vardaman had refused to favor declaring war against Germany, one of just six senators to vote no. Afterward, some in Mississippi ridiculed him as "Kaiser Vardaman." He knew all the politicians speaking at the reunion would attack Germany, praise Wilson, and promote the war effort. Yet when

Roziene invited him to deliver his own speech, he could hardly refuse to meet Civil War veterans.[102]

While Vardaman did not refuse to give a speech at Vicksburg, he never spoke to the gathered veterans. Vicksburg's rival newspapers delivered sharply different explanations about how this happened. Vardaman, all agreed, had been scheduled to speak at 11:00 on Thursday, October 18. According to the *Vicksburg Evening Post*, when he arrived at the camp, he found it nearly deserted. This became a contentious point between Vicksburg's rival newspapers when the *Vicksburg Herald* claimed that the camp had been crowded but that few veterans wanted to hear the famously antiwar senator. The *Post* initially explained that the camp had been empty because the veterans' parade ran behind schedule. The *Post* reported that Vardaman walked through the empty camp, greeting warmly those few veterans he encountered. The *Post* argued that even northern soldiers liked Vardaman by quoting one old Illinois soldier as telling the Mississippi senator, "I read all your speeches and like them." Roziene and Newbill both tried to persuade Vardaman to stay and make his speech at a later time, but the senator begged off, saying his schedule would not permit it.[103] The *Herald*, a less friendly paper, charged that Vardaman left in a huff because so few veterans wanted to hear him.[104] A few days later, the *Post* returned to Vardaman's defense, but with a different story than it had initially presented. Now the *Post* put the blame on Roziene. Roziene, the *Post* told its readers, "eighty years old and almost overwhelmed with the responsibilities and anxieties of arranging for and conducting the splendid reunion," had forgotten about the parade when scheduling Vardaman's speech. Vardaman, the *Post* explained, could not stay because he had to tend to sick kinfolk living north of Jackson.[105]

Mississippi's other senator, John Sharp Williams, had once been a Vardaman ally. The two fell out when running against each other for the Senate in 1907. Unlike Vardaman, Williams had supported Wilson's preparedness program and voted to declare war against Germany. Like all the other speakers at the reunion, Williams delivered a patriotic address, one that focused far more on the world war than the Civil War. Watching the parade of old veterans, Williams said, had stirred his heart. Just knowing that those old men had fought against each other as young boys, in "a truly un-unified country," but now stood together against the Germans stirred confidence in his breast. And the Civil War soldiers, Williams claimed, had fought "a chivalrous warfare" that did not harm women for military advantage—unlike the Germans. The boys in the present conflict, Williams went on, "stood shoulder to shoulder, brother by brother . . . rich or poor, married or single, white or black, high or low" against the Germans.[106]

Williams endorsed Woodrow Wilson for his courage. He tweaked those, like Vardaman, who did not support the president. "It is the duty of every true American to uphold the nation's policy," the senator said. Williams did not mention Vardaman by name but declared that he did not want to see Mississippi become an object of suspicion. After reminding his audience that he stood for Mississippi on the national stage, Williams implied that Mississippians had a special duty to be patriotic. He said that he would dread "the finger of scorn" pointed at the state.[107]

To those who opposed the war, Williams suggested the alternative was a German invasion of America, much as the North had invaded the South. The Yankees had preferred fighting in Tennessee, Alabama, Georgia, and Mississippi, and the South would rather have fought in the North. The result was massive devastation. Americans, Williams said, should trust their government as the best judge of where its army should fight.[108]

No doubt white Americans fought over two contending memories after the Civil War. Whites rejected black narratives of the Civil War, stories that made the war a tale of liberty and racial revolution. Reunion and reconciliation edged out race, and sentiment triumphed over ideology. The sections reconciled, but the races divided.[109] The Gettysburg reunion was all about reconciliation over emancipation. The Pennsylvania affair was "a Jim Crow reunion."[110]

Vicksburg's reunion was, of course, also a Jim Crow affair. In Mississippi, no Civil War celebration could be all white. African Americans would not allow it. Black veterans paraded with the whites, separately, but they could not be ignored altogether. Racial segregation contrasted with the nation's need for sectional reconciliation as it marched into Europe's bloody trench warfare. Speaker after speaker ignored racial disharmony to hail the nation's sectional unity, suggesting that geographic reconciliation made an effective war effort possible.

The complicated collision of sentiments at the 1917 reunion rehearsed the South's later bifurcated view of its Civil War memories. In 1962, Strom Thurmond would come to Vicksburg seeking to mobilize Confederate memories on behalf of the nation's war against Communism. Thurmond wanted to "stem and reverse the tide of the cold war," or "we find ourselves encircled . . . like the besieged Confederates within Vicksburg." Thurmond identified Vicksburg's Confederate defenders with all Americans (and the North Atlantic Treaty Organization [NATO] too) in the fight against the encroaching Communist enemy. Perhaps forgetting that the besieged Confederates lost, Thurmond wanted the nation to take heart and draw strength from the Vicksburg metaphor.

Just a year later, George Wallace went to Gettysburg, where he used the Civil War metaphor to attack the federal government. Wallace carried out his fight for states' rights under the Confederates' Civil War battle flag, which he literally ran up the flagpole over his capitol. Thurmond invoked the Civil War on behalf of the nation's war against a foreign enemy; Wallace did not like Communists either, but in Gettysburg he used the same history to bolster southern resistance to the national power.[111]

In 1917, Vicksburg saw its Civil War memory converted to the national cause, directed into patriotic channels toward nationalism and against the hated German enemy. Once again, national military power triumphed on the Vicksburg battlefield. And again, black Vicksburgers went home, still segregated, still barred from jury service, and still fearful of white mobs and vigilantes. Perhaps they could forget these disabilities, if only for a moment, when the news of America's triumph over Germany reached Mississippi.

Notes

1. *Vicksburg Evening Post,* May 21, 22, 23, 24, 26, 27, 28, 29, 30, 31, 1890.

2. C. Vann Woodward launched historical studies of segregation with *The Strange Career of Jim Crow* (New York: Oxford University Press, 1955). See also Howard Rabinowitz, *Race Relations in the Urban South, 1865–1890* (New York: Oxford University Press, 1978); and Joel Williamson, *The Crucible of Race: Black-White Relations in the American South since Emancipation* (New York: Oxford University Press, 1984).

3. *Vicksburg Evening Post,* May 30, 1890.

4. *Vicksburg Evening Post,* May 24, 1890.

5. *Vicksburg Evening Post,* April 27, 1893.

6. *Vicksburg Evening Post,* April 27, 1895; May 1, 1896; April 24, 26, 27, 29, 1897; May 11, 1898; May 1, 1899; May 9, 1900; April 27, 1901; May 5, 1902; April 29, 1902; April 23, 25, 1903; April 24, 1906; April 27, 1907; April 27, 1908; April 24, 1909; April 23, 1910; April 20, 1918; April 24, 1920; April 9, 1921; April 25, 1923; April 19, 21, 1924; April 8, 1925; April 19, 1926; April 25, 1931; April 20, 1935.

7. *Vicksburg Evening Post*, May 11, 1898.

8. *Vicksburg Evening Post*, May 14, 1898.

9. David W. Blight, *Race and Reunion: The Civil War in American Memory* (Cambridge, Mass.: Harvard University Press, 2001), 8–9.

10. Blight, *Race and Reunion*, 6–12.

11. *Vicksburg Evening Post*, August 16, 1913.

12. "Memorial to the Congress of the United States," n.d., box 20, letters received, VNMP, National Archives, East Point, Georgia.

13. *Vicksburg Evening Post*, August 16, 1913.

14. Frederick Roziene pension application, 1186027, National Archives, Washington, D.C.

15. Roziene to Rigby, June 18, 1915, box 19, letters received, and D. J. Morrison to Rigby, August 31, 1914, box 19, letters received, VNMP, National Archives, East Point, Georgia.

16. *Peace Celebrations at Vicksburg, Miss.*, Hearings before the Subcommittee of House Committee on Appropriations, 63rd Cong., 3rd sess., 1915.

17. William F. Holmes, *The White Chief: James Kimble Vardaman* (Baton Rouge: Louisiana State University Press, 1970), 297.

18. Martin B. Madden to John Sharp Williams, August 24, 1914; Thomas S. Martin to John Sharp Williams, August 22, 1914; John Sharp Williams to Thomas S. Martin, August 20, 1914; and John Sharp Williams to F. A. Roziene, August 20, 1914, box 19, letters received, VNMP, National Archives, East Point, Georgia; James L. McCorkle, Jr., "Mississippi from Neutrality to War (1914–1917)," *Journal of Mississippi History* 43 (1981): 82–125.

19. "Union and Confederate Reunion," *Illinois Central Magazine* 3 (July 1914): 53–57; Williams to D. J. Morrison, June 16, 1914, box 19, letters received, VNMP, National Archives, East Point, Georgia.

20. Washington Gardner to Rigby, August 13, 1914, box 19, letters received, VNMP, National Archives, East Point, Georgia.

21. A. M. Trimble to Rigby, March 15, 1915, box 19, letters received, VNMP, National Archives, East Point, Georgia.

22. Roziene, form letter, n.d., box 19, letters received, VNMP, National Archives, East Point, Georgia.

23. *Vicksburg Evening Post*, June 22, 1918; McCorkle, "Mississippi from Neutrality to War," 108.

24. *Vicksburg Evening Post,* June 22, 1918.
25. *Vicksburg Evening Post,* June 5, 1917.
26. *Vicksburg Evening Post,* October 12, 1917.
27. *Vicksburg Evening Post,* October 22, 1917.
28. Wilson, "A Statement in the American People," July 26, 1918, in Arthur Link, ed., *The Papers of Woodrow Wilson,* 69 vols. (Princeton, N.J.: Princeton University Press, 1966–1994), 49:97–99; Christopher Capozzola, "The Only Badge Needed Is Your Patriotic Fervor: Vigilance, Coercion, and the Law in World War I America," *Journal of American History* 88 (March 2002): 1354–82.
29. *Congressional Record,* January 25, 1922, 67th Cong., 2nd sess., vol. 62, 1742. Historians of the Civil War in American memory have quite rightly recognized lynching as a component of that memory. Blight, *Race and Reunion,* 108–13, 335–51; Cecilia Elizabeth O'Leary, *To Die For: The Paradox of American Patriotism* (Princeton, N.J.: Princeton University Press, 1999), 215–17; David Goldfield, *Still Fighting the Civil War: The American South and Southern History* (Baton Rouge: Louisiana State University Press, 2002), 56–57.
30. James D. Schmidt, *Free to Work: Labor Law, Emancipation, and Reconstruction, 1815–1880* (Athens: University of Georgia Press, 1998), 93–121.
31. David L. Cohn, *The Mississippi Delta and the World: The Memoirs of David L. Cohn,* ed. James C. Cobb (Baton Rouge: Louisiana State University Press, 1995), 6, 64; Neil R. McMillen, *Dark Journey: Black Mississippians in the Age of Jim Crow* (Urbana: University of Illinois Press, 1989), 210–16; Schmidt, *Free to Work,* 165–93.
32. *Vicksburg Evening Post,* January 22, 1894.
33. *Strauder v. West Virginia,* 100 U.S. 303 (1880); *Ex Parte Virginia,* 100 U.S. 347 (1880); *Neal v. Delaware,* 100 U.S. 370 (1880); *Virginia v. Rives,* 100 U.S. 339 (1880).
34. W. E. Mollison, *The Leading Afro-Americans of Vicksburg, Miss., Their Enterprises, Churches, Schools, Lodges and Societies* (Vicksburg, Miss.: Biographia Publishing Co., 1908).
35. *Vicksburg Evening Post,* September 8, 1904.
36. *Vicksburg Evening Post,* February 18, 1908.
37. *Vicksburg Evening Post,* February 13, November 7, 1907; February 20, 21, April 7, 1908.

38. *Vicksburg Evening Post*, July 7, 1891; *Natchez Banner*, quoted in *Vicksburg Evening Post*, August 8, 1891.

39. *Vicksburg Evening Post*, July 5, 1928.

40. *Vicksburg Evening Post*, July 5, 1907.

41. Annie L. Pierson, "T. Dabney Marshall" Subject File, Mississippi Department of Archives and History, Jackson.

42. *Vicksburg Evening Post*, August 16, 1884.

43. *Vicksburg Evening Post*, August 9, 1895.

44. *Vicksburg Evening Post*, November 14, 1895; November 6, 1896; July 9, 1901.

45. *New Orleans Picayune*, quoted in *Vicksburg Evening Post*, August 12, 1895.

46. *Vicksburg Evening Post*, July 7, 1891.

47. *Vicksburg Evening Post*, August 13, 1895.

48. *Vicksburg Evening Post*, August 13, 1895.

49. *Vicksburg Evening Post*, August 15, 1895.

50. *Vicksburg Evening Post*, August 23, 1895.

51. *Vicksburg Evening Post*, December 14, 1895.

52. *Vicksburg Evening Post*, November 11, 1895.

53. *Vicksburg Evening Post*, December 17, 1895.

54. *Vicksburg Evening Post*, December 17, 1895. For the South's honor culture, see James C. Klotter, *Kentucky Justice, Southern Honor, and American Manhood: Understanding the Life and Death of Richard Reid* (Baton Rouge: Louisiana State University Press, 2003); Richard F. Hamm, *Murder, Honor and Law: Four Virginia Homicides from Reconstruction to the Great Depression* (Charlottesville: University Press of Virginia, 2003); Edward L. Ayers, *Vengeance and Justice: Crime and Punishment in the 19th-Century American South* (New York: Oxford University Press, 1984); Grady McWhiney, *Cracker Culture: Celtic Ways in the Old South* (Tuscaloosa: University of Alabama Press, 1988); and Dickson D. Bruce, Jr., *Violence and Culture in the Antebellum South* (Austin: University of Texas Press, 1979). The classic work remains Bertram Wyatt-Brown, *Southern Honor: Ethics and Behavior in the Old South* (New York: Oxford University Press, 1982).

55. *Vicksburg Evening Post*, November 11, 1895.

56. *Vicksburg Evening Post*, July 8, 1901.

57. *Vicksburg Evening Post*, August 7, 1901.

58. *Vicksburg Evening Post*, February 13, 1907.

59. *Vicksburg Evening Post*, March 21, 1905; June 2, April 7, 22, 1908.

60. J. L. Hyland testimony, bill of exceptions, transcript of evidence, *State of Mississippi v. Joe Hill*; T. C. Childs, testimony; W. E. Mollison testimony; and "Abstract of Facts and Brief," *Joe Hill v. State of Mississippi*, April term 1906, March 22, 1906, case 12017, box 14359, Mississippi Supreme Court records, Mississippi Department of Archives and History, Jackson.

61. "Abstract of Facts and Brief," *Joe Hill v. State of Mississippi*, April term 1906, *State of Mississippi v. Joe Hill*, March 22, 1906, case 12017, box 14359, Mississippi Supreme Court records, Mississippi Department of Archives and History, Jackson.

62. *Joseph Hill v. State of Mississippi*, 89 Miss. 23 (1906).

63. *Joseph Hill v. State of Mississippi*, 89 Miss. 23 (1906).

64. *Vicksburg Evening Post*, May 24, 1907; *George Lewis v. State of Mississippi*, 91 Miss. 505 (1907).

65. J. William Harris, "Etiquette, Lynching, and Racial Boundaries in Southern History: A Mississippi Example," *American Historical Review* 100 (April 1995): 387–410.

66. *New Orleans Picayune*, January 16, 1885.

67. *New Orleans Picayune*, May 8, 1888.

68. *New Orleans Picayune*, July 8, 1891.

69. *New Orleans Picayune*, December 28, 1892.

70. *New Orleans Picayune*, December 10, 1894.

71. *New Orleans Picayune*, October 23, 1900.

72. *New Orleans Picayune*, May 2, 4, 5, 6, 1903.

73. *Vicksburg Herald*, July 29, 1907; *Vicksburg Evening Post*, July 29, 1907; *Vicksburg American*, July 29, 30, August 5, 1907

74. *Vicksburg Evening Post*, March 28, 1886.

75. *Vicksburg Herald*, May 2, 1888; *Vicksburg Evening Post*, May 1, 1888; *New Orleans Picayune*, May 1, 1888.

76. *Vicksburg Evening Post*, February 23, 1889; *Vicksburg Herald*, February 23, 1889; *New Orleans Picayune*, February 23, 1889.

77. *Vicksburg Evening Post*, July 4, 1903; January 20, 1915; *Vicksburg American*, July 8, 1903.

78. *Vicksburg Evening Post*, July 10, 1918.

79. *Vicksburg Evening Post*, April 5, 1918.

80. *Vicksburg Evening Post*, April 16, 1918.

81. Harry Grey testimony, December 19, 1919, transcript of the record, *King et al. v. State*, case 21095, Supreme Court of Mississippi, Mississippi Department of Archives and History, Jackson; J. A. Miller to Shillady, October 29, 1918, part 7, series A, reel 14, NAACP Papers, Library of Congress, Washington, D.C. (microfilm); *Vicksburg Evening Post*, July 24, 1918.

82. McMillen, *Dark Journey*, 245–51.

83. This conclusion is based on a reading of every *Vicksburg Evening Post* published by John G. Cashman from 1883, when he started the paper, until 1914, when he became a federal marshal. His son Frank continued his father's opposition to mob law thereafter.

84. William C. Hunt, comp., *Fourteenth Census of the United States Taken in the Year 1920*, vol. 3, *Population 1920* (Washington, D.C.: U.S. Government Printing Office, 1922), 540.

85. *Vicksburg Evening Post*, May 17, June 6, 1917.

86. *Vicksburg Evening Post*, May 14, June 3, 1898.

87. *Vicksburg Herald*, November 11, 1906.

88. *Vicksburg Herald*, November 11, 1906; January 9, 22, February 19, August 17, September 11, 1907; April 12, 1908.

89. *Vicksburg Evening Post*, October 16, 1917; Colonel Willard D. Newbill, *General Report of the National Memorial Celebration and Peace Jubilee (National Memorial Reunion) Vicksburg, Mississippi, October 16 to 19, 1917* (Washington, D.C.: U.S. Government Printing Office, 1917), 6–15.

90. Newbill, *General Report*, 6–14; *Vicksburg Evening Post*, October 3, 1917.

91. *Vicksburg Evening Post*, October 6, 1917.

92. *Vicksburg Evening Post*, October 3, 1917.

93. *Vicksburg Herald*, October 18, 1917; *Vicksburg Evening Post*, October 23, 1917.

94. *Vicksburg Evening Post*, October 15, 16, 17, 1917.

95. *Vicksburg Evening Post*, October 16, 1917.

96. Jack E. Davis, *Race against Time: Culture and Separation in Natchez since 1930* (Baton Rouge: Louisiana State University Press, 2001), 24.

97. *Vicksburg Herald*, October 21, 1917.

98. *Vicksburg Evening Post*, October 16, 17, 1917.

99. *Vicksburg Evening Post*, October 17, 1917.

100. *Vicksburg Evening Post*, October 17, 1917.
101. *Vicksburg Evening Post*, October 17, 1917.
102. Holmes, *The White Chief*, 294–327.
103. *Vicksburg Evening Post*, October 18, 1917.
104. *Vicksburg Herald*, October 19, 1917.
105. *Vicksburg Evening Post*, October 23, 1917.
106. *Vicksburg Herald*, October 19, 1917.
107. *Vicksburg Herald*, October 19, 1917.
108. *Vicksburg Herald*, October 19, 1917.
109. Blight, *Race and Reunion*.
110. Blight, *Race and Reunion*, 9.
111. Robert Cook, "(Un)Furl That Banner: The Response of White Southerners to the Civil War Centennial of 1961–1965," *Journal of Southern History* 68 (November 2002): 906–9.

A Farewell to Arms

THE state and the press often promote heroic myths about war. Celebrating heroism and imagined glory universally fulfills any government's need to defend itself or launch adventures—or so writes the veteran war correspondent Chris Hedges, finding Shakespeare, *The Iliad*, and *The Odyssey* applicable to twenty-first-century Bosnia and every other war. Contrast the journalist with the historian. Cecilia O'Leary finds that in World War I, the state, "for the first time . . . became a major participant in articulating the nationalist discourse." Both authors cannot be right; the first sounds suspiciously ahistorical, while the second excessively historicized. Journalists mythologize "enduring" truths, while academics eagerly find "turning points" to make their research significant.[1]

In the Civil War, it has been said, governments delivered armies to the slaughter. "No war of the nineteenth century pointed more clearly to the future," Thomas C. Leonard writes. Andrew Delbanco says the Civil War divided a "culture of faith" from "a culture of doubt." According to Delbanco, Grant previewed "the dead-eyed murderers one meets in fictional and factual twentieth-century texts." Yet because the Civil War generation told of a "clean and uplifting war," the nation failed to grasp fully what industrialized combat really meant.[2]

Perhaps, though, the Civil War did not divide faith from doubt so perfectly. World War I brought such horrors home to

235

Vicksburg so shockingly that, for a time, Mississippians bade farewell to arms. World War I discomforted even combat veterans of the Civil War, or so claimed Vicksburg's newspapers. In the wake of gas warfare, celebrations of Civil War valor, what Edmund Wilson has called "warlike cant," dimmed noticeably.[3]

In 1916, three months after Pancho Villa's raid on Columbus, New Mexico, Mississippi women saw their men off to war. The scene almost eerily recalled 1861. In that Civil War year, thirteen Vicksburg ladies had presented a Confederate flag to the Volunteer Southrons as they prepared for war. When Vicksburg regiments had shipped out, doting mothers and loving sisters cried. Sweethearts shrieked. But the *Vicksburg Citizen* solemnly intoned that "stoic indifference . . . seemed engraved upon the countenances of the brave soldiers."[4]

The same scenes played out in 1916. Once again, young Vicksburgers joined the Volunteer Southrons. Vicksburg recruits filled out the ranks of Companies A and D. The Young Women's Business Club of Jackson presented a large silk flag to the soldiers. Trixie Nelson, representing Mississippi women, called on the assembled soldiers to remember "that your cause is just, that your object humanitarian, that it is you who are carrying liberty to an ignorant and prejudiced race." Just in case someone missed the point, another orator recalled that an earlier generation of southern women had presented flags to Confederate regiments as they marched off to war. According to the newspapers, when the mayor of Jackson spoke, "he grew eloquent and his frame trembled with patriotic fervor."[5]

The 1st Mississippi spent five months on the Mexican border without fighting any Mexicans. One soldier voiced his discontent with doggerel:

> I went and joined the Army to fight in Mexico,
> They put me on the Border, where I didn't want to go.
> With centipedes and rattlesnakes as thick as they could be
> And with sagebrush and cactus plants as far as you could see.

This soldier concluded,

I thought I loved my country on the 19th day of June,
So I signed up for six years, to cross the border soon,
We stayed four months in Jackson, then we moved in San Antone,
But you bet I won't love my country, when I get back home.[6]

Another soldier declared that the 1st Mississippi always obeyed orders, adding, "And it's a fact, that they will stick by their State and Colors too," and then pledging, "The Old First will stand by the Nation/Whether it happens to be right or wrong."[7] They then returned to Jackson, were mustered out, and then mustered back in for European service, becoming Company A of the 155th Infantry. One Vicksburger recalled proudly that as the Volunteer Southrons, the unit had fought the Mexican War, the Civil War, and the Spanish-American War. "Now we are in the World Series war and hope to keep up the high standard set up by our predecessors," Sergeant Charles Davis wrote home.[8]

The United States declared war on Germany on April 6, 1917. Through the summer, contingents of Vicksburgers shipped out for France. The nation scrambled to find housing, uniforms, and officers for a two-million-man army. Not until the summer of 1918 would the bulk of U.S. Army troops arrive in France. The first letters young Vicksburg soldiers wrote home reported on the strange and alien French culture, so different from the Mississippi delta. One soldier found the heavy wooden shoes worn by French peasants peculiar and amusing.[9] Lieutenant Lloyd Kiernan thought all French girls fell into two categories: the respectable and the other kind. Kiernan assured the folks back home that French girls were not as witty as Americans, having only narrow interests. Reassured on that score, Vicksburg newspaper readers must have been a bit shocked by what Kiernan revealed next. Going into a French shop, the Mississippi soldier discovered a perfectly composed but only half-clad French woman.[10]

As Kiernan and other soldiers negotiated French culture, the German war machine seemed unstoppable, the demoralized French prepared to evacuate Paris, and the Americans struggled to prevent disaster. In June, the U.S. Marines drove the Germans from the Belleau Wood. By the end of July, American soldiers had taken the offensive across a wide front. British, French, and German observers criticized the hastily trained Americans for bunching up and taking unnecessary casualties, but they agreed that the fresh American troops made all the difference. The war-weary Europeans noted the Americans' buoyant enthusiasm. In fact, these Americans sometimes seemed reckless.[11]

The 155th Regiment became part of the 39th Infantry Division. The 39th never saw combat but farmed its soldiers out to other units as replacements. For the first time, the Volunteer Southrons would not fight as a unit. Shortly after the 155th arrived in France, the only Vicksburgers still in the ranks were its sergeants. The privates who took the place of the Mississippi boys came from New York, Ohio, and other random places. Like other Americans, the Mississippi soldiers who made their way to the front (most did not) found trenches infested with formidable rats, lice, bedbugs, stench, death, and mud. "Dead horses and dead men," one writer related, "were sometimes not buried for months and often simply became an element of parapets and trench walls." The front line stunk for miles.[12] By August, the first reports of American casualties appeared in the Vicksburg papers. One headline read, "Mangled by Shell, Gassed, Minus Noses and Ears, Bodies Raked with Bullets and Racked with Pain, Our Boys Return." Writing for the International News Service (INS), Ernest Orr described a trainload of wounded unloaded in Paris from the front. Orr wrote that he had seen French, British, and Belgian wounded for two years, but that did not prepare him for the shock of seeing mangled American flesh.[13] Another INS report suggested that the war hardened the minds and spirits of American soldiers as well as mutilating their bodies. One American soldier told an INS reporter that he routinely shot Germans trying to surrender.[14]

Through 1918, parents, wives, and girlfriends waited anxiously for word from the front. Lieutenant George C. McCabe wrote his sister that he had been gassed. "I hope the next time I will get wounded all right with blood and bandages and all like that instead of just feeling like I am smothering."[15] J. J. Hirsch wrote that combat was like deer hunting. You expect to be scared, Hirsch wrote home, "but that is not so, in fact you don't want to leave it."[16] In October, the Allein family learned that both their sons had perished. Henry Allein, an aviator, had been shot attacking a German aircraft. When he tried to land his own plane to get medical attention, he crashed and died. A German artillery shell struck Private William Allein as he attacked a machine gun emplacement October 4. He died in a small corner of the Argonne Forest, according to a comrade who wrote the family. The army buried both Allein boys in France, but their parents begged that the bodies be returned to Vicksburg. If possible, T. H. Allein wrote one army officer, please return both brothers at the same time. "The trial on my wife would be very great if Henry and Billie came at different times." In both cases, the brothers' officers and comrades assured the Alleins that their sons had successfully killed the Germans they attacked.[17]

Military censorship kept the details of gas warfare from Vicksburgers until 1919. In France, soldiers learned that the Germans and British had been gassing each other since 1915. But the Americans arrived just as the two nations learned to rely on chemical warfare in earnest, making it their primary means of killing each other. Germany introduced mustard gas in July 1917, just as American troops joined the battle. Vicksburg's Southrons confronted unbridled chemical warfare at its most sophisticated.[18] Sam Peatross told the homefolk that the combat was "hell on earth" and described fighting through "constantly rolling gas mists."[19] While Peatross avoided being gassed himself by keeping his face covered with his hot and uncomfortable gas mask, others were not so lucky. Lieutenant McCabe got caught with his mask off in a mustard gas attack. "You feel a little prickling in your eyes and nose, not sufficient to distress you much," he recalled. The nausea and vomiting came later. So did the burning. McCabe warned that even slight exposure could prove fatal. Men brushing against foliage coated with mustard spray caught it on their skin. On "every part of the body where there is perspiration, sores result. . . . Men have actually lost their limbs from the burns of mustard gas," McCabe said.[20]

Through the summer of 1919, Vicksburg soldiers returned home from France. New horror stories circulated. Herbert Heckler told of being hustled to the Marne front within hours of landing. "I never will forget my first night under shell fire, which came as soon as we reached our positions," Heckler said. He thought the German artillery barrage that night, July 14, 1918, was the biggest of the war, covering the entire American front. Then the poison gas came. As soldiers struggled with their masks, they realized the artillery became more accurate, closing in on the Americans' positions. "It is hard to describe our feelings," Heckler said, "with the boys dropping around us and being shattered by the exploding shells, when we couldn't even see a German."[21]

Heckler saw his first Germans, dead on the battlefield, when he went "over the top." And he found "plenty of our brave boys lying cold on the field" too. For Heckler, the most gruesome and sickening scene of the war came when he found a platoon of more than twenty American soldiers, all dead and unmarked by any wound. Some corpses stood against the trench wall. "Others were lying on their knees and face with one hand stretched out in front and still others were lying around in a crumbled heap or stretched out flat on their backs with the sun blazing into their sightless eyes." Heckler supposed that German gas had caught and suffocated the soldiers before they could don their masks.[22] He experienced more horrors, but the civilians left behind may not have heard the worst stories. Three years after the armistice, one newspaper editor wrote that the world war veterans would not talk about what they had seen. "What really happened . . . in France will in large part forever remain a secret."[23]

240

Warren County sent about 500 African American soldiers to France. These young men also returned through the summer of 1919. The *Vicksburg Evening Post* insisted that returning black troops should be treated with respect. Some white southerners feared "friction" when the blacks returned, the *Post* acknowledged, but, the paper continued, "So far as we have heard there has not been a single instance of the sort."[24] In May, Vicksburg's white civic leaders planned downtown celebrations for "colored" soldiers on Memorial Day. But then white residents living near the courthouse complained that they did not want their peace and quiet disturbed by celebrations for black veterans. So, on Memorial Day, black Mississippians celebrated much as they always had, at the National Cemetery. Aging Civil War veterans from Vicksburg's two Grand Army of the Republic (GAR) posts turned out. Crowds were no larger than usual, perhaps a bit smaller.[25]

In the 1920s, World War I raised questions about militaristic patriotism generally. Europeans expected American veterans to return to old battlefields much as northern Civil War vets returned South. The French tire company Michelin commenced its famous tour guides as early as 1917, hoping to cash in on tourists eager to see the Western Front. One hotel businessman expected "our glorious battlefields" would lure 700,000 American tourists to France the first year alone. Anticipating this rush of tourism, Touring-Club of France erected granite markers in war zones. And tens of thousands of visitors did come. Some writers thought the World War I tourists differed from their Civil War counterparts by being "modern." Travelers to the European battlefields felt disconnected, while Civil War veterans found attachment, forging bonds not only with old comrades but even with former enemies. The novelist R. H. Mottram describes a World War I veteran visiting Flanders as an isolated figure seeking some link with his past, but, finding none, he hurries away in the dusk, as much (if not more) a stranger as when he arrived.[26]

The Civil War and World War I generated novels, poetry, memoirs, and plays—every kind of literature imaginable. The most important Civil War literature, though, came in the memoir form. No novelist matched Ulysses S. Grant for capturing the essence of how Victorian America wanted to remember the Civil War. Grant's memoir perfectly replicated the popular rags-to-riches stories of Horatio Alger. Grant, the quintessential ordinary man, lived at the birth of enormous bureaucracies. Like many Americans of his time, he never fully identified himself with his organization, but, unlike most, he did master it. Alger's fictional *Ragged Dick* became real-life Ragged Ulysses.

World War I veterans best expressed their experiences through fiction. Grant's World War I counterpart, John J. Pershing, also wrote a memoir of his experiences.[27] Unlike Grant's book, Pershing's literary efforts could not articulate the American public's sense of what the world war should mean. Both Grant and Pershing graduated from West Point, but Pershing was a different sort of soldier than Grant. Grant left the army and had life experiences outside its bureaucracy. He described himself as only nominally a military man; he was a citizen soldier. The slouching Grant triumphed over discipline and bureaucratic authority. Pershing spent his life in the army, serving in western outposts, in the Philippines, Japan, and Mexico—wherever the army sent him. He lived a separate life from most Americans, a world confined to "the little constricted familylike U.S. Army."[28] Contemporaries thought him aloof, distant. "No one looked or acted the soldier more than John Pershing," one admiring biographer wrote. His supporters complimented his cold, hard discipline. The men would never call him "Papa," one subordinate wrote, thinking that Pershing had hard eyes and thin lips. Pershing liked his soldiers in rows, anonymously lined up. When Pershing inspected the troops, anyone caught looking at him had to stand alone at attention with eyes front for half an hour. Pershing was a product of military bureaucracy. Grant did not really learn the most fundamental principles of life from the army, or so he suggested in his memoir. Pershing, though, presented himself as truly an organization man. What he understood about life came from a dusty military outpost.[29]

The literature that captured the essence of what became the American take on the world war rebelled against such martinets. In a novel titled *Three Soldiers* (1921), John Dos Passos indicted soldiers' patriotism as misguided. "The Star Spangled Banner" sifted into one soldier's consciousness "through a dream of what it would be like over there." Dos Passos ridiculed the soldier for imagining flags in the wind, a band playing "The Yanks Were Coming." In the fevered imagination of this misguided soul, soldiers marched very fast, as though in a movie. By the end of the novel, the character based on Dos Passos himself tells a friend he no longer has any patriotism left. History simply narrates "organizations growing and stifling individuals, and individuals revolting hopelessly against them."[30]

Dos Passos valued the individual over the bureaucratic, militaristic state. Other writers picked up the same theme. A year after *Three Soldiers*, e. e. cummings's more obviously autobiographical *The Enormous Room* recounted that author's vigorous individualism run afoul of the French security apparatus. On his first page, cummings scoffs at "Our Great President" and his crusade to save "civilization from the clutches of Prussian tyranny." The rest of the novel celebrates individualism—and human will—matched against a mindlessly stifling prison bureaucracy. When cummings is arrested, one of the officers pronounces his name accurately, "the first and last time my name was correctly pronounced by a Frenchman." The guards seem determined to assault cummings's individualism, his very identity, by mangling his name: "Vous etes uh-ah KEW-MANGZ?"[31] In 1923, Thomas Boyd's *Through the Wheat* has a character declare the war "damned ridiculous." The anonymity of the fighting demoralized the soldiers. A full battalion is mostly wiped out and "we never even saw a German. . . . That's hell." When a general gives a patriotic speech, sending men pointlessly to their deaths, he "wondered irresistibly whether his impending rise to lieutenant-general would give his wife access into the more imposing houses of Washington." Boyd summed up the literary judgment of World War I when he has his main character's mother write, "This war is not like the war that grand-papa used to tell you about."[32] World War I seemed to reveal bu-reaucratic violence at its most horrible and patriotic rhetoric as nothing but a cover for blind institutional loyalty. The war killed anonymously; Dos Passos, cummings, and Boyd rebelled by stress-ing their individuality.

Rigby very likely never read Dos Passos, cummings, or Boyd. In any case, he did not slacken his labors on behalf of his beloved park. In 1920, he worked to put statues of Abraham Lincoln and Jefferson Davis in the park. He initially planned to put Davis di-rectly opposite the center of the Memorial Arch. The aging Fred-erick Roziene objected. Roziene harbored proprietorial feelings for the Arch. He had, almost alone, pursued the campaign that fi-nally led to the 1917 jubilee and had led efforts to persuade Con-gress to provide money for the reunion. His endeavors produced a surplus of funds that would be used to construct a Memorial Arch, dedicated October 18, 1920. Now he found that Rigby planned to put a Jefferson Davis statue right in front of "his" arch. This was a "a surprise indeed," the old Union veteran wrote. Roziene feared that the Davis statue would "mar the impression of grandeur of the Arch." Visitors would see Davis as "a promi-nent scheme of intended adornment added to the Arch."[33] He pointed out that Lincoln had been relegated to the interior of the park. The park was a big place, Roziene observed. Could not Davis go somewhere else?[34]

Rigby remained adamant even when Roziene wrote the secre-tary of war. He had personally selected the spot where he wanted Jefferson Davis to stand. Roziene just could not see the logic. Davis deserved a prominent place to memorialize Vicksburg's de-fenders "for the reason that he was a citizen of this county." And, Rigby told the War Department at the end of February 1921, Lincoln was where he should be, near a statue of Grant.[35]

Roziene would not give up. He went to work mobilizing other veterans against placing the Davis statue so close to the Memorial Arch. He contacted members of Congress and the GAR and persuaded northern state legislatures to petition the War Department. To show that he was not prejudiced against Davis or southerners in general, Roziene demanded that no statues of any kind be placed within 200 feet of the Arch. In March, the War Department "compromised" and forbade the erection of any statues within 150 feet of the Arch.[36] Rigby agreed to move the statue to a site "not less than 150 feet distant from" the Arch. He wanted that statue as close to Roziene's Arch as possible.[37]

A decade or so before, Rigby's quarrel with Roziene might have ignited a public debate. And if North Carolina had dedicated its Vicksburg monument before World War I, all of Vicksburg would have turned out in a vast celebration. In 1925, 500 Confederate veterans stopped off at the Vicksburg dedication on their way to the national reunion. In his speech presenting the monument, J. H. Dillard rehearsed the familiar arguments: slavery had nothing to do with the Civil War, and southerners fought for constitutional principles and law. Rigby hailed Confederate valor as "unsurpassed." Rigby read from park monuments, all approved by the federal government, to show that the nation recognized that both sides fought with "unselfish devotion to duty" and patriotism.[38]

Familiar rhetoric. Yet there is evidence that beneath the rhetoric, things changed after World War I. Vicksburg whites had faithfully celebrated Confederate Memorial Day every April 26 since 1893—until the 1920s. In that decade, Vicksburgers began celebrating Confederate Memorial Day on the Sunday nearest April 26, a sure sign that schools and businesses were no longer willing to shut their doors to honor the Confederacy.[39]

Vicksburg's Fourth of July celebrations also changed after World War I. A Civil War television series once said that after Vicksburg surrendered on the Fourth of July 1863, the holiday "would not be celebrated in Vicksburg again for 81 years."[40] And for some time after 1863, southerners generally—and Vicksburgers in particular—sometimes did not celebrate the Fourth. In 1890, the *Vicksburg Commercial-Herald*, recalling Vicksburg's surrender, scolded that year's celebrants, warning them not to do it again. The *Commercial-Herald* thought the festivities the work of ignorant people, mere laborers, and complained that most "did not know what the Fourth of July is, would not know when it came but for their leaders, white and colored, informing them." The *Commercial-Herald* still resented the surrender, but the reference to "leaders, white and colored" hints that racial prejudice really explained the *Commercial-Herald*'s objections to Fourth of July festivities. Two years before, the *Commercial-Herald* had "very much" regretted "the necessity for lynch law" but went on to say that when such a "necessity" existed, "there should be no hesitation about resorting to it."[41]

The *Vicksburg Commercial-Herald* did not speak for all of Vicksburg when it called for an end to Fourth of July celebrations. The *Vicksburg Evening Post* did not think that the city's 1863 surrender had so tainted the Fourth as to require a boycott. Instead, the *Post* countered the *Commercial-Herald* by saying that if most of the celebrators did not know the meaning of the Fourth, "Is [it] not a good idea to celebrate the day anyhow, and instruct them as to its meaning? Let them learn the meaning by reading the Declaration of Independence," the *Post* suggested.[42]

The *Vicksburg Evening Post* suspected that "many of the people who celebrated the day have a pretty good general idea of what the Fourth of July signifies." They know it means "liberty," the *Post*'s editor ventured, pointedly adding that there were Vicksburgers with a special understanding of that word. "Some of them who have been in slavery know how sweet liberty is," the editor continued, commenting that "we believe that there never was a slave who did not have a longing and a hope for liberty."[43]

The *Post* concluded by urging Vicksburgers to continue celebrating the Fourth and to read the Declaration of Independence, learn its truths, and study the Constitution. "Secure your rights under it," the *Post* advised its black and white readers.[44]

In 1904, the *Vicksburg Evening Post* carried news of Fourth celebrations in Jackson but not Vicksburg. Vicksburg honored the

Fourth by shutting its businesses and government buildings.[45] In 1907, Vicksburg's fraternal organizations went all out, with music, parades, and speeches. "The people turned out for the parade just like they do on circus days," the *Post* happily reported. T. Dabney Marshall served as master of ceremonies and gave the principal address, offering his explanation that both the North and the South fought for liberties promised in the Declaration of Independence. Northerners, fearing the southern states would lose their liberty outside the Union, "shouldered their guns and marched as to holy war." Southerners thought their right of secession guaranteed by the Declaration.[46] The *Vicksburg Herald*, now reconciled with the Fourth, called the parade "commendable" and told its readers that "everyone enjoyed an old time Fourth of July." The *Herald*, in fact, editorialized that southerners should again make the Fourth a custom as they had before the Civil War. Perhaps to help everyone remember how it was done, the *Herald* reprinted an article describing an 1860 Fourth celebration.[47]

A year later, the *Vicksburg Evening Post* reported that Fourth celebrations rang out all over Mississippi, more generally celebrated than ever before.[48] In Vicksburg, the parading continued. In 1909, live eagles with streamers for each of the thirteen original states embellished the merrymaking.[49]

After World War I, Fourth celebrations slowly faded. In 1923, a Vicksburg newspaper reported that fireworks had been banned—saving many lives. But celebrations went on in other ways, with ball games, boxing matches, and barbecues. By the end of the decade, though, the Fourth once again no longer seemed a gala day in Vicksburg. A year before Ernest Hemingway published *A Farewell to Arms*, the *Vicksburg Evening Post* urged its readers to celebrate the Fourth quietly by reading the Declaration of Independence. *A Farewell to Arms* became the greatest World War I novel and forms the intellectual backdrop to Vicksburg's fading interest in patriotic bombast. "I don't believe in victory anymore," Hemingway has one of his disaffected characters say. Hemingway's narrator remarks that the words "sacred, glorious, and sacrifice" embarrassed him. Apparently, Vicksburgers felt the same way. Fourth of July speeches, with their appeals for glorious sacrifice, faded at the same time that Hemingway's novel circulated.[50]

And Dabney Marshall died. Marshall had so often delivered patriotic speeches at Vicksburg's Fourth of July observances because Vicksburgers liked hearing him speak. His reputation for articulate, modest, wide-ranging intelligence drew passersby into his office just to hear him talk. Marshall left Vicksburg for North Carolina, probably at the end of 1926. He lived with his niece. On July 2, 1928, he died; Vicksburg's newspapers carried the news of his passing on July 5.[51]

Thereafter, the Fourth did not go unobserved in Vicksburg. Banks and other businesses closed. Vicksburg athletes challenged neighboring towns to baseball games. For several years, though, the Vicksburg newspapers used the occasion to tally the holiday death toll, near 400 in 1939 and 233 in 1941. In 1942, the *Vicksburg Evening Post* reported that Vicksburgers celebrated the holiday at home, with picnics and fishing trips.[52]

North–South reunions declined along with Fourth celebrations. Aging Confederates and Union men continued to hold reunions, but they did so separately through the 1920s. After rejecting the idea in 1928, the United Confederate Veterans endorsed another Blue–Gray reunion in 1929, but only conditionally. The Union veterans had to admit the Confederate flag to the festivities, the old Confederates declared. The GAR rejected the terms, and the idea of a new reunion faded. Furthermore, the national government saw no reason to fund a reunion as it had done in World War I. In 1928, Congress considered appropriating money for another North–South reunion, but the proposal died in committee, one congressman explaining that sentiment just did not exist for another reunion.[53]

World War I alone does not explain the declining interest in the Civil War memory. The people most invested in promoting the Civil War as a vital public memory passed from the scene at an increasingly rapid rate. By 1928, fewer than 80,000 Civil War pensioners survived in the United States. Union soldiers died at the rate of 1,200 a month. Only 600 Confederate veterans still lived in Mississippi, just 20 in Warren County. In 1929, this was brought home to Vicksburg residents most directly when William T. Rigby, the park's great champion, succumbed.[54]

The real reason that interest in sentimentalizing the Civil War declined—the reason the old Confederates and Yankees lost their facility for reconciliation—lay in the profound isolationism that gripped the nation and Vicksburg after World War I. In the 1920s and into the 1930s, the great bulk of Americans feared another bloody European carnage. Vicksburgers watched the rise of Hitler uneasily but still desperately hoped to avoid involvement in another European war. Such feelings also contributed to the prevailing hostility toward sentimentalizing warfare, even the Civil War. In Vicksburg, the Veterans of Foreign Wars circulated petitions calling on Congress and the president to keep the United States out of foreign wars. The local newspaper asked editorially, "Do we want to tie our hands that way? At a time when international gangsters are on the prowl . . . do we want to make it plain that no matter what they do we shall not lift a hand to stop them?" The newspaper answered its own question: "Well— why not?" The editor explained that the nation had learned that war was the wrong way to solve problems.[55]

This antiwar sentiment generated a powerful distaste for romanticized feelings about the Civil War or any war. Congress proved stubbornly unsympathetic when World War I veterans asked for a bonus for their service. *Literary Digest* decried "professional patriotism." Religious leaders denounced "strident patriotism" as the greatest threat to world peace. An *Atlantic Monthly* writer remembered being taught "introverted patriotism" as a boy. "I imagine it is not so easy to bamboozle the modern skeptical youth as it was our generation," Earnest Elmo Calkins wrote.[56] In this environment, H. L. Mencken attracted leading southern journalists to his hard-boiled writing style.

Mencken's skepticism, which seemed so emblematic of the age, reached foreign adventures; he hated Franklin Roosevelt as a warmonger. The tough-minded of the 1920s despised the sentimental element so prevalent in previous Civil War parades and love feasts. In the 1920s, turning the Civil War into "an affair of moonlight and romance" seemed more revolting than ever before. The new realists saw the war as grim, hard, and bloody. When the same veterans who had once turned out for reunions now scorned such affairs, this seemed to document a wisdom wrung from hard experience. Actual soldiers consider battlefields cruel and bloody, a "bit of hell on earth," Vicksburgers decided. Some in Vicksburg urged everyone to remember this truth and desist from sentimentalizing the conflict.[57]

It hurt Vicksburg National Military Park when "moonlight and romance" fell from favor. "Seeing America first" became a popular slogan in the 1920s, accelerating tourism and putting more travelers in search of interesting destinations. Henry Ford and John D. Rockefeller, Jr., began collecting historical artifacts and buying historic sites.[58] But the new tourists did not often travel to the Vicksburg battlefield. Shabby housing encroached on the park's boundaries. Vandals and picnickers defaced the monuments.[59] On the once-sacred ground where soldiers fought and died, where soaring oratory once celebrated their valor, cattle grazed under the eyes of indifferent park officials. The animals cut trails across historic lunettes and redans that allowed erosion to destroy the earthen remnants of valor. Rain dug deep gullies into the battlefield; the very soil soldiers fought over washed away.[60] In 1927, the Mississippi State Guard built a tent city on the park to shelter 1,000 white refugees from the big flood that year. And, of course, state authorities did not admit black flood victims to their camp.[61] One of the observation towers deteriorated so much that the few tourists venturing onto park grounds did not dare mount it.[62] The park's custodian, the War Department, maneuvered to unload its responsibility, hoping to transfer the park to the Interior Department. Given the War Department's indifference, this was a sensible idea. The Interior Department administered such scenic treasures as Yosemite and Yellowstone. History, rather than natural beauty, had always been Vicksburg's strength. History had, of course, always been central to the park's purposes. At the same time, Vicksburg's champions had consistently advertised the battleground as a beautiful place for tourists to visit. Nonetheless, the transfer idea languished in Congress for years, leaving the park in the hands of an agency with declining interest in its development.[63]

Changing attitudes about Memorial Day also signaled a decline in sentimentalism. Decorating graves and honoring the Civil War dead now seemed more maudlin than deeply felt.[64] A frightening crime wave, including a national epidemic of kidnappings and urban gangster violence, seemed proof that Civil War values had faded. Confederate soldiers fought for law, Judge Harris Dickson lectured his audience on Confederate Memorial Day 1927. Now, he continued, the children of Civil War soldiers tolerated lawlessness and actually trampled on the law when it suited their purposes to do so. Judge Dickson scolded his listeners that they should stand ashamed and silent before the graves of Civil War soldiers. Dickson delivered a bitter conclusion: "We have not carried on. We have not held aloft the torch."[65]

It was in the 1920s that the Ku Klux Klan revived in Warren County. The Klan did arouse old memories of Civil War and Reconstruction; the masked order held meetings on the national park grounds. One Klan chapter consciously evoked memories of the war by calling itself the Jefferson Davis Ku Klux Klan. While the Klan could certainly be called a "Civil War organization," it is not clear how many Vicksburgers thought this connection particularly salient.[66] If the Klan's revival documented the level of white Vicksburg's continuing Civil War sentiment through the 1920s, then it must also be recognized that a majority rejected it. In 1924, the Klan posted a full slate of candidates for the membership on the Warren County Democratic Executive Committee. The Klan candidates went down to defeat by large majorities.

The Klan became so unpopular that Vicksburg's civic leadership feared association with it. When rumors circulated that local leaders had joined the Klan, they published articles in the newspaper denouncing the Klan, distancing themselves from the Invisible Empire.[67] In 1926, the *Vicksburg Evening Post* pronounced the Klan "kaputt" in Vicksburg.[68]

In World War I, the federal government did ratchet up its support for Civil War commemorations. Vicksburg's youth hurried off to war, anxious to test their mettle against a Southron mythology forged in the Mexican War, the Civil War, and the Spanish-American war. They encountered chemical warfare and gory horrors for which their parents and grandparents had not prepared them. Through the 1920s, interest in celebrating Civil War valor seemed to decline in Vicksburg. If the federal government turned a corner in 1917, it seemed to retreat for a time thereafter. It would take a new crisis before the federal government again moved to rejuvenate interest in Vicksburg's Civil War history.

Notes

1. Chris Hedges, *War Is a Force That Gives Us Meaning* (New York: Public Affairs, 2002), 83–121; Cecilia Elizabeth O'Leary, *To Die For: The Paradox of American Patriotism* (Princeton, N.J.: Princeton University Press, 1999), 220–45. G. Kurt Piehler, *Remembering War the American Way* (Washington, D.C.: Smithsonian Institution Press, 1995), 4, calls World War I "a watershed in attempts by the federal government to encourage a national pattern of remembrance." But Piehler also describes the Civil War as a watershed, the beginning of efforts to commemorate ordinary soldiers.

2. Thomas C. Leonard, *Above the Battle: War-Making in America from Appomattox to Versailles* (New York: Oxford University Press, 1987), 9–24; Andrew Delbanco, *The Death of Satan: How Americans Have Lost the Sense of Evil* (New York: Farrar, Straus & Giroux, 1995), 138–39.

3. Edmund Wilson, *Patriotic Gore: Studies in the Literature of the American Civil War* (New York: Oxford University Press, 1962), xiii.

4. *Vicksburg Citizen*, April 4, 11, 12, 1862.

5. *Vicksburg Evening Post*, June 29, 1916.

6. T. Mitchell Robinson and Harold E. Gardiner, eds., *Invasion of Texas: First Mississippi Infantry* (Jackson, Miss.: Authors, 1917), not paginated.

7. Robinson and Gardiner, *Invasion of Texas*.

8. *Vicksburg Evening Post*, October 23, 1918.

9. *Vicksburg Evening Post*, October 23, 1918.

10. *Vicksburg Evening Post*, January 29, 1919; Gary Mead, *The Doughboys: America and the First World War* (Woodstock, N.Y.: Overlook Press, 2000), 191–207. Another World War I veteran, e. e. cummings, made the same judgment of French women. See e. e. cummings, *The Enormous Room* (1922; rev., New York: Liveright, 1978), 102.

11. Mead, *The Doughboys*, 66–126; Edward M. Coffman, *The War to End All Wars: The American Military Experience in World War I* (New York: Oxford University Press, 1968), 212–61.

12. Colonel M. J. Mulvihill, Sr., *First Mississippi Regiment—Its Foundation, Organization and Record* (Vicksburg, Miss., 1931), 38; Paul Fussell, *The Great War and Modern Memory* (New York: Oxford University Press, 1975), 49.

13. *Order of Battle of the United States Land Forces in the World War: American Expeditionary Forces: Divisions*, 3 vols. in 5 (1931–1949; repr., Washington, D.C.: Center of Military History, U.S. Army, 1988), 2:246–53; Coffman, *The War to End All Wars*, 255; *Vicksburg Evening Post*, October 23, August 23, 1918.

14. *Vicksburg Evening Post*, July 5, 1918.

15. Lieutenant George McCabe to sister, July 16, 1918, Works Progress Administration papers, box 426, series 447, RG 60, Mississippi Department of Archives and History, Jackson.

16. J. J. Hirsch to sister, October 18, 1918, Works Progress Administration papers, box 426, series 447, RG 60, Mississippi Department of Archives and History, Jackson.

17. M. Buchanan to T. H. Allein, January 7, 1919; Charles Douglas to T. H. Allein, January 7, 1919; L. C. Windsor to T. H. Allein, April 18, 1919; and T. H. Allein to Col. C. L. Dasher, February 22, 1921, Old Court House Museum, Vicksburg.

18. Hugh R. Slotten, "Humane Chemistry or Scientific Barbarism? American Responses to World War I Poison Gas, 1915–1930," *Journal of American History* 77 (September 1990): 476–98.

19. *Vicksburg Evening Post*, May 15, 1919.

20. *Vicksburg Evening Post*, June 11, 1919.

21. *Vicksburg Evening Post*, July 11, 1919.

22. *Vicksburg Evening Post*, July 11, 1919.

23. *Vicksburg Evening Post*, December 8, 1921.

24. *Vicksburg Evening Post*, April 12, 1919.

25. *Vicksburg Evening Post*, May 9, 14, 30, 1919.

26. Modris Eksteins, "War, Memory, and the Modern: Pilgrimage and Tourism to the Western Front," in Douglas Macaman and Michael Mays, eds., *World War I and the Cultures of Modernity* (Jackson: University Press of Mississippi, 2000), 151–60; Paul Dickson and Thomas B. Allen, *The Bonus Army: An American Epic* (New York: Walker & Co., 2004).

27. John J. Pershing, *My Experiences in the World War*, 2 vols. (New York: Frederick A. Stokes, 1931).

28. Gene Smith, *Until the Last Trumpet Sounds: The Life of General of the Armies John J. Pershing* (New York: John Wiley & Sons, 1998), 133.

29. Pershing, *My Experiences in the World War*. Pershing's biographers emphasize this point. Smith, *Until the Last Trumpet Sounds*, 1–136, 70 (quotation); Richard Goldhurst, *Pipe Clay and Drill: John J. Pershing, the Classic American Soldier* (New York: Thomas Y. Crowell, 1977), 39–226.

30. John Dos Passos, *Three Soldiers* (1921; repr., Boston: Houghton Mifflin, 1947), 37, 420–21.

31. cummings, *The Enormous Room*, 3, 5, 40, passim.

32. Thomas Boyd, *Through the Wheat* (New York: Charles Scribner's Sons, 1923), 215, 221.

33. Roziene to Rigby, January 18, 1921, box 74, Records of the War Department Relating to National Parks, Records of the National Park Service, RG 79, National Archives, College Park, Maryland.

34. Roziene to Rigby, February 16, 1921, box 74, Records of the War Department Relating to National Parks, Records of the National Park Service, RG 79, National Archives, College Park, Maryland.

35. Rigby to Assistant Secretary of War, February 25, 1921, box 74, Records of the War Department Relating to National Parks, Records of

the National Park Service, RG 79, National Archives, College Park, Maryland.

36. W. R. Williams to Rigby, March 1, 1921, box 74, Records of the War Department Relating to National Parks, Records of the National Park Service, RG 79, National Archives, College Park, Maryland.

37. Rigby to Assistant Secretary of War, August 26, 1921, box 74, Records of the War Department Relating to National Parks, Records of the National Park Service, RG 79, National Archives, College Park, Maryland.

38. Rigby to Quartermaster General, May 19, 1925, box 74, Records of the War Department Relating to National Parks, Records of the National Park Service, RG 79, National Archives, College Park, Maryland; *Vicksburg Evening Post*, May 18, 1925.

39. *Vicksburg Evening Post*, April 8, 1926; April 19, 1928.

40. Ken Burns, *The Civil War*, episode 5: "1863: The Universe of Battle" (Alexandria, Va.: Florentine Films, 1989).

41. *Vicksburg Commercial-Herald*, quoted in *Vicksburg Evening Post*, July 5, 1890; *Vicksburg Commercial-Herald*, May 2, 1888.

42. *Vicksburg Evening Post*, July 5, 1890.

43. *Vicksburg Evening Post*, July 5, 1890.

44. *Vicksburg Evening Post*, July 5, 1890.

45. *Vicksburg Evening Post*, July 4, 1904.

46. *Vicksburg Evening Post*, July 5, 1907.

47. *Vicksburg Daily Herald*, July 4, 5, 1907.

48. *Vicksburg Evening Post*, July 4, 1908.

49. *Vicksburg Evening Post*, July 5, 1909.

50. *Vicksburg Evening Post*, July 4, 1923; June 14, 17, 1924; July 4, 1928; Ernest Hemingway, *A Farewell to Arms* (1929; repr., New York: Scribner, 1997), 165, 169.

51. *Vicksburg Evening Post*, July 5, 1928.

52. *Vicksburg Evening Post*, July 2, 4, 1928; July 1, 3, 5, 1929; July 2, 5, 1930; July 4, 6, 1931; July 5, 1934; July 4, 1935; July 3, 1936; July 5, 1937; July 3, 4, 1938; July 4, 1939; July 5, 6, 1941; July 3, 5, 6, 1942.

53. *Vicksburg Evening Post*, February 10, April 6, 17, May 10, 11, 1928; September 21, 1929.

54. *Vicksburg Evening Post*, January 14, July 21, 1927; May 9, 1928; May 13, 1929.

55. *Vicksburg Evening Post*, December 15, 1937; William E. Cain, "A Lost Voice of Dissent: H. L. Mencken in Our Time," *Sewanee Review* 104 (spring 1996): 229–47.

56. "Dangers of False Patriotism," *Literary Digest* 96 (January 14, 1928): 30; "The '100-Per-Cent. American' as a Peril to Peace," *Literary Digest* 99 (November 17, 1928): 31; Earnest Elmo Calkins, "My Country, Right or Wrong?" *Atlantic Monthly* 148 (December 1931): 681.

57. *Vicksburg Evening Post*, October 5, 1932. For Mencken's influence, see Ann Douglas, *Terrible Honesty: Mongrel Manhattan in the 1920s* (New York: Farrar, Straus & Giroux, 1995), 31–72; Marvin Kenneth Singleton, *H. L. Mencken and the American Mercury Adventure* (Durham, N.C.: Duke University Press, 1962).

58. Michael Kammen, *Mystic Chords of Memory: The Transformation of Tradition in American Culture* (New York: Knopf, 1991), 338–62.

59. *Vicksburg Evening Post*, August 20, 1926.

60. *Vicksburg Evening Post*, October 11, 1933.

61. *Vicksburg Evening Post*, May 6, 1927.

62. *Vicksburg Evening Post*, October 20, 1933.

63. *Vicksburg Evening Post*, April 30, 1928.

64. *Vicksburg Evening Post*, May 30, 1928.

65. *Vicksburg Evening Post*, April 26, 1927.

66. *Vicksburg Evening Post*, August 5, 7, 1922.

67. *Vicksburg Evening Post*, February 19, March 13, 1923; July 12, August 6, 8, 20, 21, 1924.

68. *Vicksburg Evening Post*, October 14, 1926.

A New Deal

O N October 13, 1936, Governor Hugh L. White came to Vicksburg to celebrate the opening of the new M. Fine and Company shirt factory. The high school band celebrated the occasion by parading through Vicksburg's business district, accompanied by the Boy Scout drum and bugle corps. Vicksburg's Chamber of Commerce industrial committee—it was remarkable that the town now *had* an "industrial committee"— urged citizens to come see how the new factory would make shirts. In his speech, Governor White pictured Mississippi's industrial future. The *Vicksburg Evening Post* sketched out the glorious details. "Two million Mississippians," the paper reported, owned untapped mineral resources and virgin forests ready to be exploited by industrialists. A tractable and cooperative workforce, one accustomed to hard work, stood ready for industrial labor. On that October day in 1936, anything seemed possible. Vicksburg businessmen could see "an unfolding of the industrial crusade" that would transform the Magnolia State into "a southern industrial empire."[1]

By the time M. Fine and Company opened its Vicksburg shirt factory, Franklin D. Roosevelt's New Deal had already consolidated its hold over Vicksburg's battleground. During the Great Depression, the federal government—northerners—would emerge more firmly in control of the park symbolically, culturally, and socially. Not only that, but the Roosevelt administration successfully made Vicksburg's military park into the city's central feature, the defining expression of its past, present, and future. Vicksburg women turned out to work in the shirt factory (M. Fine and Company did not expect men to make shirts). Blanche Terry, as feisty and independent as her great-grandfather, John "Red Jack" McGuiggan, took a job as inspector to make enough money to buy her first house. Blanche Terry got her house, but the city was destined to be a tourist mecca more than the capital of an industrial empire. The battleground would be Vicksburg's focal point, not its industrial base. At least as effectively as M. Fine and Company, the chamber of commerce, and Governor White sold industrialization to Vicksburg's population, New Dealers pedaled history. While Blanche Terry worked in Vicksburg factories most of her life, her husband took a job at the Vicksburg National Military Park as a guide.[2]

Grand struggles can begin with small skirmishes. On March 30, 1932, the Vicksburg Park superintendent, Major J. Broadus Holt, told Alivia Davis that he planned to establish a flagpole at the Illinois monument. Alivia had been working at the Illinois monument, but Holt had no intention of allowing her to raise and lower the American flag each day. "This is not properly the duty of a lady," Holt explained. He arranged for a male war veteran to handle the flag duties. He told Alivia to hand over her key the next day.[3] It was just a small change in policy.

When Holt dismissed Alivia Davis from her Illinois monument duties, he began a long quarrel with Alivia and her husband, Zack M. Davis, one that illustrated the government's changing attitudes toward the park. In 1914, the Davises had erected a souvenir stand right at the edge of park property, selling cold Coca-Colas and other goods to park visitors. Davis made himself central to the park's tourist trade, even publishing and selling his own battleground tourist guide. Through the 1920s, the Davises had sold their Cokes and souvenirs with no objection from park officials, even though they exhibited garish advertisements on park property. In 1932, Holt decided that the Davis shop insulted the park's "high-class" memorials. He thought that he could eject the Davises on a technicality: their building encroached on park property by several inches. Moreover, there was a traffic problem. Tourists stopping to buy a cold drink or a souvenir from the Davises frequently parked on the public road, blocking park visitors wishing to pass. Holt erected "no parking" signs, which the Davises promptly took down. Holt complained that Zack Davis "is trying to make a personal persecution case of it." In fact, the feud between Holt and Davis became very personal. Davis at one point flew "into a fit of rage and high temper, making various threats," according to Holt. Zack Davis told Holt "that he was from Kentucky where matters were settled quickly." Holt responded by matching his own manhood against Davis's Kentucky bluster. Davis sued Holt, and the United States sued the Davises. In 1938, the U.S. attorney dropped the government's suit. Rigby's old deeds were not accurate enough to sustain a suit over inches, he explained.[4]

Holt's fight with the Davises reveals in microcosm the government's desire to remake the park. The Davis souvenir stand is an artifact from a time when the veterans came back to "their" battlefield and wanted something cold to drink. In one of his letters, Holt writes that the trouble started when "it was found out that the display of commercial signs did not coincide well with the Park management idea." Holt thought the Davises' "antagonism to Park ideas is revolting." He gave as an example the fact that Davis had constructed a ten-foot Coca-Cola sign just a few feet from the Logan Memorial, "this patriotic piece of art."[5]

Holt brought a new "park management idea" to Vicksburg. Dignity had to be bestowed on the park by professionals enforcing decorum. He rejected the old idea that the battleground should simply host the old soldiers' patriotism. Davis, in contrast, still clung to this notion, which tolerated commercial vendors who could service the old veterans much as sutlers had provided refreshments for the troops. While the old soldiers had lent a

The National Park Service claimed Zack Davis's store encroached on park grounds by several inches. Old Court House Museum photograph.

solemn dignity to the park, the new generation of tourists, Holt and other park officials thought, brought no patriotic nobility themselves; they had to learn it from the park.

In July, Holt tried to persuade the Davises' lawyer that his clients should not remove traffic signs he put up around the Davis store. As Holt fought for his "hand painted 'Slow' sign," the country prepared itself to elect a new president, one that promised a new style of governing. On July 2, after the Democratic National Convention nominated him for president, Franklin D. Roosevelt broke with tradition and personally appeared before the delegates. At the conclusion of his speech, he declared, "I pledge you—I pledge myself—to a new deal for the American people." By the end of the campaign, this pledge had become Roosevelt's theme. He asked voters to make him president as "the humble emblem" of "the new deal."[6]

In Vicksburg, the New Deal meant to hallow the battle-ground. Roosevelt's storm of legislation in his first hundred days included a law authorizing creation of the Civilian Conservation Corps (CCC), proposed March 21 and enacted March 31. On April 5, Roosevelt issued an executive order setting up the CCC. Roosevelt envisioned a force of 250,000 men, employed in "simple work" that would not compete with industry. He included forestry, combating soil erosion, and flood control in that goal. He wrote later that he wanted to both "save a generation" of young men and restore endangered natural resources. Some critics have characterized the CCC as a surreptitious crime control program designed to take the most criminally inclined element in the population out of the cities and incarcerate them in country compounds. Roosevelt did say that he wanted to take young men off city street corners and place them in the woods, but his critics have never explained why the CCC booted out anyone the New Dealers considered deviant if Roosevelt so wanted his new agency to warehouse criminally inclined youth.[7]

Roosevelt directed four federal departments—War, Agriculture, Labor, and Interior—to implement the CCC program. The Army organized the CCC camps, detailing an officer to command each. The volunteers were called "enrollees," given physical exams, issued uniforms, and housed in army tents or barracks. Perhaps to make sure the CCC did not become too militaristic, Roosevelt named as director labor leader Robert Fechner. Fechner aimed to make illiterate enrollees literate, teach work discipline, and educate the unemployed.[8]

This challenged white southerners' conservatism. While Mississippi white folks championed states' rights, Fechner headed a federal program intended to reform and uplift individual citizens, the largest such effort since Reconstruction.[9] If the Civil War pitted state against national power, then the white South went into the Great Depression unrepentant and unreconstructed. National economic calamity, though, made the sacred mantra of states' rights seem a dubious proposition. Mississippi's

1890 constitution had established a structure allowing the governor few powers; this left counties and villages to face an international economic disaster with only their local resources. In the Great Depression, Mississippi made some small strides toward centralizing state power on its own, establishing, for example, an Oil and Gas Board and a Fish and Game Commission for the first time. Such minor reforms did little to relieve the Magnolia State's economic suffering. Perhaps their state's faltering response helps explain why many white Vicksburgers excitedly welcomed the New Deal. In 1933, the most determined proponent of states' rights could hardly contend that Mississippi would ever shrug off economic collapse without federal help.[10] The most conservative whites now largely welcomed as necessary the sort of federal intervention they had once rejected.[11]

The National Industrial Recovery Act (NIRA) became a cornerstone of Roosevelt's initial plan for recovery. It authorized the administration to establish codes for industry to follow. In Vicksburg, businessmen heartily endorsed the NIRA. Merchants displayed the NIRA Blue Eagle logo in their stores or in their newspaper advertisements. The *Vicksburg Evening Post* attached the Blue Eagle to its masthead. Since violators enjoyed unfair advantages, Blue Eagle businessmen had a vested interest in making certain that all their competitors, regardless of race, followed the NIRA code.

As whites rallied around Roosevelt's program, African Americans recognized the NIRA as a new opportunity to combat their oppression. Black Vicksburgers warned whites that any plan neglecting African Americans would not "fulfill Mr. Roosevelt's dream of economic benefit to all the citizens of our common country." In Vicksburg, black leaders negotiated with their white counterparts. The *Vicksburg Evening Post*'s column "Among the Colored Folks," authored by an anonymous black writer, described the whites as "patriotic southern white men" but defined patriotism as not ignoring the interests of local African Americans. This masterfully put pressure on the white leaders. And the black negotiators had leverage. Whites needed black cooperation for the NIRA to apply to every business in town. After meetings with white leaders where "different points of view were presented," black ministers gave the whites what they wanted, instructing their congregations to support the NIRA.[12] When Vicksburg's white leadership began registering CCC volunteers, they accepted blacks. On April 27, a committee that included the sheriff and other local leaders enrolled nearly one hundred local unemployed Vicksburg workers. A month later, fifty-five Vicksburg men, both black and white, shipped out for an Alabama CCC camp. It was an achievement, albeit one limited by prevailing racialism. The CCC maintained segregated camps.[13]

Vicksburg's military park became the focus of CCC efforts. On April 13, Holt wrote his superiors asking that a camp of fifty or a hundred men be assigned to Vicksburg. Holt expected the men to plant trees; he argued that since the park was "well laced up with highways," the people would "get a close up view of governmental care of this growing forest." Holt reassured his superiors that the battleground had appropriate sites for camps.[14] A few weeks later, National Park Service (NPS) officials learned that the matter "is now being thrashed out in Washington."[15] In June, word came that the president had approved a 200-man camp for Vicksburg, more than Holt had requested. Along with the good news came a disturbing peculiarity: the NPS would supervise the work, but the Army would actually install and maintain the camps.[16] On June 23, five passenger cars disembarked 175 CCC men, commanded by Captain W. R. Burns. The CCC men set to work erecting twenty-nine army tents.[17] At once the divided command structure led to trouble. Stuart Cuthbertson, NPS historian, objected that the Army's camp threatened Civil War trenches. Holt sided with the Army, and Cuthbertson quarreled with Holt. When Holt ignored the NPS man's objections, Cuthbertson fired off a telegram to his superiors in Washington. That really irritated Holt. Holt soon learned to despise Cuthbertson, a man so helpless he could not even read a map, or so

Holt complained. Holt had understood that he and the Army were in charge and that technicians, like Cuthbertson, were just there to pick up any Civil War "souvenirs" that might turn up. Cuthbertson's efforts to protect "historic" ground seemed completely impractical to Holt. "Every part of this Park is historic," Holt complained, and if historic ground could not be disturbed, then the CCC could not camp anywhere. Holt further grumbled that Cuthbertson "kill[ed] time . . . by asking a thousand and one useless questions." In short, the NPS historian endangered the whole project.[18] The root of Holt's anger at Cuthbertson, as the superintendent himself saw it, lay in the divided command structure. "This technician reports frequently to his superior, who is not *my* superior," Holt pointed out.[19]

The trouble between Holt and the NPS really ran deeper than that. The War Department soon would hand the Vicksburg battleground to the NPS. The NPS historians had arrived in Vicksburg a week or so before the CCC men, coming without prior warning. They probably shocked Holt a bit with their news that the Interior Department would soon be taking over the park. According to Holt, the NPS men explained they had come "to instruct and enlighten me" on how the Interior Department operated. They wanted to see Holt's budget for the year and said that NPS technicians would be coming soon to "help." Holt's response that he did not really need their help left the young men undeterred. When Cuthbertson started sending his complaining telegrams to Washington, Holt suggested that in the future he, as park superintendent, should initial all outgoing correspondence. Cuthbertson countered by suggesting that in the future he, Cuthbertson, should initial all of Holt's outgoing correspondence. "These Technicians are a most impractical type of young men," Holt fumed.[20]

The official transfer from the War Department to the NPS took place August 10. This move launched the federal effort to revive interest in the Civil War. Roosevelt issued a new executive order, consolidating administration of all national parks, cemeteries, and monuments in the Department of the Interior. The president abolished numerous commissions and agencies, expecting to save $25 million annually, he claimed. For Vicksburg, Roosevelt's order meant that the national park and the National Military Cemetery would finally be transferred from the War Department to the NPS.[21]

The takeover came after the NPS had already begun to redefine itself. The energetic Horace Albright had taken over as NPS director in 1929. In a flurry of activity, Albright pushed education and historical research, hiring Verne E. Chatelain as the first NPS historian. Chatelain wrote the letter Roosevelt sent to Congress on behalf of the 1935 Historic Sites Act. Speaking through Roosevelt, Chatelain claimed that historic sites would stimulate patriotism, "the respect and love of the citizen for the institutions of his country." The NPS would strengthen citizens' "resolution to defend unselfishly the hallowed traditions and high ideals of America." Interestingly, Albright and Chatelain launched their public history program at precisely the same moment that John D. Rockefeller, Jr., opened Colonial Williamsburg.[22]

Rockefeller expected Colonial Williamsburg to "sell" patriotic history to the American public, and NPS officials picked up this idea and brought it to Vicksburg. Selling history was nothing new, really. Boosters had been marketing Gettysburg since the battle ended, if not before. Some unkind observers charged that greedy Gettysburg entrepreneurs gouged soldiers with overpriced whiskey, water, and bread, and even charged the wounded for transportation. One way to explain Gettysburg's success is that entrepreneurs vigorously and skillfully blended the sacred and the profane, tourism with patriotism. David McConaughy and John Bachelder recognized Gettysburg's tourist potential and consciously marketed the battlefield to tourists and gawkers.[23]

In Vicksburg, New Dealers' marketing schemes encountered generational complications. The War Department had organized its interpretation for veterans, based largely on veterans' memories, as old soldiers made up the bulk of the first wave of visitors.

This resulted in numerous detailed markers devoted to individual units. For example, one marker read,

Steele's Division: Assault, May 22, 1863

Thayer's Brigade, except the 4th Iowa Infantry, took position the afternoon and evening of May 19, under cover of the spur extending north from the Confederate line at this point. Wood's Brigade, except the 78th Ohio, and Manter's were moved from the right and passed in rear of Thayer's on May 22. About 4:00 p.m. the advance was ordered by Gen. Steele, and the three regiments of Thayer's Brigade moved forward in line, followed by Wood's Brigade in column by regiments—the 12th Missouri leading. Thayer's regiments approached close to the Confederate line; the 12th Missouri of Wood's Brigade, climbed the north face of the spur and advanced in support of the leading brigade—the four right companies reaching a position near the Confederate line. The ground gained was held until after dark, when the division retired under orders—Wood's and Manter's Brigades returning to their respective positions on the right. This tablet marks the furthest advance of the 9th Iowa of Thayer's Brigade. Casualties: 13th Illinois, killed 1, wounded 1, total 2; 30th Missouri, wounded 3; 31st Missouri, killed 1, wounded 1, total 2; Lieut. William Robinson killed; aggregate Manter's Brigade, killed 2, wounded 5, total 7; 25th Iowa, killed 5, wounded 27, missing 5, total 37; 31st Iowa, killed 3, wounded 19, total 22, Lieut. Robert Anderson mortally wounded; 3d Missouri, killed 3, wounded 12, missing 3, total 18; 12th Missouri, killed 26, wounded 82, total 108, Major Gustavus Lightfoot, Capt. Christian Andel, Lieuts. Charles L. Kasten and George Eggart killed; aggregate, Woods' Brigade, killed 37, wounded 140, missing 8, total 185; 9th Iowa, killed 18, wounded 60, total 78, Lieuts. Edward Tyrell and Jacob Jones killed, Capts. Florilla M. Kelsey and Frederick S. Washington and Lieut. Leonard L. Martin mortally wounded; 26th Iowa, killed 4, wounded 23, total 27; 30th Iowa, killed 13, wounded 36, missing 1, total 50; Col. Charles H. Abbott, Lieut. James P. Milliken killed, Lieut. David Letner mortally wounded; aggregate Thayer's Brigade killed 25, wounded 119, missing 1, total 155.[24]

No doubt the men of Thayer's Brigade appreciated the detail and contributed to it. By the 1930s, though, the park rarely serviced Civil War veterans. The new generation of visitors had less interest in such precise, detailed information. "They are out for a good time," one guide observed. The NPS staff thought the visitors fell into roughly two groups: "Garden Club people—high class; Mardi Gras people—not so high." Naturally, such folk knew little about the battle. One staffer described visitors' knowledge as "pretty scant."[25]

These tourists often needed help understanding the big picture in a way that earlier visitors had not. As they wandered through the park, they discovered that the hundreds of detailed historical markers made no effort to distinguish the less critical from the more important. For veterans, it was essential not to designate one unit's experience as more vital than the others. Ordinary visitors needed their information hierarchically arranged. One NPS inspector complained that "no general narrative and interpretive markers" existed despite an "obvious need."[26] While some in the NPS called for simplified marking systems, others worried that less complicated interpretations risked criticism from Civil War buffs, who still made up a significant and influential portion of visitors.[27]

The NPS replaced Holt with a new man, L. G. Heider from Connecticut. The local press tried to suggest that little had changed by emphasizing that Heider, like Holt, was a military man. From the perspective of the local population, the big news was that the NPS announced plans to pave thirty miles of park roads and construct a history museum and an administration building. While the locals never openly questioned the reconstruction program, the NPS actually had a checkered history with buildings on historic sites, sometimes blurring the line between the bogus and the authentic.[28] In Vicksburg, the NPS would construct a replica of a plantation mansion, supposedly based on a Natchez building. The NPS built visitors' centers based on local architecture in several of the Civil War parks it took over. The Fredericksburg Visitors' Center went up at roughly the same time as the one in Vicksburg and resembled the local brick architecture.[29]

Holt's nemesis, Stuart Cuthbertson, headed a new history department at the park. Cuthbertson did not wait for the new building but immediately opened a temporary museum underneath the Shirley House, exhibiting uniform buttons and various types of bullets and shell fragments. He also distributed new brochures advertising the park. Like Rigby, he recognized and appreciated that the Illinois Central Railway had "always manifested a particular interest in this park." Cuthbertson credited Illinois Central officials as the "prime movers in securing federal and state legislation, the appropriations, and appointments of the first officials." Like Rigby, the NPS still depended on the Illinois Central to print and distribute "complete and attractive" pamphlets about the park. "Here in Vicksburg," the NPS man wrote, "we are in constant and close contact with the state and district railroad officers."[30]

Cuthbertson planned both historical research at the park and an educational program reaching out to the community.[31] This was no southern operation. Northerners made up the NPS staff stationed at Vicksburg. It seems an almost bizarre thing to say given the South's supposed dedication to its past and history, but Heider and his men passionately believed that they had to sell their park and its history to indifferent locals. The NPS staff organized meetings with civic leaders seeking to excite city residents about Civil War history and the park. Heider explained that he expected his planned program would educate the locals about the park's history so that they could better "sell" it and themselves to outside visitors. But first, native Vicksburgers had to be convinced, Heider recognized. "The primary aim of our educational

VICKSBURG
FOR
THE TOURIST

THE VICKSBURG
NATIONAL
MILITARY PARK
COMMEMORATING THE SIEGE AND
DEFENSE OF THE HISTORIC CITY,
A MOST INSTRUCTIVE AND IMPRESSIVE
OBJECT PAGE OF ONE OF THE
NATION'S MOST INTERESTING
HISTORICAL INCIDENTS

THE NATIONAL
CEMETERY
ONE OF THE MOST PARK-LIKE, LARGEST
AND PLEASINGLY IMPRESSIVE OF
ALL THE NATIONAL CEMETERIES

THE CITY
PICTURESQUELY
OVERLOOKING THE MISSISSIPPI
FROM ITS COMMANDING SITE

Compliments of ILLINOIS CENTRAL SYSTEM Passenger Department
Revised Edition, 1929-1930

The Illinois Central Railroad promoted and advertised Vicksburg National Military Park as a way of promoting travel on its passenger trains. National Archives.

work," Heider explained, "is to awaken in the minds of visitors at the Park new interests in American History." Heider wanted to generate appreciation for "our development as a nation."[32]

Just a month after the NPS took over the park, officials met with Vicksburg's mayor and aldermen to determine just what the New Deal might mean for Vicksburg.[33] Verne Chatelain, the new NPS chief historian, came to Vicksburg, speaking to local businessmen. Chatelain, former chair of the Department of History and Social Sciences at Nebraska State Teachers College, expected to raise professional standards among his rangers. The NPS head Horace Albright aggressively sought historic sites, including Mount Vernon (but not Frederick Douglass's home: he was not significant enough). Chatelain's professional ambitions did not sway him from his chief goal of popularizing American history. He wanted to "breathe . . . life into American history" by offering ordinary Americans "the color, the pageantry, and the dignity of the country's past."[34]

In Vicksburg, Chatelain's vision for the military park went far beyond merely commemorating the Civil War. Chatelain envisioned a park where he could interpret the Mississippi valley's entire history, starting with French and Spanish explorers. To make this happen, Chatelain called for cooperation between locals, state officers, and the federal government. Mississippi must build better highways, Chatelain declared, complaining that Mississippi's rough roads had forced him to leave his car in Memphis rather than risk the drive. No doubt with the Davises' souvenir stand in mind, the NPS said that the city had to clean up neighborhoods around the park. "Uncouth, sloppy, shaggy looking shacks abutting the park" had to be discouraged, Chatelain said. The federal man frankly told Vicksburg's business leaders that Vicksburg was not a city of many beauties. Visitors had to look hard to find beauty in Vicksburg. Instead, Chatelain urged, "The beauty complex of our people could be developed." Vicksburgers often told outsiders they lived in a pretty place indeed. Nonetheless, Chatelain's tough talk won over his audience. According to press accounts, local business leaders liked Chatelain's candor. Vicksburg Mayor John Brunini contacted the Mississippi State Highway Department to plead for better roads. "I will do my best to take care of you," the Mississippi highway man responded, while insisting his highways were not really so bad as Chatelain imagined. Chatelain should have given them a try instead of taking the train, he observed.[35]

Cuthbertson headed a staff of two. All three NPS historians learned their Civil War and southern history at northern institutions. Cuthbertson had earned his A.B. degree at the University of Illinois in 1925, then had finished all the course work necessary for a Ph.D. except writing his dissertation. He had gone to some of the nation's very best graduate schools, studying at the University of Chicago and Columbia. Before coming to Vicksburg, he had worked as an assistant professor of literature at Washington and Jefferson College. Cuthbertson's assistant, J. Walter Coleman, earned his B.S. degree at Pennsylvania State Teacher's College before teaching in Pennsylvania high schools. He earned his M.A. degree at Pennsylvania State College in 1931. Cuthbertson's other assistant, Olaf T. Hagan, came from Minnesota, where he had worked as a junior high school principal before winning his M.A. degree at the University of Minnesota in 1930. Hagan had been working as a teaching assistant at the University of Minnesota's Department of History before joining the NPS.[36]

What these students of history understood about the nineteenth-century South came primarily from Ulrich B. Phillips and William Archibald Dunning. Phillips had published *American Negro Slavery* in 1918 and *Life and Labor in the Old South* in 1929. For decades, historians regarded Phillips's work as the most authoritative scholarship on slavery. Born in Georgia in 1877, Phillips held professorships at the University of Michigan and Yale. He viewed slavery as a "school" for barbaric Africans. "The civilizing of the Negroes was not merely a consequence of definite schooling but a fruit of plantation life itself," he wrote. "Notoriously primitive, uncouth, improvident and inconstant," blacks needed

The National Park Service photographed the park's entrance to show that shabby and abandoned commercial structures crowded close to the battleground. National Archives.

the help whites offered through slavery, according to Phillips, writing in 1929.[37] W. E. B. Du Bois dismissed Phillips's work as "a defense of American slavery."[38] William Archibald Dunning's 1907 book *Reconstruction: Political and Economic* was no less authoritative and no less racist. Born in New Jersey, Dunning taught at Columbia from the 1880s into the 1920s. The Ku Klux Klan, Dunning wrote, was "the inevitable extra-legal protest" of whites "against their subjection to the freedmen and northerners."[39] The students of these two scholars often expressed a racism even more candid than that of their mentors. After studying under Dunning, James W. Garner griped about the "unreliable character of negro labor." "Even now," Garner observed, "the negro is not a model of industry, frugality, and foresight."[40]

If NPS historians sought information about Mississippi, they could turn to Garner's *Reconstruction in Mississippi*. While Garner taught at the University of Illinois from 1904 to 1938, Cuthbertson never took one of his classes. A political science professor, Garner taught "American National Government," "Continental European Government," and "International Law: Law of War and Neutrality."[41] That Cuthbertson never set foot in Garner's classroom matters little. The influence of Phillips and Dunning was pervasive; Cuthbertson apparently learned little about slavery, the Civil War, and Reconstruction that would contradict Phillips and Dunning. He might have read Du Bois's revisionist *Black Reconstruction*, but only if he encountered an unusually unorthodox professor. If Cuthbertson had not already read Garner's *Reconstruction in Mississippi* before he started building the Reconstruction portion of his museum, he likely sought it out while researching the topic.

In fact, there is not much evidence that Cuthbertson took his research beyond Vicksburg's Civil War military experience. By 1935, Cuthbertson had ensconced himself in Study Room 4 at the Library of Congress, searching for material on the Vicksburg siege. His reports indicate how totally the military side of the siege absorbed his attention. Cuthbertson went to the Adjutant

General's Office, Old Records Division, to find the names of Vicksburg soldiers. He searched the logbooks of naval vessels stationed around Vicksburg at the naval War Records Division. He identified diaries, journals, memoirs, and collections of letters relevant to the siege. At the Library of Congress, Cuthbertson found the Comstock collection, notebooks with sketches of federal positions. The Porter Collection occupied twenty-one boxes, thirty-six packages, and one wooden case, all "thoroughly disarranged."[42] Using such records and others, Cuthbertson labored through the summer of 1935, constructing a roll of Confederate and federal military organizations present during the siege.[43] In the fall, Cuthbertson journeyed down to Richmond, visiting the Virginia Historical Society, the Virginia State Library, and the Confederate Museum, looking for source materials on Vicksburg's siege.[44]

Cuthbertson wanted to make the park a "tourist mecca." After studying the numbers of park visitors, Cuthbertson decided that attracting half a million visitors yearly to his story of slavery, Civil War, and Reconstruction was "no pipe dream." He planned to contract with a movie company to make travelogues about historic Vicksburg to be shown in movie theaters all over the country. He organized a children's essay contest and systematically cultivated contacts with civic organizations. Universities should send classes to the park, Cuthbertson thought. Park personnel would compile mailing lists and produce brochures and tourist maps.[45]

In addition to Cuthbertson's ambitious outreach programs, park staff continued Rigby's research among veterans, sending form letters to surviving veterans asking for recollections. Heider announced his intention to recreate "the Vicksburg scene in 1863 in its entirety." More than Rigby, Heider sought information about ordinary soldiers' day-to-day existence during the siege.[46]

Cuthbertson preached what he called the gospel of relics. One relic, Cuthbertson lectured Vicksburg residents, might provoke more thought than an entire lecture. "Dilettantes" had been collecting relics for years; this would not be like that. Instead of cabinets of curios, Cuthbertson would display pictures, models, maps, and charts in "carefully planned and organized interpretive and stimulating exhibits." The result would not just be "interesting" but "significant and purposeful." The heart of the museum would be a large relief map of the park, constructed by the NPS, showing fortifications and troop positions. Four more models would illustrate troop movements through the campaign.[47] Cuthbertson expected to build not only a museum but a reference library as well. He considered persuading Vicksburgers to join him to be vital to this effort to rejuvenate the park. Local advisory groups would assist the federal men, and thousands of school children would tour the park. By December, the NPS had published a detailed guide to the park, summarizing its historical features. Impressed with the whole NPS effort, Vicksburg's mayor announced that a new day had dawned in the park's history. Heider and Cuthbertson's enthusiasm and their earnest presentation impressed the Vicksburgers.[48]

Using some of the CCC enrollees as guides, the NPS designed a new tour to show off the rejuvenated park. On December 15, the NPS inaugurated its tour program. By noon, the service estimated that 900 persons, traveling in sixty-eight cars and fourteen school buses, had begun touring the park. Heider stationed his staff at key points along the route to explain the history of the siege.[49]

The northerners running the park wrote a Civil War narrative that southerners found appealing. In a lecture to a local high school, for example, Cuthbertson told the students that slavery had little to do with the Civil War. The real struggle, he explained, pitted states' rights against national power. At the same time, Cuthbertson wanted to promote national patriotism. In Cuthbertson's narrative, human history became a story of ever-increasing loyalties. Men first devoted themselves to their families, then to tribes, "and finally to the loyalty that exists today to national government and to one's fellowmen the world over." The Vicksburg siege, Cuthbertson opined, had not only decided the

Civil War but had also been a turning point in the rise of national loyalty.[50]

In another lecture, Junior Park Historian H. C. Landru explained that a clash of economic interests had caused the Civil War. Northern industrial interests determined their region's course both at the outset of the war and after, in Reconstruction. Whatever humanitarian feelings northerners felt, Landru said, could just as easily have been directed toward "the congested conditions of the slums, dangerous factory conditions and similar industrial abuses." They were not, however, because "politically the north reflected the views of its wealthiest group," Landru charged.[51] The northern historians had accepted the southern mythology as incorporated in the historical works of the time.

The NPS did not confine its efforts to the park. They identified historic sites worthy of preservation outside the park, in the city of Vicksburg, and planned to use CCC men to refurbish these sites.[52] The NPS used Natchez's famous pilgrimage as a model, hoping to replicate that success in Vicksburg.[53] In 1931, members of Natchez garden club had organized a tour of homes for the second annual convention of the Mississippi State Confederation of Garden Clubs. The next year, the first official pilgrimage opened twenty-six homes to visitors from thirty-seven states. These tourists, according to Natchez officials, spent $50,000 in local restaurants, hotels, and shops. Katherine Grafton Miller, originator and general chairman of the Natchez Pilgrimage, came to Vicksburg, dressed in her antebellum costume, showing slides of Natchez mansions. White Vicksburgers hoped Miller's success in Natchez might transfer to their city. Miller agreed to organize a new group called the "Descendants of the Participants of the Campaign, Siege, and Defense of Vicksburg." Miller expected to organize chapters all across the country filled with people eager to spread the word about Vicksburg.[54] She also wanted to institute a Vicksburg Pilgrimage similar to the Natchez operation. Miller predicted that her new organization, combined with the Vicksburg Pilgrimage and the NPS-organized free park tours, would generate a feeling of excitement in Vicksburg not seen since the 1917 reunion.[55]

Miller's siege descendants held their first meeting in 1936. The meeting included a historical pageant with "interludes," or scenes depicting significant moments in Vicksburg's history. The pageant actors performed scenes from 1698, 1802, 1830, and the Civil War. The Civil War scene focused on fraternizing between "Johnny and Yank," showing soldiers from the opposing armies meeting between the lines at night. At their meeting, the descendants announced that their first goal was to commemorate the heroism of soldiers fighting at Vicksburg, one of the great battles of modern times. The descendants also hoped to promote tourist visitation of the Vicksburg battleground by descendants and the citizenry.[56]

The NPS brought history to Vicksburg with the latest audiovisual technology. A Department of the Interior photographer filmed the park in April 1934, making movies that could be used to create a travelogue of the park. At the same time, the park historians received a slide projector that would allow them to illustrate their lectures to local groups.[57]

While NPS personnel busily drafted their historical narrative of the Vicksburg campaign, the CCC sculpted the landscape. Going far beyond Holt's original idea of planting trees, the CCC enrollees filled in gullies, smoothed over cavernous washouts, terraced the land, and laid sod. Anyone riding through the park would have noticed a dramatic transformation. To a considerable extent, the Vicksburg battleground today is the product of CCC landscaping.[58]

The NPS quickly won over Vicksburg's press. In October, the *Vicksburg Evening Post* urged its readers to interest themselves in their city's Civil War history.[59] By the spring of 1934, the first phase of the NPS plan to "sell" the park seemed to be paying off. "Vicksburg," the *Evening Post* announced, "is rapidly becoming 'Military Park Conscious.'" Statisticians of the NPS documented the success of efforts to spark a revival of interest in the park. In November 1933, only 245 visitors ventured into the park. In

The Civilian Conservation Corps landscaped the battleground, filling in gullies, laying sod, and building terraces. National Archives.

March 1934, 2,395 visitors made the trip. The number of school groups increased dramatically, from sixteen in the first four months of 1935 to thirty-two for the same four months in 1936 and forty-seven in 1937.[60]

In 1934, white Vicksburgers celebrated national Memorial Day on park grounds for the first time. Heider organized a Robert E. Lee birthday celebration. The local high school band performed, and the United Daughters of the Confederacy provided a tribute. Heider also organized segregated Memorial Day celebrations. Blacks held their observances from 6:00 A.M. until 2:00 P.M., while whites started at 2:30 P.M. "Comment on all sides was positive," Heider wrote.[61] Mayor J. C. Hamilton described it as a historic day in Vicksburg, "The first general community observance of National Decoration Day." Whites had already commemorated the Confederate dead on Confederate Memorial Day. On National Memorial Day, the mayor explained, "We come . . . to honor their gallant foes" as well as American soldiers who perished in other wars.[62]

But while Hamilton emphasized the novelty of white people celebrating National Memorial Day, Judge Harris Dickson took satisfaction that the "general community observance" did not include African Americans. Whites intended to appropriate what had been a black-dominated celebration. Dickson traced the origins of commemorating fallen soldiers to "the first faint dawn of time" when "the white savage from whom we are descended" set up memorials. In 1927, Dickson had scolded his audience for failing to live up the ideals of the Confederate dead. Now Dickson imagined the Civil War dead arising from their graves, 17,000 strong, and once again asking, "My son, are you carrying on?" The answer, Dickson believed, was quite different than had been the case in 1927. Truthfully, Dickson said, white Vicksburg citizens could now say, "'We are.'" The fight now attacked poverty and unemployment, Dickson said, a battle as fierce as the Civil War.[63]

The NPS had won over Dickson, an important achievement in Vicksburg. Dickson was Vicksburg's most accomplished writer,

The National Park Service made this photograph of the last Confederate veteran of the Vicksburg siege, James W. Hazelett, with Mississippi Governor M. S. Conner. National Archives.

an author of historical novels, including *The Black Wolf's Creed* and *The Ravenels*, as well as articles in the *Saturday Evening Post*. Dickson collaborated with NPS personnel to produce a walking-tour script for the Vicksburg park, "A Story-Telling Ramble with Harris Dickson." In his talk, Dickson praised the park's organization as "compact and efficient." He pronounced the NPS's work "marvelous." Vicksburg's battlefield "is perhaps the most interesting on the globe." The CCC boys, Dickson wrote, behaved themselves, did not get into trouble, and fought erosion to preserve the terrain. "A bully bunch of kids," Dickson said. Dickson's narrative does not mention Gettysburg but compares Vicksburg to Hannibal's campaigns, Omdurman, and Waterloo. Speaking from his own travels, Dickson knowledgeably and favorably compared Vicksburg's state of preservation with those other, more exotic battlefields. Dickson's script is interspersed with notes to the NPS historians requesting information. "Col Heider will give me data," he writes at one point. Later: "Mr. Landru will give me data on Railroad redoubt for insertion here." He was using the park's staff as his research assistants, and they were using him as their dramatist.[64]

Vicksburg whites petitioned Congress to allow the National Cemetery to inter Confederate soldiers as well as the Union dead and build a marker commemorating the ideals of the Confederacy.[65] That effort failed, but when the NPS opened its new museum on November 21, 1936, Heider made sure the first visitors were Confederate descendants. Heider escorted the ladies of the United Daughters of the Confederacy through the museum, built to resemble "the typical ante-bellum home of Southern romance." The ladies found Vicksburg's history from European exploration to the present on display. Heider boasted that his new exhibits represented the latest in museum development, the first "complete" NPS museum east of the Mississippi River. Just as Cuthbertson had promised, Heider explained that the museum did not merely display relics but also interpreted events. "Ideas dramatically visualized rather than a junkshop array of miscellaneous and unrelated objects" was the museum's aim, according to one Vicksburg newspaper.[66]

If the ladies worried about this Connecticut Yankee's interpretation of their history, their tour quickly reassured them. Bringing "moonlight and romance" back with a vengeance, Heider transported his guests into another age. "Vivid coloring" and "graphic illustration of the stately homes and colorful life of the period" carried them into the antebellum era. The ladies encountered the NPS's picture of the "Southern chivalric ideal," a system based "on personal honor between gentlemen and kindness and sympathy for those of inferior position." Mannequins posed as a gentleman and a lady, wearing aristocratic dress from 1850. Another exhibit showed slaves picking cotton under the watchful eye of an overseer, "sitting quietly by under a tree covered with Spanish Moss."[67]

The museum did not overlook the harsher realities of southern life. Another exhibit explained the South's "negro problem." The

The National Park Service built a replica of an antebellum mansion for its museum. Courtesy Vicksburg National Military Park.

ladies read a label that told them that "at the close of the war the vote was extended to the negro. Being illiterate they were easily swayed by unscrupulous whites. Told that the land would be divided among them and that they were the equals of the whites, the negroes refused employment, turned to vagrancy and committed many crimes against their former masters." The exhibit went on to say that blacks "monopolized" political offices, voting themselves exorbitant salaries. "Relief" came in 1874 when whites reclaimed city offices in an election. Subsequently, whites ousted Peter Crosby, the illiterate black man serving as sheriff. In this "history," inaccuracies ran amok. African Americans never "monopolized" Mississippi political offices. Crosby was quite literate.[68]

Later, as World War II raged in Europe and across the Pacific, visitation into Vicksburg's park declined. Gas rationing took its toll. Young male employees at the park, eager to join the military, could hardly concentrate on their work. The superintendent, James R. McConaghie, found himself so shorthanded that he had to patrol the park personally and sometimes stand at the museum doorway to collect entrance fees from those few tourists stopping by. By 1945, though, McConaghie had figured out how to win national attention for the park. The superintendent organized a Fourth of July celebration, the first, he falsely claimed, since July 4, 1863. The NPS always carefully tracked its press clippings, and Heider's Fourth celebration hit the papers coast to coast. The Vicksburg papers reported that the festivities marked the first "wholehearted" and "all-out" Fourth celebration. The Associated Press quoted an address delivered by Major General Edward H. Brooks boasting of Vicksburg's new spirit of unity. Officials of the NPS congratulated McConaghie for his initiative.[69] In 1946 and 1947, Vicksburg again celebrated the Fourth but called the festivities its "Carnival of the Confederacy." Dwight Eisenhower came to town in 1947, drawing thousands to hear his speech.[70]

It sometimes seems that the white South ultimately rebuffed the New Deal. But the New Deal further implanted the national government in Vicksburg's Civil War memory. Federal officers sentimentalized the Old South and the Confederacy, presenting a history the most determined Lost Cause enthusiast could admire. The federal government emerged as a more permanent fixture on Vicksburg's Civil War landscape.

Notes

1. *Vicksburg Evening Post*, October 12, 1936.
2. Author's interview with Blanche Terry, August 20, 1997.
3. Holt to Alivia Davis, March 30, 1932, file 601, box 2570, NPS/ Vicksburg records, National Archives, College Park, Maryland. For the NPS decision to limit guide service to males, see W. H. Noble, "Employment of Women as Park Guides," March 17, 1933, file 230.14, box 77, NPS/Vicksburg records, National Archives, College Park, Maryland.
4. Holt to Z. M. Davis, May 17, 1932; John Brunini to Holt, July 1, 1932; Holt to Brunini, July 8, 1932; Ben F. Cameron to Holt, July 9, 1932; L. G. Heider to director, NPS, February 2, 1935; Heider to director, NPS, March 28, 1935; John Brunini to Heider, January 9, 1936; and

Toxey Hall to Attorney General, Lands Division, December 1, 1938, file 601, box 2570,NPS/Vicksburg records, National Archives, College Park, Maryland. Z. M. Davis, *History of the Siege of Vicksburg and Maps of the Vicksburg National Military Park* (Vicksburg, Miss.: n.d.). A copy of this tourist brochure is in the Old Court House Museum collection, Vicksburg.

5. Holt to Brunini, July 8, 1932, file 601, box 2570, NPS/Vicksburg records, National Archives, College Park, Maryland.

6. Holt to Brunini, July 1, 1932, file 601, box 2570, NPS/Vicksburg records, National Archives, College Park, Maryland; *New York Times*, July 3, November 8, 1932.

7. Samuel I. Rosenman, comp., *The Public Papers and Addresses of Franklin D. Roosevelt*, vol. 2, *The Year of Crisis, 1933* (New York: Random House, 1938), 80–81; 48 Stats. 22–23; John A. Pandiani, "The Crime Control Corps: An Invisible New Deal Program," *British Journal of Sociology* 33 (1982): 348–58; Eric Gotham, "The Ambiguous Practices of the Civilian Conservation Corps," *Social History* 17 (1992): 229–49.

8. Conrad L. Worth, *Parks, Politics, and the People* (Norman: University of Oklahoma Press, 1980), 65–157.

9. Forrest McDonald, *States' Rights and the Union: Imperium in Imperio, 1776–1876* (Lawrence: University Press of Kansas, 2000).

10. *Vicksburg Evening Post*, June 23, 1933; John Ray Skates, "From Enchantment to Disillusionment: A Southern Editor Views the New Deal," *Southern Quarterly* 5 (1967): 363–80; Daniel C. Vogt, "Government Reform, the 1890 Constitution, and Mike Conner," *Journal of Mississippi History* 48 (1986): 43–56.

11. *Vicksburg Evening Post*, September 12, 1933.

12. *Vicksburg Evening Post*, September 4, 1933. African Americans had experience in playing this game. In World War I, whites had also felt they had to call on blacks to support the federal program, in that case to preserve food for the war effort. See P. M. Harding to B. W. Griffith, October 9, 1917, Old Court House Museum, Vicksburg.

13. *Vicksburg Evening Post*, April 27, May 22, July 27, September 4, 1933.

14. J. B. Holt, "Reforestation for Vicksburg National Military Park," April 13, 1933, file 688, box 78, Records of the War Department Relating to National Parks, Records of the National Park Service, RG

79, National Archives, College Park, Maryland. Hereinafter cited as NPS/CCC records.

15. Kramer, Memorandum Carrier Sheet, May 4, 1933, NPS/CCC records.

16. Horace M. Albright to J. B. Holt, June 2, 1933, NPS/CCC records.

17. There would ultimately be four CCC camps on the Vicksburg battlefield.

18. Holt to O. G. Taylor, June 24, 1933, NPS/CCC records.

19. Holt to Quartermaster, IV Corps Area, June 27, 1933, NPS/CCC records.

20. Holt to Quartermaster, IV Corps area, June 30, 1933, NPS/CCC records.

21. Rosenman, *The Public Papers and Addresses of Franklin D. Roosevelt*, 223.

22. Barry Mackintosh, "The National Park Service Moves into Historical Interpretation," *Public Historian* 9 (spring 1987): 54; Cary Carson, "Colonial Williamsburg and the Practice of Interpretive Planning in American History Museums," *Public Historian* 20 (summer 1998): 20–21.

23. Jim Weeks, *Gettysburg: Memory, Market, and an American Shrine* (Princeton, N.J.: Princeton University Press, 2003), 13–53.

24. William T. Rigby, "Siege and Defence of Vicksburg and the Vicksburg National Military Park" (pamphlet published by the Illinois Central Railroad, 1909). This pamphlet contains the text of all position markers in place in 1909.

25. "Vicksburg National Military Park—Inspection by Ronald F. Lee, May 18–19, 1940," Vicksburg National Military Park correspondence, 1940–1959, History Park Files, National Park Service, Washington, D.C.

26. "Vicksburg National Military Park—Inspection by Ronald F. Lee, May 18–19, 1940," Vicksburg National Military Park correspondence, 1940–1959, History Park Files, National Park Service, Washington, D.C.

27. Mackintosh, "The National Park Service Moves into Historical Interpretation," 56.

28. The service inherited a bogus George Washington "birthplace" but as late as 1956 hesitated to admit the ersatz replica had been built

over the wrong foundation. As late as 1984, the service would not admit that its Abraham Lincoln birthplace was inauthentic. Mackintosh, "The National Park Service Moves into Historical Interpretation," 57.

29. *Vicksburg Evening Post*, March 20, 1934.

30. Stuart Cuthbertson to Miss Story through Mr. Chatelain, April 5, 1935, file 504, box 2560, NPS records, National Archives, College Park, Maryland.

31. *Vicksburg Evening Post*, October 20, 1933.

32. Superintendent's Monthly Report, November 1932, file 207-002.4, part 1, box 2560, NPS records, National Archives, College Park, Maryland.

33. *Vicksburg Evening Post*, September 21, 1933.

34. John Bodnar, *Remaking America: Public Memory, Commemoration, and Patriotism in the Twentieth Century* (Princeton, N.J.: Princeton University Press, 1992), 175–77.

35. *Vicksburg Evening Post*, September 22, 1933; Brown Williams to John Brunini, October 17, 1933, file 618, box 2572, Vicksburg National Military Park, National Military Parks, RG 79, National Park Service Central Classified File, National Archives, College Park, Maryland.

36. *Vicksburg Evening Post*, January 1, 1934.

37. Ulrich B. Phillips, *Life and Labor in the Old South* (Boston: Little, Brown, 1929), 198–200; Merton L. Dillon, *Ulrich Bonnell Phillips: Historian of the Old South* (Baton Rouge: Louisiana State University Press, 1985); John Herbert Roper, *U. B. Phillips: A Southern Mind* (Macon, Ga.: Mercer University Press, 1984). For a useful collection of writings about Phillips, see John David Smith and John C. Inscoe, eds., *Ulrich Bonnell Phillips: A Southern Historian and His Critics* (Athens: University of Georgia Press, 1993).

38. Du Bois, "Reviews of American Negro Slavery," in Smith and Inscoe, *Ulrich Bonnell Phillips*, 86.

39. Dunning, *Reconstruction: Political and Economic, 1865–1877* (New York: Harper and Brothers, 1907), 121–23.

40. James W. Garner, *Reconstruction in Mississippi* (1901; repr., Baton Rouge: Louisiana State University Press, 1968), 137.

41. *University of Illinois Annual Register, 1923–1924* (Urbana: University of Illinois, 1924), 330–33; *University of Illinois Annual Register, 1924–1925* (Urbana: University of Illinois, 1925), 332–35; *University of*

Illinois Annual Register, 1925–1926 (Urbana: University of Illinois, 1926), 332–35; Masatomo Ayabe to Vernon Burton, October 22, 2002, e-mail in possession of the author (thanks to Vernon Burton for this information).

42. Stuart Cuthbertson, "Report of Historical Technician, Vicksburg National Military Park, July 15–July 30, 1935," Vicksburg National Military Park correspondence, 1934–1959, History Park Files, National Park Service, Washington, D.C.

43. Stuart Cuthbertson, "Progress Report, Continuation of Search, Federal Records of Events," September 20, 1935, Vicksburg National Military Park correspondence, 1934–1959, History Park Files, National Park Service, Washington, D.C.

44. Cuthbertson to Chatelain, October 7, 1935, Vicksburg National Military Park correspondence, 1934–1959, History Park Files, National Park Service, Washington, D.C.

45. Cuthbertson to W. N. Miner, December 23, 1933, folder 133, box 6, Administrative Series, Vicksburg National Military Park, Vicksburg, Mississippi.

46. Heider to Seth W. Jones, February 9, 1936, folder 136, box 6, Administrative Series, Vicksburg National Military Park, Vicksburg, Mississippi.

47. Stuart Cuthbertson and Ralph Lewis, "Interpreting the Vicksburg Story," not dated, Vicksburg National Military Park Papers, Missouri Historical Society, St. Louis.

48. *Vicksburg Evening Post*, November 15, December 14, 1933.

49. *Vicksburg Evening Post*, December 15, 1933.

50. *Vicksburg Evening Post*, March 23, 1934.

51. *Vicksburg Evening Post*, March 19, 1936.

52. *Vicksburg Evening Post*, November 13, 1933.

53. *Vicksburg Evening Post*, March 30, 1934.

54. Jack Davis, *Race against Time: Culture and Separation in Natchez since 1930* (Baton Rouge: Louisiana State University Press, 2001), 51–57; *Vicksburg Evening Post*, January 22, March 16, 1936.

55. *Vicksburg Evening Post*, March 19, 1936.

56. *Vicksburg Evening Post*, March 28, 1936.

57. *Vicksburg Evening Post*, April 11, 1934.

58. Park officials went to great lengths to document their landscaping. Numerous photographs show gullied sections of the park before

and after CCC work. See, for example, boxes 2572, 2573, and 2574, National Military Parks, Vicksburg, National Park Service Classified File RG 79, National Archives, College Park, Maryland. The CCC also launched Mississippi's state park system, which did not exist prior to the New Deal. Justin C. Eaddy, "Mississippi's State Parks: The New Deal's Mixed Legacy," *Journal of Mississippi History* 65 (summer 2003): 147–68.

59. *Vicksburg Evening Post,* October 20, 1933.

60. *Vicksburg Evening Post,* March 10, April 23, 1934; May 2, 1937.

61. *Vicksburg Evening Post,* January 16, 1935; Heider to director, January 18, 1935, file 502, box 2567, NPS/NARA records; Heider to director, June 2, 1934, file 502, box 2567, NPS records, National Archives, College Park, Maryland.

62. *Vicksburg Evening Post,* May 31, 1934.

63. *Vicksburg Evening Post,* May 31, 1934.

64. Harris Dickson, "Vicksburg National Military Park," Works Progress Administration Papers, RG 60, Mississippi Department of Archives and History, Jackson. For Dickson, see "Warren County Historical Research Project No. 27—the Bar," in Dickson, "Vicksburg National Military Park."

65. *Vicksburg Evening Post,* June 8, 1935.

66. *Vicksburg Evening Post,* November 23, 1936; May 19, 1937.

67. H. C. Landru, January 18, 1937, "The Vicksburg National Military Park Museum," folder 39, box 3 Vicksburg National Military Park (VNMP).

68. Landru to Ned J. Burns, January 16, 1937, folder 40, box 3 Vicksburg National Military Park (VNMP); Eric Foner, *Freedom's Lawmakers: A Directory of Black Officeholders during Reconstruction* (New York: Oxford University Press, 1993), 54.

69. James R. McConaghie, Monthly Narrative Report, August 10, 1945, file 207-02.3, box 2564; and Hillory A. Tolson to McConaghie, August 24, 1945, file 502, box 2567, RG 79, National Park Service Central Classified File, National Military Parks, Vicksburg, Mississippi, National Archives, College Park, Maryland; *Vicksburg Evening Post,* July 2, 1945; *Chicago Tribune,* July 5, 1945.

70. *Vicksburg Herald,* June 30, July 4, 1946; and July 2, 5, 1947; *Vicksburg Evening Post,* July 4, 1947.

EPILOGUE

I N June 1863, an army doctor named Thomas Hawley walked about one of the battlefields around Vicksburg. He was not alone, but nonetheless he found the landscape achingly empty. Hawley told his parents that he felt "two hundred miles south away from the haunts of men." Hawley tried to explain why he felt so lonely: "Who cares to linger or live near the scene of bloody carnage where the ground is saturated with the life current of our fellow men?" Hawley looked about; every hill was a cemetery and every gully a grave for tens or even hundreds of corpses, "once the grace of vigorous manhood but now their limbs devoid of flesh, refused a covering by mother earth protrude as if they would fain be monuments of fallen heroes who died victims to a false idea." Hawley saw long mounds of earth with a plain board giving an officer's name or simply saying that twenty-five or a hundred Union men lay buried there. As he walked over the tortured earth, Hawley could see where the battle raged hottest by counting the dead. Hawley gauged the soldiers' marksmanship by looking at the trees: "These [shots] are but seldom higher than a mans head, recording distinctly the shur aim . . . of the men engaged." Hawley gazed into the faces of Union dead and wrote, "Our men mostly old veterans and I think the enemy fought well."[1]

Eighty years later, Hawley would not have recognized the Vicksburg battleground. True, even now a ranger will occasionally come across an unexploded Civil War shell and call on Army Ordinance Disposal soldiers for help. At the end of the twentieth century, Civil War relic hunters still found human remains.[2] Woods and underbrush still cover some areas. Much of the park, though, is not rough at all. The tourists glide through smoothly crafted glades, neatly sodded and terraced by the Civilian Conservation Corps. For the average visitor, the gullies and hills once filled with Civil War dead are hard to find. The scene that greets most tourists is one of neatly mowed hills and dales, dotted with detailed markers spelling out the exact position of many regiments. Majestic state monuments glisten in the bright sun. The national government has remade the landscape, crafting the earth and interpreting the meaning of what it has made.

For a generation after Appomattox, patriotic orators like John A. T. Hull invoked the North's Civil War victory, "the swelling triumph of that moment," to kindle patriotic feelings in a new generation:

> How the proud huzzas rang out as the cavalry dashed by to complete the work of the Infantry and artillery,
>
> Singing in Grand Chorus "We will rally around the flag boys, rally once again." We went forever forward until the victorious armies of the west struck hands with the brave men of the army of the Potomac. . . .
>
> Let the young be taught the lesson of patriotism, and standing with uncovered heads by the side of the graves of our dead, hearing the story of how and for what they died, light the fire of patriotism in their young hearts and make them vow fealty to liberty and union.
>
> Let the father teach his child that the flag of his country represents more than a pleasing blending of colors. . . .
>
> Wherever it floats, it dissolves the chains of slavery, breaks down oppression and ennobles man.[3]

All nations treasure their soldiers' valor. The mythology of war is a source of strength, a resource for any nation or national movement. For this reason, every marker on the battleground went in only after approval by the War Department or the Park Service. Federal officers carefully guard the Vicksburg battleground to this day. National Park Service historians design the exhibits in the new visitor's center.

As it sculpted Vicksburg's Civil War landscape, the national authority mostly surrendered whatever weak and timid vision it had of the Civil War as an act of racial justice. The federal government hosted festivities where racists proclaimed their creed. Federal officers told schoolchildren that slavery had nothing to do with the Civil War. The National Park Service celebrated Robert E. Lee's birthday, organized a segregated Memorial Day, and hosted a Jim Crow Fourth of July celebration that it trumpeted to the world as fresh evidence of American patriotism and unity. The federal government "won" at Vicksburg, but it did so by embracing every element in the white southern racial creed. When white southerners' interest in the Lost Cause flagged, the national government stirred it up again.

Yet the fact remains that, however compromised, the national government emerged from the Civil War and its celebrations and remembrances more deeply embedded in ordinary Americans' lives than before the war. The campaign to make Gettysburg the essential Civil War battlefield illustrates the North's early and firm grasp on the Civil War commemoration effort. Northern writers swiftly anointed Gettysburg as central to the war. More than that, it had to be the greatest battle in human history, surpassing Waterloo. William Rigby did not begin buying the Vicksburg battlefield until 1899; David McConaughy started the Gettysburg Battlefield Memorial Association and purchased East Cemetery Hill, Culp's Hill, and the Round Tops in 1863. Major General John Reynolds's staff commenced collecting funds to honor their fallen commander within months of his falling. The Reynolds monument did not go up until 1872, a delay that allowed the First Minnesota volunteers the honor of putting up the first Gettysburg monument—in 1867.[4] Even twenty years after the battle, anti-Confederate feeling animated the Gettysburg commemorators. To be sure, LaSalle Pickett came along to celebrate the Lost Cause with her forgeries[5] and plagerisms.[6] But the northern/federal effort to enshrine Gettysburg could absorb the Lost Cause and even turn such Confederate efforts to the greater good: making Gettysburg preeminent. One writer explains Gettysburg's popularity by pointing out that it featured dramatic infantry movements, while Vicksburg, a city under siege, had to surrender eventually.[7] This hardly seems a satisfactory explanation: Grant's daring movement through Louisiana on a single road was not boring. Untrained and outnumbered black troops pitted against determined attackers is a story that does not lack drama.

The South's invasion of the North, white men fighting other white men in Pennsylvania, became a better Civil War symbol than a campaign across Louisiana and Mississippi that included Sherman's Chickasaw Bayou disaster, black soldiers, slavery, Grant's failed attacks of May 19 and 22, the plodding siege, and emancipation. The North's Vicksburg victory was inelegant. For a nation seeking to see the Civil War in nonracial terms, as a white man's contest, a battle in Pennsylvania worked better than one in Mississippi. Making Vicksburg the representative Civil War battle ran the risk that someone might make Milliken's Bend the high-water mark of northern racial egalitarianism—better to mythologize Confederate General George E. Pickett's failed Gettysburg charge as the white South's "high-water mark." Vicksburg's second-place finish to Gettysburg was no happenstance. It records the North's command of Civil War memory.

So, too, does the National Park and National Cemetery in Vicksburg, a permanent federal presence in the Deep South city. The war shifted the balance of power between the states and the national authority; the Vicksburg park memorializes many things, but it marks that shift of power too.

Local historians did have an alternative to the park. In 1937, the Warren County Board of Supervisors adopted plans for a new courthouse building. Two years later, the county abandoned the old courthouse, a striking structure on a hill dominating the town since its construction between 1858 and 1860. When word circulated that the supervisors might demolish the old structure, the United Daughters of the Confederacy registered a protest.

The most serious fight to save the building, though, came from Mrs. Eva Whitaker Davis. She moved quickly and determinedly to turn the old building into a history museum dedicated to Jefferson Davis. She saw it as "a hallowed shrine of historical interest." Rumors circulated that the federal government might take the building and turn it over to the National Park Service. The very idea revolted Davis, and she fought back, peppering her senator with a flurry of mail.[8]

Davis had long been interested in Vicksburg's history. She had worked at the 1917 reunion, providing information to visiting veterans. "I live here," she declared in 1952, "I grew up with the park and you might say 'communed with God and Nature in its environs.'" Davis completely agreed with Park Service officials that the park needed to be "sold" to an indifferent public. "I am sorry that our people have not been taught to revere" the park, she lamented.[9] Davis probably saw park promotion as a tool to encourage patriotism. She admired Joe McCarthy and feared that "America is being insidiously sold down the communist drain."[10]

Her letters on behalf of the old courthouse went unanswered, but in 1947, Davis's efforts bore fruit when the supervisors finally and reluctantly agreed to turn the building over to Davis's Warren County Historical Society. Davis herself sifted through the trash, scrubbing away the dirt, searching for relics she could put on display. One newspaper explained that Davis had rolled up her sleeves and saved the building "from sheer love of the old and historic." In fact, she turned it into a monument to the Confederacy and Jefferson Davis.[11] Insofar as the Confederacy had an alternative to the National Park Service and Vicksburg National Military Park, the Old Court House Museum was it, becoming a shrine to Jefferson Davis and the center for local history in Vicksburg.

The Old Court House Museum could be seen as a monument to white southerners' continuing commitment to the Lost Cause. Or perhaps it marked the Park Service's success at "selling" history to white Vicksburgers. The Park Service came to Vicksburg wanting to sell Civil War history. Eva Davis might have found her interest in history without the Park Service. She was, without question, "sold" on history and commemorating the Confederacy. The year Eva Davis opened her doors was a "Confederate Carnival" year, a Fourth of July celebration inspired by the National Park Service's 1945 Fourth festivities. But even the Old Court House Museum is a compromised alternative to the park. Visitors often go to both. And Eva Davis agreed that the park had to be sold to locals. She helped in the selling herself to promote patriotism and fight communism.

Another Vicksburger, Myrlie Beasley, remembered her hometown as having a reputation for good race relations. She could not understand why, "but it was there, bragged about, referred to on special occasions, believed in proudly by the whites and hopefully by the Negroes."[12] In 1950, Beasley went to college at Alcorn, where she soon had a boyfriend. Her boyfriend surprised her family by calling her home in Vicksburg and then hitchhiking down from his home to visit.[13] Medgar Evers stayed at Vicksburg's Negro YMCA. He later told a reporter that he courted Beasley at Vicksburg's National Military Park. It was, after all, "one of the state's most beautiful spots." Later, after joining the National Association for the Advancement of Colored People (NAACP), the battlefield still drew him back to Vicksburg; he liked showing it to his children and friends. In 1958, he took a magazine reporter to the battleground, walking with other tourists over the soil where Civil War soldiers fought and died. For Evers, Vicksburg's battlefield was a very special place.[14]

Evers had been a soldier himself, serving in World War II, stationed in England and then Le Havre, Liege, Antwerp, and Cherbourg. Back in Mississippi, he finished college, married Myrlie, and moved to Mound Bayou, where he sold insurance. Though born and raised in Mississippi, Delta poverty shocked Evers. He came home "bursting with stories" and increasingly angry at the injustice he found. All through 1952, as Evers sold insurance, he studied Delta society and its racial hierarchy, "a stu-

294

dent driven by horror to learn more." In 1954, he became the first NAACP field secretary. Angrily driven to make his beloved Mississippi a better place, Evers cast about for models. There were false starts. He learned of Jomo Kenyatta, leader of the Mau Mau in Kenya. He toyed with the idea of a secret black army, fighting for freedom in the Delta. "I am sure," Evers wrote later, that Medgar never realized that his dream of black vigilantes "was straight out of the Southern tradition . . . the Ku Klux Klan, the lynch mob, the terrorist police turned black."[15]

The landscape that shaped Evers included Vicksburg National Military Park, the place he loved to visit. Perhaps John A. T. Hull did not have the likes of Evers in mind when he orated, "Let the young be taught the lesson of patriotism," and declared that the flag "dissolves the chains of slavery." When a society transforms itself, Maurice Halbwachs wrote, "At the beginning it does not foresee the consequences of the new principles that it asserts." Hull wanted the battleground to teach America's youth patriotic values, but he could not fully control what those values might be, what it would really mean to "dissolve" slavery. As a young man, Evers stood on the battleground that Hull helped make into a national park and tried to understand what it meant, what the lesson Hull and his generation left behind. When a society rethinks core beliefs, Halbwachs writes, it must persuade itself that its members already carried within themselves the new values. What Evers discovered—or imagined he discovered—as he walked across the Vicksburg park did not entirely come from the battleground itself.[16]

From its beginnings, African Americans, sometimes by the thousands, migrated to Vicksburg's military park on Memorial Day. These segregated people listened to orators read Lincoln's Gettysburg Address. They looked at the rows of white tombstones; standing over black and white Union soldiers, they gazed at the majesterial Illinois monument and other state monuments. And like Warren County's majority on January 26, 1861, they knew why the artillery boomed.

Notes

1. Hawley to parents, June 7, 1863, Thomas Hawley Papers, Missouri Historical Society, St. Louis.

2. *Vicksburg Post*, March 27, 1997; July 13, 17, 1998; March 2, 1999.

3. John Albert Tiffin Hull, undated speech, folder 7, file 2, part 4, box 2, John Albert Tiffin Hull Papers, State Historical Society of Iowa, Des Moines.

4. Carol Reardon, *Pickett's Charge in History and Memory* (Chapel Hill: University of North Carolina Press, 1997), 66–72; Benjamin Yarber Dixon, "Gettysburg, a Living Battlefield" (Ph.D. diss., University of Oklahoma, 2000), 44–76.

5. LaSalle Pickett, ed., *The Heart of a Soldier: As Revealed in the Intimate Letters of General George E. Pickett, C.S.A.* (New York: Seth Moyle, 1913); Lesley J. Gordon, *General George E. Pickett in Life and Legend* (Chapel Hill: University of North Carolina Press, 1998), 2, 100–101; Gary W. Gallagher, "A Widow and Her Soldier: LaSalle Corbell Pickett as Author of the George E. Pickett Letters," *Virginia Magazine of History and Biography* 94 (July 1986): 329–44.

6. LaSalle Pickett, *Pickett and His Men* (Atlanta, Ga.: Foote and Davies, 1899); Walter Harrison, *Pickett's Men: A Fragment of War History* (New York: D. Van Nostrand, 1870); Gordon, *General George E. Pickett in Life and Legend*, 2, 172.

7. Amy J. Kinsel, "'From These Honored Dead': Gettysburg in American Culture, 1863–1938" (Ph.D. diss., Cornell University, 1992), 521.

8. *Vicksburg Evening Post*, May 2, 1937; Gordon A. Cotton, *The Old Court House* (Raymond, Miss.: Keith Printing, 1982), 47–48.

9. Davis to William C. Everhart, September 24, 1952, Old Court House Museum, Vicksburg, Mississippi.

10. Davis to Douglas MacArthur, February 20, 1952; and Davis to Joseph McCarthy, March 31, 1952, Old Court House Museum, Vicksburg, Mississippi.

11. Cotton, *The Old Court House*, 48.

12. Mrs. Medgar Evers with William Peters, *For Us, the Living* (Garden City, N.Y.: Doubleday, 1967), 34.

13. Evers, *For Us, the Living*, 49–50.

14. Medgar Evers, as told to Francis H. Mitchell, "Why I Live in Mississippi," *Ebony* 14 (November 1958): 65–70.

15. Evers, *For Us, the Living*, 24, 79, 85, 90–92.

16. Maurice Halbwachs, *On Collective Memory*, ed. and trans. Lewis A. Coser (Chicago: University of Chicago Press, 1992), 86.

Herman Lieb's Report on the Battle at Milliken's Bend

AFTER the Milliken's Bend battle, Colonel Henry Lieb wrote a report of the battle never published in *The War of the Rebellion: A Compilation of the Official Records of the Union and Confederate Armies* (Washington, D.C., 1880–1901). David Cornwell included a version of it in his unpublished memoir, explaining that Lieb transmitted his report to General Elias S. Dennis, who used it in writing his report, which does appear in the *Official Record*. Cornwell writes, "I do not hesitate to denounce Gen. Dennis' report of that fight as a contemptible theft and fraud." Cornwell adds, "If he had been a gentleman he would have forwarded Lieb's report to Grant with a letter of transmittal. It would then have got into the Army Records."

Cyrus Sears published his version of the Lieb report in his booklet *The Battle of Milliken's Bend*. Sears interspersed Lieb's text with his own commentary, disputing minor points. Edwin Bearss cites Lieb's report in his three-volume history of the Vicksburg campaign as "'After Action Report of Colonel Hermann Lieb,' files VNMP." I am informed by the current historian of Vicksburg National Military Park that this document was stolen some time after Bearss published his book. (Edwin Cole Bearss, *The Campaign for Vicksburg*, 3 vols. [Dayton, Ohio: Morningside, 1986], 3:1176n48;

Terrence J. Winschell to Christopher Waldrep, March 21, 2003, author's collection.)
Cornwell's version:

Head Quarters, African Brigade
Milliken's Bend, La., June 8th, 1863.
General.

I have the honor to report that pursuant to orders and instructions from Brig. Gen. E. S. Dennis, commanding Dist., of N.E. La., I made a reconnaissance in the direction of Richmond. Leaving camp at two o'clock A.M. of June 6th, I came up with a small force of our cavalry encamping in the timber three miles from the Bend, under command of Captain Anderson.

It was agreed that he should take the left side of Walnut Bayou and pursue it as far as Mrs. Armus' Plantation, while I with my command—250 strong—proceed along the Richmond Road.

I then started marching leisurely forward to the railroad deep within three miles of Richmond, where I encountered the enemy's pickets and advance which we drove in with scarcely any opposition, but anticipating that the enemy was in strong force, I retired slowly in the direction of the Bend.

When about half way back, a squad of our cavalry came dashing madly up in our rear, badly pressed by the enemy's cavalry, reported to be in strong force.

I immediately drew up my regiment in line across an open field and fired one volley, which was sufficient to send them back in disorder, but anticipating a flank movement in order to context our passage over Walnut Bayou bridge, I again took up my line of march to the camp, where I arrived without further incident at 12:40 P.M.

I immediately dispatched a courier with intelligence of the facts to General Dennis, who immediately started to my assistance the gunboat *Choctaw*, and a detachment of the 23rd Iowa Infantry.

Shortly after my arrival in camp I proceeded to double my pickets, and sent a squad of mounted infantry from my regiment to act as videtts. Immediately issued orders to the different regiments of African Descent in my command, to be in line of battle within the intrenchment at 2 A.M., leaving the 23rd Iowa—who were without tents or other shelter until 2:53 A.M., when I ordered them to move in double quick time to the breastworks.

All my orders were promptly obeyed. After a few minutes the pickets came in reporting the enemy rapidly advancing in strong force on the main Richmond road, at the same time heavy firing was heard in that direction verifying the report. I immediately disposed my regiments in the rifle pits as follows.

The 9th La. Infty. 285 strong and the 23rd Iowa, 105 strong in the center, and the 11th La. 395 strong on the right.

The enemy advanced on the left of our front, with a strong force of cavalry on his right flank, marching in close column by division, until within 3/4 of a mile of our works in an open field, when they deployed to the right and left marching boldly on our works.

Our men were ordered to hold their fire until the enemy was within musket shot. The first volley was delivered when they were about in this range, which made them waver and recoil—a number running in confusion to the rear—the balance pushing on with intrepidity soon reached the levee, where a charge was ordered by the leaders and they came madly on with cries of 'No quarters for white offices, kill the damned Abolitionists, but spare the niggers' &c.

Our men being unaccustomed to the use of muskets—some having drilled only two days—the most proficient not more than three weeks in the manual of arms, they succeeded in getting up to our works and a number of them on top of the levee before any of our men could succeed in reloading their pieces. Many of our guns were Austrian Rifles and failed to fire, owing to deficiency in manufacture.

Here ensured a desperate hand to hand fight of several minutes duration with bayonets and clubbed muskets, the blacks exhibiting unprecedented bravery, and standing the charge nobly until the enemy in vastly overwhelming numbers succeeded in gaining a position on the levee on our extreme left from which they poured murderous enfilading along our line, directing their fire chiefly to our officers who fell in numbers. Then, and not until they were overpowered and forced from their position, were the blacks driven back, when numbers of them sought shelter behind wagons, piles of boxes and other objects. The others sought shelter behind the river bank and all poured volley after volley into the advancing enemy, and doggedly contested every inch of the ground.

At this juncture a broadside from the gunboat checked the enemy who soon disappeared behind the levee—keeping up a constant fire on our men, and appeared to be extending their lines to our extreme right, although keeping up the heaviest fire on the left. They however attempted to cross the levee on our extreme right but were held in check by two companies of the 11th La. Infty. which I had posted behind cotton bales and part of the old levee. In this position the fight continued until near noon, when the enemy suddenly withdrew. Our men seeing this movement on the left, rushed after them and poured into their retreating ranks volley after volley while they remained within gunshot.

The old gunboat *Lexington* gave the retreating rebels her farewell compliments, their scattering masses showing where the shot and shell struck with telling effect. All thanks to the staunch and noble boats, *Choctaw* and *Lexington*: they will long be remembered by the officers and recruits of the African Brigade.

My entire force, officers and men, are deserving of high compliment and special notice. Such a hand to hand conflict, such feats of daring, especially when we take in consideration that they were raw recruits and opposed to vastly superior number of veteran Texan troops, has never in the annals of this war been equalled. The endurance of the men after being wounded, their persistence in doggedly fighting—after having been driven from the breastworks, and their eagerness to resume the conflict, can never be surpast.

I would gladly mention the names of some of the officers who made themselves conspicuous by acts of dareing, but for fear of doing injustice to others, I will omit mentioning them here. The majority acted nobly.

The enemy had in action one brigade of infantry, and about 200 cavalry, commanded by Brig. Gen. McCulloch—nearly treble our number—with two brigades in reserve. His loss is over 100 killed, and a large number wounded. They succeeded in getting a large number of wounded off the field. Among their killed is Colonel Allen of the tenth Texas.

The losses in my command are as follows,

9th La. Infantry.

Lieutenants, J. Bruner, H. Wetmore and Thomas L. Walters, and 1st Sergeants John J. Wine, B. F. Perrine and C. F. Cady, killed. Captains Hisseng, Hammond and Dewitte, and Lieutenants C. M. Clark, Dave Cornwell, R. T. Pains, M. M. Miller, W. A. Skillen, and 1st Sergeant John W. Ayers wounded. Captain Heath is a prisoner now in the negro prison at Richmond. 60 privates killed, 90 wounded and 21 missing.

1st Miss. Infty.

2 killed, 21 wounded, 3 missing.

13th La. Infty.

5 wounded.

11th La. Infty.

2 officers killed, 7 wounded, and 1 missing. 31 privates killed. 112 wounded and 242 missing.

I can only account for the very large number reported missing from the 11th La. Infty., by presuming that they were permitted to stray off after the action, as I am confident that none of them were taken prisoners.

Soon after the engagement, Col. Smith of the 54th Ohio Infty., arrived at the Bend, and kindly proffered the use of his boat, the *American*, for the wounded and sick, extending great courtesy and attention to officers and men.

This report is in main a resume of regimental reports, I myself having in the early part of the action received a not severe but very painful gunshot wound in the thigh, which soon incapscitated me for action. The command then devolved on Colonel Chamberlain of the 11th La. Infty., who was nowhere to be seen on the field. Lieut. Col. Page of the 9th La. Infty. then assumed command. The 23rd Iowa Infty. left the field soon after the enemy got possession of the levee, headed by their Colonel, and was seen no more.

The detachment of Ill. Cavalry, commanded by Maj. Shaw, although posted quite near, took no part in the action.

H. Lieb, Col. 9th La. Infty.

Commanding African Brigade

Source: David Cornwell, "Dan Caverno: A True Tale of American Life on the Farm in a Country Store and in the Volunteer Army" (U.S. Army Military History Institute, Carlisle, Pennsylvania, 1908).

Cyrus Sears's version:

This report is in main, a resume of regimental reports, I myself having, during the early part of the action, received a not very severe but painful gunshot wound in the thigh, which soon incapacitated me for action. The command then devolved upon Colonel Chamberlain of the 11th La. (my regiment) "who was nowhere to be seen on the field." Lieut. Col. Payne of the 9th La. Infty. (Lieb's regiment) "then took command."

After mentioning his return to camp at 12:40 P.M. from a skirmish of the day before, he says:

I immediately dispatched a courier with intelligence to Gen. Dennis (at Young's Point) who immediately started to my assistance the gun-boat *Choctaw*, and a detachment of the 23rd Iowa Infantry. Shortly after my arrival in camp I proceeded to double my pickets and sent a squad of mounted infantry to my regiment to act as vedettes.

I immediately issued orders to the different regiments of African descent in my command to be in line of battle behind the intrenched works at 3 A.M., leaving the 23rd Iowa, who were without tents or other shelter, on board the transports until 3:53 A.M. when I ordered them to move in double quick time within the breast works.

After a few minutes the pickets came in, reporting the enemy rapidly advancing in strong force on the Main Richmond road, at the same time heavy firing was heard in that direction

303

corroborating the report. I immediately disposed the forces in the rifle pits as follows: The 9th La. Infantry, 285 strong, on the extreme left, the 1st Miss., 153 strong, the 13th La. Infantry, 108 strong, and the 23rd Iowa, 105 strong, in the center, and 11th La., 395 strong, on the extreme right.

"The enemy advanced on the left of our line" (I saw on our whole line) "throwing out no skirmishers in front, with a strong force of cavalry on the right flank, marching in close column by division until within three-fourths of a mile of our works.

"My men were ordered to withhold their fire until the enemy was within musket shot; and the first volley was delivered when they were within that range, which made them waver and recoil; a number running in confusion to the rear, the balance pushing on with intrepidity, soon reaching the levee, where a charge was ordered by their leaders and they came madly on with the cries—kill the d—d Abolitionists, spare the Niggers. Our men being unaccustomed to the use of Muskets, some having had but two days drilling, the most proficient not more than three weeks" (hardly that within the sixteen days mentioned) "the enemy succeeded in getting up to our works, a number of them on top of the Bend" (levee) "before many of our men succeeded in reloading their pieces, while many of them (Austrian Rifles) failed to fire.

A desperate hand to hand fight of several minutes duration then ensued; the blacks exhibiting unprecedented bravery, standing the charge nobly, until the enemy in overwhelming numbers had succeeded in gaining a position on the levee at our extreme left, from which they poured murderous enfilading fire—chiefly upon the officers—who fell in numbers; but not until overpowered by numbers and forced from their position, were the blacks compelled to fall back, seeking shelter behind wagons, piles of boxes, and other obstructions and behind the banks of the river, pouring volley after volley into the ranks of the enemy.

At this critical juncture, a broadside from the *Choctaw* checked the enemy's progress, who soon disappeared behind the levee, but keeping up a constant fire upon our men and apparently extending their line toward our extreme right though keeping up the heaviest fire on our left. They however attempted to cross the levee on our extreme right but were held in check by two companies of the 11th La. which I had posted behind cotton bales and a part of the old levee." (I say by the whole 11th) "In this position the fight continued until near noon, when the enemy suddenly withdrew. Our men seeing this movement on the left rushed after them and poured volley after volley into them while they remained within gun-shot range."

(I had a splendid view of the situation and opportunity to hear and see, but did not see this rushing nor hear these volleys.)

"My entire force of officers and men are deserving of special notice as such hand to hand conflict, such daring feats against vastly superior forces of Texas troops, has never in the annals of this war, been equaled. The endurance of the men after having been wounded, their persistence in doggedly fighting after having been driven from their breastworks, and their eagerness to resume the conflict, can never be surpassed."

(To be candid, I don't remember that "eagerness," but that we were glad to be authors of the pattern followed by Meade a short time afterward at Gettysburg: by letting the enemy go in peace, kissing them goodbye, hoping they would never call again, and thanking God it was no worse.)

Lieb continued:

"The enemy had in action one brigade of infantry and about 200 cavalry, commanded by Brig Gen McCullough, or nearly treble our number, with two brigades in reserve. His loss is over 100 killed and a large number wounded. They succeeded in getting the majority of their wounded off the field. Among the killed is Col. Allen of the 16th Texas."

. . . Lieb's report says nothing of the killed and wounded in the 13th La., which he says went into the fight 108 strong; says nothing of its killed and wounded for the very good reason that he was mistaken about any such regiment being there. Only the other regiments he mentions were "in it." And he says nothing of the killed and wounded of the 105 strong 23rd Iowa. All he says about them after stating his disposition of them, is this:

"The 23rd Iowa Infantry left the field soon after the enemy had gained possession of the levee, headed by their Colonel and were seen no more."

I think it may be taken for granted he wrote this of the 23rd Iowa from his own knowledge; and, therefore, that it took place early in the engagement—before he was disabled. . . .

To be candid,—and with due deference, I am of the opinion that there are some mistakes in Lieb's report;—I know the 13th La. was not there—I believe he has the casualties too high—though, by no means high enough to rightfully deprive the 9th La. of the honor of having sustained the highest per cent loss in killed *and mortally wounded* in a single engagement of the Civil War. . . .

Source: Cyrus Sears, *The Battle of Milliken's Bend* (Columbus, Ohio: F. J. Herr Printing Co., 1909), 8–11.

"The Battle of Milliken's Bend," by David Cornwell

Editor *National Tribune*: The following is an extract from an article that appeared in the *National Tribune* of Oct. 10, 1907:

"Col. Cyrus Sears, 49th U.S.C.T., Harpster, O.

"He afterward became Lieutenant-Colonel of the 49th U.S.C.T., and owing to the bad conduct of his Colonel, became ranking officer in the bloody fight at Milliken's Bend, where most of the officers present of his regiment were killed or afterward hanged by the rebels. In spite of the overwhelming numbers and the vicious charges of the enemy, Col. Sears managed so well that he got his men together behind the last levee and made a determined stand, repulsing the enemy with great loss. The regiment lost 62 killed, which Comrade Sears believes is the largest proportion of killed in any regiment in a single engagement."

As soon as I read the above I wrote Col. Sears, and at his request sent him a copy of it, and he denies its authorship and responsibility for its publication. And it has occurred to me that possibly the *National Tribune* might accept for publication a candid and truthful account of this unique fight, provided I can throw new light on the affair, and make clear some points upon which the historians are a trifle hazy. I will be as brief as possible and commence at the attack, and end with the withdrawal of the Confederate forces.

The diagram accompanying this article will show the situation in less space and much clearer than I could describe it in words, and so I will try and avoid repeating here what is plainly shown there.

Unfortunately, while Col. Herman Lieb, of the 9th La., who was in command of the forces there, was absent with his own regiment the day before, some one cut down a few rods of the hedge on our left, which made this the weak point in our line. Opposite here were stationed two companies, which made about 25 files, to watch this gap and to act as a reserve. And a lucky precaution it was, too.

The enemy advanced over this smooth level field as if on parade, took the double-quick at a distance of a couple of hundred of paces from us, and reached the hedge in front of us before a shot was fired upon them.

We had no artillery, and the little gunboat that lay at the bank had no steam on and could not move.

When the enemy's line struck us their right was advanced and hit us first. Where the hedge was down they at once sailed up the exterior slope of the levee and met our thin line on the top. Those of them who hit the hedge near this big gap rushed around thru it and up on the levee with the others, and they swept our line away with the greatest ease.

As they came cautiously down the interior slope, many of them loading their pieces, I signaled up the reserve, of which I had command, and they bounced forward with the fury of a cyclone, and went into that gang with their bayonets. It was a furious, a terrible struggle for a few minutes, but these darkies were as savage as tigers when it came to bayonet fighting, and they forced them back on their own side of the levee and made them stay there.

For about two hours the fight continued by spasmodic shooting over the crest of this levee, and we were getting much the worst of it, for these Texans were good shots and our men could not hit the broad side of a cotton gin. There was nothing for it but to go to the river bank before we were all picked off. We

308

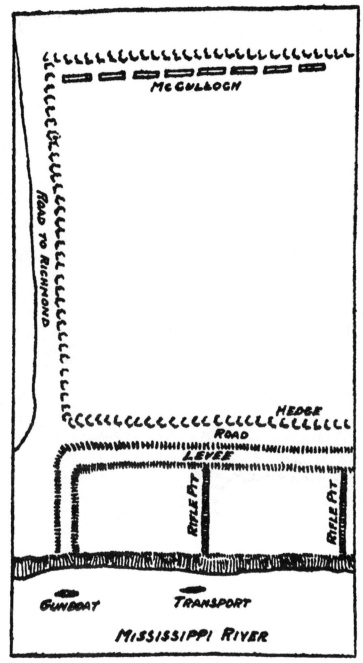

David Cornwell's map of the Milliken's Bend battlefield.

were no longer afraid of their bayonets, for their officers could not by threats or coaxing induce them to try that game again.

Col. Lieb, who was the only mounted officer on our side of the levee, and who got a bullet in his hip early in the fight, rode up and told me of this move, and he had no more than got away from there before I saw them break to the rear from about the center of our line. I notified my Lieutenant of what was taking place, and at once started back, as my arm had been broken at the shoulder by a bullet directly after the bayonet fight and I could not run.

Of course, it is unusual to stay in a fight after being seriously wounded, but this was an unusual fight, and it was better to die game than to be shot to pieces after throwing up your hands. We pretty well understood what was in store for us, and did not propose to lie down as long as we were able to stand up.

A concerted effort was not made to follow us—only two or three spasmodic rushes—but as soon as our men would jump up from behind the river bank and start to meet them with the bayonet, they would go back as if so many devils were after them. Our men were now where they could stand upright and load their pieces and only expose their heads and shoulders while firing, and as the enemy had failed to follow us to the river bank and shoot us into the river, as they might have done if they had had the sense and sand, the fight was practically won. It was now only a question of time when they would withdraw.

Now, mark, up to this time the gunboat had not fired a shot, and for the very good reason that they were so low in the river that the levee was not in their line of sight. And if it had been they could not have used their guns upon it till we got away from there. But now as we were under the bank they commenced sending them over into the field, way beyond, but their only effect was a moral one, for they couldn't hit anybody.

Col. Lieb turned the command over to our Lieutenant-Colonel (Page), and proceeded to bathe his hip at the water's edge. It may have been an hour and it may have been more when the enemy concluded they were gaining nothing by lying there behind the levee, and so hastily withdrew. The gunboats—one or two more had run up on the last end—scared the Johnnies all they could, but it is unlikely that they killed any of them, for at no time could they see them.

Col. Lieb was helped to his tent, and remained a few days in the old camp, received reports from the battalions of their losses, and sent in his official report. The losses were: 9th La.— Killed 6 officers and 60 men; wounded, 9 officers and 90 men; missing, 2 officers and 21 men. 1st Miss—Killed, 2 men; wounded, 21 men; missing, 3 men. 13th La.—Wounded, 5 men. I cannot give the loss of the 23d Iowa, as they did not make a report to Col. Lieb, but it was very severe. By much campaigning and hard fighting they had been reduced to just a skeleton of a regiment, and it was the cruelest of fate that this gallant little band should have been shoved into such a terrible fight and nearly annihilated. 11th La.—Killed, 2 officers and 31 men; wounded, 7 officers and 112 men; missing, 1 officer and 242 men.

There was quite a mistake in reporting to Col. Lieb that this last regiment put only 395 men into the fight, for that is exactly the number they claim to have lost. Capt. Frank Orm, of Burlington, Iowa, under date of April 6, 1902, says they put into the fight about 685 men, and that there were 85 in his own company (B). Their companies must have been quite full, for most of them were mustered in, while none of the 9th was able to muster a First Lieutenant.

The percentage of killed and wounded was about as follows: 9th La., 53 per cent; 1st Miss., 14 per cent; 13th La., 4½ per cent; 11th La., 22 per cent.

I will not venture to say of the 23rd Iowa what their percentage of loss was, but it must have amounted almost to annihilation.

Col. Chamberland, of the 11th La. is said to have gone about the gunboat and remained there till the fight was over, when he came ashore and took command of his regiment again. He did not remain long, but was soon compelled to resign. While a large portion of the regiment straggled off during the fight, which would indicate they were not well officered, yet Lieut. Col. Sears was allowed to remain, and one Van E. Young was picked up somewhere and put in command of this regiment, which later became the 49th U.S.

David Cornwell

Brevet Lieutant Colonel, U.S. Vols, Allegan, Mich.

Source: *Washington National Tribune*, February 13, 1908.

Reported Lynchings in Warren County, Mississippi

THE only source for lynching violence comes from newspapers. This source is deeply flawed, as the inventory of Warren County "lynchings" here shows. Nonetheless, such accounts of white mob violence against former slaves and their descendants stands as one kind of memorial to the North's failure to achieve racial justice in the Civil War and after.

1. Daniel Carnahan. January 15, 1885.

"A large Negro, representing himself as an escaped convict, called at the house of a widow lady named Mrs. Lindergreen, who, with her daughter, resides in the Red Bone neighborhood," January 13. "The negro is known by the description given of him by the ladies as one Dan Carnahan, living on the Will cotton plantation." He "followed and overtook" the daughter "and then choked her down and outraged her." Neighbors held a meeting January 15 and scoured the country "and my informant states that he has reason to believe that the black ravisher has already paid the penalty of his crime with his life." *New Orleans Picayune*, January 16, 1885.

2. Frederick Villarosa. March 28, 1886.

Fred. Villarosa attempted on Thursday to commit a criminal assault upon a little girl, daughter of a well-known citizen. *Vicksburg Evening Post*, March 27, 1886.

March 28: party of masked men forced the jail; hanged Fred Villarosa to a tree on Grove Street. *Vicksburg Evening Post*, March 29, 1886.

3. Thomas Harris. April 30, 1888.

April 29: "three negroes" broke into Thomas King's store, awakening two ladies asleep there. One burglar "brutally outraged" one lady. "Through shame this was suppressed until a late hour this morning. The black fiend was about to assault Miss Weatherly when her companion remonstrated and was herself attacked." *Vicksburg Evening Post*, April 30, 1888.

April 30: Thomas Harris is the negro who entered Thomas King's store. He was arrested by police and then taken from jail by mob, interrogated, and hanged from tree, east side of courthouse. *Vicksburg Evening Post*, May 1, 1888; *New Orleans Picayune*, May 1, 1888; *Vicksburg Daily Commercial Herald*, May 1, 1888.

"The necessity for lynch law in any community is very much to be regretted, but when it does exist there should be no hesitation about resorting to it." *Vicksburg Daily Commercial Herald*, May 2, 1888.

4. Marley. May 8, 1888.

James Newbaker of Oak Ridge neighborhood was waylaid and shot. "It is also stated his assassination was one Mr. Marley, who lived near him and is said to be a half breed, and that short work was made of him." *New Orleans Picayune*, May 9, 1888.

5. Henry Barnes, June 11, 1888.

Vicksburg Evening Post does not call this a lynching, but reports that R. H. Iler, who claimed that Barnes had robbed him, had custody of Barnes, took him to a lonely and isolated place, and shot him in the head. "The officers who delivered Barnes to an irresponsible individual, are also worthy of censure." "The murder of Barnes was a deed of peculiar atrocity;—his hands were tied behind him, and he was shot in the back of the head." *Vicksburg Evening Post*, June 12, 1888.

R. H. Iler undergoes a preliminary examination before Justice of the Peace Loewenberg. Iler is released; charges dismissed. *Vicksburg Evening Post*, June 13, 16, 1888.

6. Wesley Thomas. February 22, 1889.

February 20: "Considerable excitement was occasioned in the city late yesterday evening by the arrest of Wes. Thomas, colored, who was charged with having attempted to violate Miss Katie Pinkston." *Vicksburg Evening Post*, February 21, 1889.

February 21: Report that a large body of men took Thomas. *Vicksburg Evening Post*, February 22, 1889.

February 22: Train passengers report seeing Thomas hanging from trestle. *Vicksburg Evening Post*, February 23, 1889; *New Orleans Picayune*, February 23, 1889; *Daily Commercial Herald*, February 23, 1889.

7. Henry Gentry. July 3, 1891.

"Meagre particulars have been received here of a lynching which took place last Friday night on Palmyra plantation, this county. The victim, a negro named Henry Gentry, had murdered another negro, George Hillyard . . . and was being carried before a magistrate for trial by two guards, when the latter were set upon by a negro mob, overpowered and their prisoner taken from them and hung." *New Orleans Picayune*, July 8, 1891; *Vicksburg Commercial Herald*, July 8, 1891.

8. Smith Tooley and John Adams. July 5, 1892.

Smith Tooley arrested, *Vicksburg Evening Post*, July 1, 1892.

Tooley identified as murderer of Benson Blake. Talk of lynching. *Vicksburg Evening Post*, July 2; *Vicksburg Daily Commercial Herald*, July 2.

John Adams arrested near Yokena. *Vicksburg Evening Post*, July 4.

Vicksburg Evening Post prints Smith Tooley's confession, July 5. *Vicksburg Daily Commercial Herald*, July 5; *Port Gibson Reveille*, July 13.

July 5: Tooley and Adams hanged. *Vicksburg Evening Post*, July 6; *Vicksburg Daily Commercial Herald*, July 7; *Jackson State Ledger*, July 8, 1892; *New Orleans Picayune*, July 6, 1892.

9. Unknown. December 28, 1892.

"A negro was lynched last Wednesday by negroes at or near Oak Ridge. . . . He had violated a negro woman." *New Orleans Picayune*, December 31, 1892.

10. Jesse Mims. December 6, 1894.

Beaten to death by Ruben Goodrum, a convict guard. "It seems that heartless brutality, on the part of some guards, is an inevitable accompaniment of convict camps. . . . Four of the convicts who were eye witnesses and who were compelled to hold the victim while he was being beaten to death, were either liberated or found opportunity to escape." *Vicksburg Evening Post*, December 10, 1894.

11. Louis Nelson. August 9, 1897.

August 9: "Louis Nelson, the negro who murdered Mrs. William Allen, at Brunswick, Miss., some weeks ago, was caught on Mr. Coleman Ducas' place, in Madison Parish, La. Yesterday evening." Officers escorted Nelson back to Mississippi but were met by a mob that hanged Nelson from a tree limb August 9. *New Orleans Picayune*, August 10, 1897; *Vicksburg Daily Commercial Herald*, August 11.

12. Gloster Barnes. October 22, 1900.

"It is rumored that Gloster Barnes, who so brutally murdered his wife on Mr. Sam Brown's plantation on Eagle Lake last Sunday night, and who was found in a small bayou with a broken hip, caused by a gun shot wound, and committed for trial without bail, was taken from the guard last night some miles south of Eagle Lake and lynched." *Vicksburg Evening Post*, October 23, 1900.

13. Ben Bryant and William Morris. May 2, 1903.

May 1: Herbert William Legg is assassinated on his plantation eight miles north of Redwood. *Vicksburg Evening Post*, May 2; *Vicksburg American*, May 2; *Vicksburg Herald*, May 3.

May 2: "Ben Bryant and William Morris, the negroes charged with the assassination of Mr. Will Legg, were summarily executed Saturday night. The prisoners were taken from the deputy sheriffs at the Haynes Bluff bridge where the death penalty was meted out." *Vicksburg Evening Post*, May 4; *Vicksburg American*, May 4.

Morris escaped when the mob's rope broke and he dropped into water. *Vicksburg Evening Post*, May 5.

Morris is really dead after all. *Vicksburg Evening Post*, May 6.

14. Cato Garrett. July 7, 1903.

July 4: "G. Harry Stout . . . had been murdered by negro man named Howard Garrett." *Vicksburg Evening Post*, July 4, 1903.

July 7: Garrett hanged to Stout's bayou bridge yesterday. *Vicksburg American*, July 8; *Vicksburg Evening Post*, July 9.

15. Sam Washington. July 29, 1907.

July 20: Sam Washington reportedly killed his father-in-law, Ollie Butler. "There is probably suspended on a rope from the side of the tall timbers in the swamps in the southern portion of this county or over in Claiborne county, all that is mortal of Sam Washington." *Vicksburg American*, July 29. Sheriff John Hyland is trying to find Sam Washington. *Vicksburg Daily Herald*, July 30.

Justice of the Peace James M. Hullum reports Sam Washington was probably not lynched. *Vicksburg American*, August 5.

16. Ed Johnson. January 20, 1915.
"Ed Johnson, negro cattle thief, was lynched by a mob last night after midnight in East Clay Street." *Vicksburg Evening Post*, January 20.

17. J. A. Miller and Dave Cook. July 23, 1918. Tarred and feathered.
June 27: "I refused, for reasons, to subscribe to One Thousand ($1,000) Dollars worth of War Savings Stamps." Miller to John Shillady, October 29, 1918, Part 7 NAACP Papers, Library of Congress, Washington, D.C.
July 23: "I was tarred and feathered on July 23rd." Miller to John Shillady, October 29, 1918, Part 7 NAACP Papers, Library of Congress, Washington, D.C.
J. William Harris, "Etiquette, Lynching, and Racial Boundaries in Southern History: A Mississippi Example," *American Historical Review* 100 (April 1995): 387–410; *Vicksburg Evening Post*, July 24, 25, 1918.

18. Ella Brooks and Ethel Barrett. July 23, 1918. Tarred and feathered.
Six white citizens, W. M. Dotson, Lem Ford, Stuart Shaw, O. R. Hoxie, Frank Patterson, and E. L. King, were each put under bond on charge of taking the law into their own hands Tuesday night and tarring and feathering two negro women. *Vicksburg Evening Post*, December 10. King, Ford, Hoxie, Shaw convicted; appeal to state supreme court. Decided October 1920. Reversed and remanded. File no. 21095, Mississippi State Supreme Court records, Mississippi Department of Archives and History, Jackson; *Vicksburg Evening Post*, July 26, 27, 29, 31, 1918.

19. Lloyd Clay. May 14, 1919.

Clay, "a negro charged with attempted rape," hanged and burned. *Vicksburg Evening Post*, May 17; *Vicksburg Daily Herald*, May 18.

20. James Brown, George Moore, and James Minor. January 6, 1930.

Lynching of three persons charged with fatally wounding an officer foiled. Monroe Work to Jessie Daniel Ames, October 8, 1890, frame 602, reel 8, Association of Southern Women for the Prevention of Lynching Papers (microfilm). *Vicksburg Evening Post*, January 6, 13, 14, 15, 1930.

21. Eli Johnson. March 29, 1931.

March 29: Johnson was alleged to have attempted to criminally assault a white lady, aged about thirty years, of the Redbone community.

A number of citizens, armed, went in pursuit of the negro and the chase lasted for an hour or so. Several shots were said to have been fired at Johnson during the chase. It was said there were about fifty in the posse.

Johnson was said to have met his death as he was climbing over a barbed wire fence. *Vicksburg Evening Post*, March 30.

22. Aaron Williams. March 19, 1932.

"Colored fireman" shot in cab in Yazoo & Mississippi Valley railroad locomotive. Auto was seen to drive by and one single shot rang out. Railroad detectives and Vicksburg police are investigating. *Vicksburg Evening Post*, March 21, 1932.

23. Wilbur Anderson. March 23, 1932.

"Colored fireman of Baton Rouge" shot and instantly killed March 23, 1932, 4:45 A.M. Sheriff and deputies investigating as are railroad detectives. He was Y & MV fireman. *Vicksburg Evening Post*, March 23, 1932.

24. James Weddington

Negro fireman on the Yazoo and Mississippi Valley Railroad shot last Saturday night. Fired at from automobile. No arrests. *Vicksburg Evening Post*, April 4, 1932.

Vicksburg Evening Post, May 6, 1932, reprints *Baton Rouge State-Times* editorial denouncing the railroad shootings.

Charles B. Coon, white fireman of the Yazoo and Mississippi Valley Railroad, arrested for murder in Natchez on May 22 of Will Harvey, negro fireman of the same railroad. Harvey was the fifth negro fireman of that railroad slain. Previously three slain in Vicksburg and one in Baton Rouge. *Vicksburg Evening Post*, June 1, 1932.

Charles B. Coon is resident of Vicksburg. Arrested June 1. Coon formerly lived in Jena, Louisiana. Has been tried in Vicksburg for murder before—murder of Marie Thompson. His fingerprints match those found on sixteen gauge shotgun shells found on street. Illinois System has posted a reward. *Vicksburg Evening Post*, June 2, 1932.

Special Agent Reed of the Illinois Central system and two detectives of Vicksburg spent the morning in Natchez and acquainted themselves with the evidence against Coon. *Vicksburg Evening Post*, June 3, 1932.

Three additional suspects brought to Natchez from Vicksburg: Lee Edward Middleton of Meadville, Vernon Campbell of Vicksburg and C. M. Bailey of Brookhaven. All three arrested in Vicksburg. *Vicksburg Evening Post*, June 4, 1932.

25. Jim Jones. January 1937.

"One of my colored friends has disappeared under very mysterious circumstances and I am almost positive that he has been lynched." J. B. Smith, Jr., to NAACP, March 13, Part 7 NAACP Papers, Library of Congress, Washington, D.C.

26. Mr. and Mrs. James "Enix" Brown and their children

Joseph (10), Robert (7), Mildred (12), Laura May (9), Doris (8), Johnny Ann (5). Burned in house fire. December 1, 1948. Henry Brown affidavit.

"Marcus C. Stewart, our editor, has done everything to help the boy [Henry Brown] but believes the story is a fabrication." Charles S. Preston, *Indianapolis Recorder*, to Walter White, December 11, 1948, box A407, Group II, Lynching General 1948-54 NAACP Papers, Library of Congress, Washington, D.C.

State Monuments on the Vicksburg Battleground

Massachusetts, dedicated November 14, 1902; cost: $4,500

New Hampshire, accepted by U.S. Government, April 20, 1904; cost: $5,000

Ohio, dedicated May 22, 1905; cost: $56,000

Illinois, dedicated October 26, 1906; cost: $194,423.92

Iowa, dedicated November 15, 1906; cost: $100,000

Pennsylvania, dedicated March 24, 1906; cost: $12,500

Minnesota, dedicated May 24, 1907; cost: $24,000

Virginia, dedicated November 23, 1907 (outside park); cost: $520

Rhode Island, dedicated November 11, 1908; cost: $5,000

Mississippi, dedicated November 13, 1909 (completed April 20, 1912); cost: $3,200

Wisconsin, dedicated May 22, 1911; cost: $90,644

Maryland, dedicated March, 1914 (outside park)

Michigan, dedicated November 10, 1916; cost: $10,000

Missouri, dedicated October 17, 1917; cost: $40,000

New York, dedicated October 17, 1917; cost: $11,636.83

Louisiana, dedicated October 18, 1920; cost: $43,500

West Virginia, dedicated November 14, 1922

North Carolina, dedicated May 18, 1925 (outside park); cost: $2,750

Indiana, dedicated June 16, 1926

South Carolina, dedicated November 22, 1935 (outside park); cost: $4,900

Alabama, dedicated July 19, 1951; cost: $150,000

Arkansas, dedicated August 2, 1954; cost: $50,000

Florida, dedicated April 17, 1954 (outside park); cost: $5,000

Kansas, erected June 1960; cost: $5,000

Texas, dedicated November 4, 1961; cost: $100,000

Georgia, dedicated October 25, 1962; cost: $7,500

Tennessee, dedicated June 29, 1996

Kentucky, dedicated October 20, 2001

THERE are two academic studies of Vicksburg and Warren County: Christopher Morris, *Becoming Southern: The Evolution of a Way of Life, Warren County and Vicksburg, Mississippi, 1770–1860* (New York: Oxford, 1995), and Christopher Waldrep, *Roots of Disorder: Race and Criminal Justice in the American South, 1817–80* (Urbana: University of Illinois Press, 1998).

Numerous books recount the Vicksburg campaign. Shelby Foote, *The Beleaguered City: The Vicksburg Campaign, December 1862–July 1863* (New York: Modern Library, 1995); James R. Arnold, *Grant Wins the War: Decision at Vicksburg* (New York: John Wiley & Sons, 1997); Richard Wheeler, *The Siege of Vicksburg* (New York: Crowell, 1978); Earl Schenck Miers, *The Web of Victory: Grant at Vicksburg* (New York: Knopf, 1955); A. A. Hoehing, *Vicksburg: 47 Days of Siege* (Englewood Cliffs, N.J.: Prentice Hall, 1969); Samuel Carter, *The Final Fortress: The Campaign for Vicksburg, 1862–1863* (New York: St. Martin's, 1980); Warren E. Grabau, *Ninety-Eight Days: A Geographer's View of the Vicksburg Campaign* (Knoxville: University of Tennessee Press, 2000); Edwin Cole Bearss, *The Vicksburg Campaign*, 3 vols. (Dayton, Ohio: Morningside, 1986); Terrence J. Winschel, *Vicksburg: Fall of the Confederate Gibraltar* (Abilene, Tex.: McWhitney Foundation Press, 1999); David G. Martin, *The Vicksburg Campaign: April 1862–July 1863* (Conshohocken, Pa.: Combined, 1994). Three new books appeared as I completed this volume: Gordon A. Cotton and Jeff T. Giambrone, *Vicksburg and the War* (Gretna, La.: Pelican Publishing Co., 2004); William L. Shea and Terrence J. Winschel, *Vicksburg Is the Key: The*

Struggle for the Mississippi River (Lincoln: University of Nebraska Press, 2003); Michael B. Ballard, *Vicksburg: The Campaign That Opened the Mississippi* (Chapel Hill: University of North Carolina Press, 2004).

For the study of memory, the starting point is Maurice Halbwachs, *The Collective Memory*, trans. Francis J. Ditter and Vida Yazdi Ditter (New York: Harper Colophon Books, 1980). A better English version is *On Collective Memory*, trans. and ed. Lewis A. Coser (Chicago: University of Chicago Press, 1992). Barry Schwartz critiques Halbwachs in "The Social Context of Commemoration: A Study in Collective Memory," *Social Forces* 61 (December 1982): 374–402. For the impact of war generally, see Chris Hedges, *War Is a Force That Gives Us Meaning* (New York: Public Affairs, 2002).

Louis Menand, *The Metaphysical Club* (New York: Farrar, Straus & Giroux, 2001), is essential for understanding this period. Jackson Lears, *No Place of Grace: Antimodernism and the Transformation of American Culture, 1880–1920* (New York: Pantheon, 1981), is equally indispensable.

There is now a rich scholarship examining vernacular Civil War history and the memory of battlefields more generally. Edmund Wilson, *Patriotic Gore: Studies in the Literature of the American Civil War* (New York: Oxford University Press, 1962), remains the classic work, though he discounts the importance of race. In 1937, Paul H. Buck explained that Civil War reconciliation allowed the South to achieve autonomy, freedom from national "interference" with its racial oppression, thus granting the nation time to heal. Buck sympathized with the South on this point. The battle over the meaning of the Civil War, Buck wrote, pitted a "people faced with the menace of Negro domination" against "people committed . . . to securing justice for the inferior race." Paul H. Buck, *The Road to Reunion, 1865–1900* (Boston: Little, Brown, 1937).

Two early reconsiderations of Wilson and Buck come from Burke Davis, *The Long Surrender* (New York: Random House, 1985); and Gaines Foster, *Ghosts of the Confederacy: Defeat, the Lost Cause, and the Emergence of the New South, 1865 to 1913* (New York: Oxford University Press, 1987). Foster warns against exaggerating the force and influence of Lost Cause enthusiasts and usefully periodizes white southerners' memorial efforts.

Gender studies have become an important site for reconsideration of Buck's reconciliationist view. Nina Silber, *The Romance of Reunion: Northerners and the South, 1865–1900* (Chapel Hill: University of North Carolina Press, 1993), finds that the "image of marriage between northern men and southern women stood at the foundation of the late-nineteenth-century culture of conciliation and became a symbol which defined and justified the northern view of the power relations in the reunified nation" (6–7). Kirk Savage, *Standing Soldiers, Kneeling Slaves: Race, War, and Monument in Nineteenth-Century America* (Princeton, N.J.: Princeton University Press, 1997), argues that the destruction of slavery did not genuinely liberate the black body but transformed the white hero. The Civil War allowed ordinary white men unprecedented access to gendered respect. Blacks had to be forgotten to better secure white soldiers' new grip on masculinity.

The most powerful critique of Buck has come from David W. Blight, *Race and Reunion: The Civil War in American Memory* (Cambridge, Mass.: Harvard University Press, 2001). Blight faults Buck for privileging reunion over race, observing that Buck documented whites' consensus about the meaning of sectional war and reconciliation before the civil rights revolution.

Numerous other writers have looked at memory and war. Jim Weeks, *Gettysburg: Memory, Market, and an American Shrine* (Princeton, N.J.: Princeton University Press, 2003), examines Gettysburg tourism. David Goldfield, *Still Fighting the Civil War: The American South and Southern History* (Baton Rouge: Louisiana State University Press, 2002); Cecilia Elizabeth O'Leary, *To Die For: The Paradox of American Patriotism* (Princeton, N.J.: Princeton University Press, 1999); Edward Tabor Linenthal, *Sacred Ground: Americans and Their Battlefields* (Urbana: University of Illinois Press, 1991); Sarah J. Purcell, *Sealed with Blood: War, Sacrifice, and Memory in Revolutionary America* (Philadelphia: University of Pennsylvania Press, 2002); G. Kurt Piehler, *Remembering War the American Way* (Washington, D.C.: Smithsonian Institution Press, 1995); Sanford Levinson, *Written in Stone: Public Monuments in Changing Societies* (Durham, N.C.: Duke University Press, 1998), John Bodnar, *Remaking America: Public Memory, Commemoration, and Patriotism in the Twentieth Century* (Princeton, N.J.: Princeton University Press, 1992); Jay Winter and Emmanuel Sivan, eds., *War and Remembrance in the Twentieth Century* (Cambridge, U.K.: Cambridge University Press, 1999); Amy J. Kinsel, "'From These Honored Dead': Gettysburg in American Culture, 1863–1938" (Ph.D. diss., Cornell University, 1992); Carol Reardon, *Pickett's Charge: In History and Memory* (Chapel Hill: University of North Carolina Press, 1997); Stephen Cushman, *Bloody Promenade: Reflections on a Civil War Battle* (Charlottesville: University of Virginia Press, 1999); Timothy Brian Smith, *The Great Battlefield of Shiloh: History, Memory, and the Establishment of a Civil War National Military Park* (Knoxville: University of Tennessee Press, 2004); Benjamin Tarber Dixon, "Gettysburg, a Living Battlefield," (Ph.D. diss., University of Oklahoma, 2000).

For the African American military experience, see Joseph T. Wilson, *The Black Phalanx* (1890; repr., New York: Arno, 1968); Thomas Wentworth Higginson, *Army Life in a Black Regiment*, ed. Howard Mumford Jones (1870; repr., East Lansing: Michigan State University Press, 1960);

Christopher Looby, ed., *The Complete Civil War Journal and Selected Letters of Thomas Wentworth Higginson* (Chicago: University of Chicago Press, 2000); George W. Williams, *A History of the Negro Troops in the War of the Rebellion, 1861–1865* (1888; repr., New York: Negro Universities Press, 1969); Benjamin Quarles, *The Negro in the Civil War* (Boston: Little, Brown, 1953); Dudley Taylor Cornish, *The Sable Arm: Negro Troops in the Union Army, 1861–1865* (New York: Longmans, Green, 1956); William Wells Brown, *The Negro in the American Rebellion* (New York: Citadel Press, 1971); Joseph T. Glatthaar, *Forged in Battle: The Civil War Alliance of Black Soldiers and White Officers* (Baton Rouge: Louisiana State University Press, 1990); Joseph T. Glatthaar, "Black Glory: The African-American Role in Union Victory," in Gabor S. Boritt, *Why the Confederacy Lost* (New York: Oxford University Press, 1992), 133–62; John David Smith, *Black Soldiers in Blue: African American Troops in the Civil War Era* (Chapel Hill: University of North Carolina Press, 2002). The previously mentioned books treat the Milliken's Bend battle. See also Cyrus Sears, *The Battle of Milliken's Bend* (Columbus, Ohio: F. J. Heer Printing Co., 1909).

Alice Fahs, *The Imagined Civil War: Popular Literature of the North and South, 1861–1865* (Chapel Hill: University of North Carolina Press, 2001).

Nineteenth-century biographies document the importance the Gilded Age attached to generals. Albert D. Richardson, *Personal History of Ulysses S. Grant* (1866; repr., Hartford, Conn.: American Publishing Co., 1885); Edward Howland, *Grant as a Soldier and Statesman: Being a Succinct History of His Military and Civil Career* (Hartford, Conn.: J. B. Burr & Co., 1868); Charles A. Dana and J. H. Wilson, *The Life of Ulysses S. Grant* (Springfield, Mass.: Gurdon Bill & Company, 1868); Henry Coppee, *Grant and His Campaigns: A Military Biography* (New York: Charles B. Richardson, 1866); Adam Badeau, *Military History of Ulysses S. Grant* (1867; repr., New York: D. Appleton and Co., 1881); John Russell Young, *Around the World with General Grant* (New York: American News Company, 1879); J. T. Headley, *The Life of Ulysses S. Grant* (New York: Perkins Book Co., 1885). For Lost Cause criticism of Grant, see Brooks D. Simpson, "Continuous Hammering and Mere Attrition: Lost Cause Critics and the Military Reputation of Ulysses S. Grant," in Gary W. Gallagher and Alan T. Nolan, eds., *The Myth of the Lost Cause and Civil War History* (Bloomington: Indiana University Press, 2000), 147–50. In fact, though, ex-Confederates in Vicksburg viewed Grant positively. For the leading Lost Cause proponent, see Jack P. Maddex, Jr., *The Reconstruction of Edward A. Pollard: A Rebel's Conversion to Postbellum Unionism* (Chapel Hill: University of North Carolina Press, 1974). For Dana, see James Harrison Wilson, *The Life of Charles Dana* (New York: Harper and Brothers, 1907); Ida M. Tarbell, "Charles A. Dana in the Civil War," *McClure's Magazine* 9 (October 1897): 1087–89; Ida M. Tarbell, *All in the Day's Work: An Autobiography* (New York: Macmillan, 1939); Charles A. Dana, *Recollections of the Civil War* (1898; repr., Lincoln: University of Nebraska Press, 1996).

The memoirs of Civil War generals (and Jefferson Davis) are critical to understanding how the Gilded Age constructed its Civil War memory. E. B. Long, ed., *Personal Memoirs of U. S. Grant* (Cleveland: World, 1952); Gen. Joseph E. Johnston, *Narrative of Military Operations During the Civil War* (1874; repr., New York: DaCapo, n.d.); Richard Taylor, *Destruction and Reconstruction: Personal Experiences of the Late War* (New York: Longmans, Green, 1955); W. T. Sherman, *Memoirs of Gen. W. T. Sherman, Written by Himself,* 2 vols. (1875; repr., New York: Charles L. Webster & Co., 1891); Jefferson Davis, *The Rise and Fall of the Confederate Government,* 2 vols. (New York: D. Appleton & Co., 1881).

The great novel of the Civil War came from an author born after Appomattox. Stephen Crane, *The Red Badge of Courage* (New York: D. Appleton & Co., 1895); Eric J. Gislason, "*The Red Badge of Courage*: An Episode of the American Civil War," http://xroads.virginia.edu/~HYPER/CRANE/reviews/ section1.html.

It is a major point of this book that Vicksburg's Civil War did not end July 4, 1863. Reconstruction is a well-trod topic for historians, but Eric Foner, *Reconstruction: America's Unfinished Revolution, 1863–1877* (New York: Harper & Row, 1988), is without doubt the best. Foner does slight constitutional issues, however. His student makes amends: Xi Wang, *The Trial of Democracy: Black Suffrage and Black Republicans, 1860–1910* (Athens: University of Georgia Press, 1997). See also Pamela Brandwein, *Reconstructing Reconstruction: The Supreme Court and the Production of Historical Truth* (Durham, N.C.: Duke University Press, 1999). For Reconstruction in Mississippi, see James W. Garner, *Reconstruction in Mississippi* (1901; repr., Baton Rouge: Louisiana State University Press, 1968). Garner was a student of William A. Dunning and reflects his racist views. William C. Harris covers Mississippi Reconstruction in two volumes: *Presidential Reconstruction in Mississippi* (Baton Rouge: Louisiana State University Press, 1967) and *The Day of the Carpetbagger: Republican Reconstruction in Mississippi* (Baton Rouge: Louisiana State University Press, 1979).

Reconstructing the history of Vicksburg's park requires a careful reading of Vicksburg newspapers, especially the *Vicksburg Evening Post* supplemented by the *Vicksburg Herald*. The park itself houses some records, but the most important are elsewhere. Vicksburg National Military Park Association minutes are in the Mississippi Department of Archives and History. The National Park Service headquarters in Washington has a useful file of Vicksburg park material. The National Archives branch in East Point, Georgia,

houses an important (and extensive) series of park correspondence, chiefly by William T. Rigby. Rigby's Papers in
the Special Collection Department, University of Iowa Library, Iowa City, are essential. National Park Service
records at the National Archives in College Park are equally
important and include War Department files relating to the
park as well. Vicksburg's Old Court House Museum com-
memorates Jefferson Davis and contains archival materials
relating to John G. Cashman and the Mississippi Memorial
as well as Eva W. Davis, founder of the Old Court House
Museum. For Thomas B. Reed and Gilded Age fiscal con-
straints, see William A. Robinson, *Thomas B. Reed: Parliamentarian* (New York: Dodd, Mead and Company, 1930);
Samuel W. McCall, *Thomas B. Reed* (Boston: Houghton Mifflin, 1914), 214; Allan Weinstein, *Prelude to Populism: Origins
of the Silver Issue* (New Haven, Conn.: Yale University Press,
1970); Barbara W. Tuchman, "Czar of the House," *American
Heritage* 14 (December 1962): 33–35, 92–102; Richard G.
Forgette, "Reed's Rules and the Partisan Theory of Legisla-
tive Organization," *Polity* 29 (spring 1997): 375–96; Randall
Strahan, "Thomas Brackett Reed and the Rise of Party
Government," in Roger H. Davidson, Susan Webb Ham-
mond, and Raymond W. Smock, eds., *Masters of the House:
Congressional Leadership over Two Centuries* (Boulder, Colo.:
Westview Press, 1998), 34–59; and Gretchen Ritter, *Goldbugs
and Greenbacks: The Antimonopoly Tradition and the Politics of
Finance in America, 1865–1896* (Cambridge, U.K.: Cambridge
University Press, 1997). The extensive William Boyd Allison
Papers (State Historical Society of Iowa, Des Moines) are a
gold mine. The John Alfred Tiffin Hull Papers, also at State
Historical Society of Iowa, are thinner but of some value for
his speeches. For Gilded Age imperialism more generally,
see David Healy, *U.S. Expansionism: The Imperialist Urge in
the 1890s* (Madison: University of Wisconsin Press, 1970);
and Ivan Musicant, *Empire by Default: The Spanish-American*

War and the Dawn of the American Century (New York: Henry Holt, 1998). For the military park idea generally, see Ronald F. Lee, *The Origin and Evolution of the National Military Park Idea* (Washington, D.C.: National Park Service, 1973). This Park Service publication is also available on the excellent Park Service website www.cr.nps.gov/history. The Vicksburg National Military Park has its own website at www.nps.gov/vick/home.htp.

The two best general histories of the Civil War are Phillip Shaw Paludan, *"A People's Contest": The Union and Civil War, 1861–1865* (New York: Harper & Row, 1988), and James McPherson, *Battle Cry of Freedom: The Civil War Era* (New York: Oxford University Press, 1988).

For ordinary soldiers, a great place to start would be: Reid Mitchell, "'Not the General but the Soldier': The Study of Civil War Soldiers," in James M. McPherson and William J. Cooper, Jr., *Writing the Civil War: The Quest to Understand* (Columbia: University of South Carolina Press, 1998), 81–95. James M. McPherson, *For Cause and Comrades: Why Men Fought in the Civil War* (New York: Oxford University Press, 1997), offers a bifurcated explanation of soldiers' motivation. Reid Mitchell has published two excellent books on ordinary soldiers: *Civil War Soldiers* (New York: Viking, 1988) and *The Vacant Chair: The Northern Soldier Leaves Home* (New York: Oxford University Press, 1993). Gerald Linderman's *Embattled Courage: The Experience of Combat in the American Civil War* (New York: Free Press, 1987) has become a classic.

My analysis of soldiers' motivations is based primarily on the diaries and letters soldiers wrote during the Vicksburg campaign. The Illinois Historical Society and the State Historical Society of Iowa are the best sites for exploring the thinking of ordinary soldiers engaged in the Vicksburg campaign. The Ohio Historical Society and the Missouri Historical Society have important materials as well. For Illinois, see William B. Tubbs, "A Bibliography of Illinois Civil War Regimental Sources in the Illinois State Historical Library: Part I, Published and Printed Sources," *Illinois Historical Journal* 87 (autumn 1994): 185–323; and William B. Tubbs, "A Bibliography of Illinois Civil War Regimental Sources in the Illinois State Historical Library: Part II, Manuscripts," *Illinois Historical Journal* 87 (winter 1994): 277–324. Regimental histories can be found in almost every midwestern library, though the state historical societies listed previously proved especially helpful.

The Virginia Historical Society has important collections relating to the Confederate Memorial Society and the founding of Battle Abbey. The Confederate Memorial Society Papers are especially valuable. For Charles Broadway Rouss, the best source is the Frederick William Holliday Family Collection (Perkins Library, Duke University, Durham, North Carolina). See also Larry A. Mullin, *The Napoleon of Gotham: A Study of the Life of Charles Broadway Rouss* (Winchester, Va.: privately printed, 1974); A. V. Mc-Cracken, *The Life of Charles Broadway Rouss* (n.p. [1896]). There is a small Rouss collection, and a useful collection of newspaper and magazine articles on Rouss, at the public library in Winchester, Virginia. Charles Broadway Rouss collection (Stewart Bell Jr. Archives Room, Handley Regional Library, Winchester, Virginia).

For the South's honor culture, see James C. Klotter, *Kentucky Justice, Southern Honor, and American Manhood: Understanding the Life and Death of Richard Reid* (Baton Rouge: Louisiana State University Press, 2003); Richard F. Hamm, *Murder, Honor and Law: Four Virginia Homicides from Reconstruction to the Great Depression* (Charlottesville: University Press of Virginia, 2003); Edward L. Ayers, *Vengeance and Justice: Crime and Punishment in the 19th-Century American South* (New York: Oxford University Press, 1984); Grady McWhiney, *Cracker Culture: Celtic Ways in the*

Old South (Tuscaloosa: University of Alabama Press, 1988); and Dickson D. Bruce, Jr., *Violence and Culture in the Antebellum South* (Austin: University of Texas Press, 1979). The classic work remains Bertram Wyatt-Brown, *Southern Honor: Ethics and Behavior in the Old South* (New York: Oxford University Press, 1982).

INDEX

Christopher Waldrep, formerly of Meridian, Mississippi, is now Jamie and Phyllis Pasker Professor of American History at San Francisco State University. He is the author of many books and articles on the American South, including *Roots of Disorder: Race and Criminal Justice in the American South, 1817–80* and *The Many Faces of Judge Lynch: Extralegal Violence and Punishment in America.*

Also by Christopher Waldrep

Night Riders: Defending Community in the Black Patch,
  1890–1915
Roots of Disorder: Race and Criminal Justice in the American
  South, 1817–80
(Editor with Donald G. Nieman) *Local Matters: Race,*
  Crime, and Justice in the Nineteenth-Century South
(Editor) *Racial Violence on Trial: A Handbook with Cases,*
  Laws, and Documents
The Many Faces of Judge Lynch: Extralegal Violence and
  Punishment in America
(Editor with Lynne Curry) *The Constitution and the Nation*

The American Crisis Series

Books on the Civil War Era

Steven E. Woodworth, Associate Professor of History,
Texas Christian University
Series Editor